Cinema and Soviet Society, 1917–1953 documents how film was used for political purposes by the Soviet government, from the revolutionary period through the death of Stalin. As Peter Kenez demonstrates, the Bolsheviks had high expectations of the film medium, believing that it would be a major vehicle for transmitting their social and political messages. Experimenting with the various ways that film could be brought to workers and peasant audiences, they achieved, in fact, some major success, although their unrealistically high expectations often led to acrimonious debate and disappointment.

Kenez also explores the roots of Soviet cinema in the film heritage of prerevolutionary Russia; the changes in content, style, technical means, and production capabilities generated by the Revolution; the constraints on form and subject imposed on artists in the name of socialist realism; the relative freedom of expression accorded to filmmakers during World War II; and the extraordinary repression during the final years of the Stalinist regime. Examining how the explicit and implicit messages in Soviet film changed over time, *Cinema and Soviet Society* also charts the evolution of the new world order created by the Soviets, through a medium where politics and culture intersected.

Cinema and Soviet Society, 1917–1953

Cambridge Studies in the History of Mass Communications

Cinema and Soviet Society, 1917–1953, Peter Kenez,
University of California, Santa Cruz

Cinema and Soviet Society, 1917–1953

Peter Kenez
University of California, Santa Cruz

CAMBRIDGE
UNIVERSITY PRESS

Published by the Press Syndicate of the University of Cambridge
The Pitt Building, Trumpington Street, Cambridge CB2 1RP
40 West 20th Street, New York, NY 10011, USA
10 Stamford Road, Oakleigh, Melbourne 3166, Australia

First published 1992

Printed in the United States of America

Library of Congress Cataloging-in-Publication Data
Kenez, Peter.
    Cinema and Soviet society, 1917–1953 / Peter Kenez.
        p.   cm. – (Cambridge studies in mass communications)
    Includes bibliographical references.
    ISBN 0-521-41671-X. – ISBN 0-521-42863-7 (pbk.)
    1. Motion pictures – Political aspects – Soviet Union.
    2. Motion pictures – Soviet Union – History.
    I. Title. II. Series.
    PN1993.5.R9K39   1992
    791.43′658′0947 – dc20   91–37125

A catalog record for this book is available from the British Library

ISBN 0-521-41671-X hardback
ISBN 0-521-42863-7 paperback

To P. K.
as always

Contents

Acknowledgments

Many friends helped me with criticisms and encouragement. Above all, I appreciate the support from Denise Youngblood, who followed the evolution of the manuscript with friendly interest and read several chapters more than once. She managed to combine warm encouragement with useful criticisms of approach and detail. Richard Stites and Richard Taylor also read the entire manuscript and made helpful suggestions. These scholars showed great generosity, for they were supportive even though their interpretations of Stalinist cinema are very different from mine. Other friends, among them Josephine Woll, Gabor Rittersporn, David Mayers, Jonathan Beecher, Sigrid McLaughlin, Charles Neider, and Boris Keyser, read parts of this work and helped me in a variety of ways. Dorothy Dalby once again, as so often in the past, saved me from numerous stylistic infelicities. My discussions with Penelope Kenez of all the major arguments presented in this book helped me to clarify my points.

Several institutions helped me in the course of writing this book. I started my work at the Pacific Film Archives of the University of California at Berkeley. The International Research and Exchange Board supported a two-month stay in Moscow in 1985 and a research trip of the same length to Budapest in 1987. My stay in Budapest was very pleasant: The staff of the Film Archives went out of its way to help. Deputy Director Janos Varga and Anna Gereb, a leading Hungarian specialist on the history of Soviet film, were particularly helpful and became my good friends. I learned a great deal from them. Through a University of California–Leningrad University exchange, I worked in Leningrad libraries in 1988. I also received support from the Research Committee on the Academic Senate of the University of California at Santa Cruz and from my own department, the History Board of Studies at UCSC.

Parts of Chapters 2–4 are taken from my book *The Birth of Propaganda State: Soviet Methods of Mass Mobilization, 1917–1929*. Chapter 5 appeared in *Slavic Review* (Fall, 1988), and a somewhat different version of Chapter 9 was published in a volume edited by K. R. M. Short, *Film and Radio Propaganda in World War II*.

ix

Introduction

This book is about films, made in a country that described itself as "revolutionary," and it is about propaganda. Most of us love movies, especially "revolutionary" movies, and we like to find evidence of manipulation of opinion, for that gives us a sense of superiority: Unlike the victims of propaganda, we can see through falsehood.

I do not want to disappoint. Although this book is a history of Soviet film from 1917 to 1953, it is written from a particular point of view. I do not hope to contribute to our understanding of the great Soviet directors' art; in any case, there are already many fine books on the works of Eisenstein, Kuleshov, Pudovkin, Dovzhenko, and Vertov. The films I will discuss in detail are not necessarily the finest, the best known, or even the most popular. For example, I will say only a few sentences about *Battleship Potemkin*, the best-known Soviet film of all time, but devote many pages to *Bezhin Meadow*, a film that was never publicly exhibited – indeed, it does not even exist today. I have little interest in modern film theory and semiotics, for these approaches do not help to answer the questions I am posing. Although most of the prominent Soviet directors were intellectuals who had many interesting things to say about the art of cinema, I will pay attention to the debates among them only when they are relevant to my topic.

My interest in cinema is that of a historian. I came to this topic while working on my previous book on Soviet propaganda.[1] Through my studies of the Bolsheviks' ideas about propaganda and the role of mass indoctrination in early Soviet society, I became interested in how cinema was used by the revolutionaries in their attempt to convey their message to the Soviet peoples, but I devoted less than two chapters to this issue. This time I will examine in more detail and over a longer time span the same question, but I also want to broaden my investigation.

The Bolsheviks were among the first politicians who appreciated the power of propaganda, became masters of the art, and had the means to create a vast apparatus. They proudly called themselves propagandists, but by propaganda they did not mean anything sinister. They assumed that they were in possession of the one true instrument for understanding social change,

1

Marxism, and that this instrument allowed them to interpret past, present, and future. Naturally, it was their duty to bring their fellow countrymen the truth, and this "truth" was to be the precondition of the development of proper socialist and revolutionary class consciousness. They did not mean to delude; they meant to educate.

The revolutionaries – as other contemporary and later observers – overestimated the power of propaganda to influence the thinking and therefore the behavior of people in general, and had too great a faith in film propaganda in particular. The Bolsheviks were particularly vulnerable to the error of overestimating the power of persuasion. As Marxists, they believed in the perfectibility of humanity, in the notion that there is only one universal truth, and in the power of reason. They were determined to create "the new socialist man." Today, in retrospect, it is evident that the Bolsheviks failed in their effort to create a new and, in their opinion, a better humanity. But the revolutionaries were not alone in their error. Attributing vast influence to propaganda and seeing its effects everywhere fulfill a useful psychological purpose for all of us: Such views enable us to deal with the inconvenient fact that many seemingly decent and intelligent people see matters that seem self-evident to us altogether differently. It is difficult to accept that our ideas, values, and beliefs do not have a universal appeal. How easy, and seemingly sophisticated, to believe that those who hold different views do so because they had been brainwashed. We can see through falsehood – but others could not.

Given their worldview, it is not surprising that the Bolsheviks were among the first to believe in the propaganda potential of cinema. At a time of great poverty they devoted scarce resources to filmmaking and oversaw the work of filmmakers with extraordinary care. But they were always disappointed. They never succeeded in harnessing what seemed to them the great power of cinema; it always just eluded them. The political story of Soviet film is, therefore, a story of unrealized hopes, disappointments, constant reorganizations, constant attempts to do something just a little differently.

To point out that many have a tendency to overemphasize the power of propaganda in general and of film propaganda in particular is not to argue that films do not make an impression on audiences. This impression, however, is usually more complex and difficult to measure than it is supposed. I am planning to examine in as much detail as possible, given the paucity of sources, how successful the propagandists were, and what ideas they managed to transmit.

But my goal is more ambitious than an examination of the propaganda role of films. I would like to contribute to our understanding of the interaction of culture and politics. I will, therefore, pay attention to Bolshevik attempts to bring cinema to the audiences, especially to the peasants, which was the most difficult task, and to the development and working of the vast censorship apparatus. My project is based on the assumption that a study of Bolshevik film policy is revealing about the nature of the regime, and about the changing mentality of the Bolsheviks. But most important, I would like to gain through a study of films some understanding of the mental world of Soviet citizens in these crucial years of great social transformation.

The Russian people in the twentieth century experienced a series of extraordinary events. Two revolutions, two catastrophic wars, industrialization and collectivization, and Stalinist terror transformed the lives of millions. As we look back at this bloody period of recent history, we want to know how people who lived through exhilaration and horror perceived and understood the changes occurring around them. Obviously, reconstructing the mental world of contemporaries of such events is an extremely difficult task. Simple people by and large leave no memoirs. But even if they did, how could we generalize about them? How could we trust works published in periods of intense repression? The sum total of subjective individual experience can never be regained; at best we can attempt to form an impressionistic picture from bits of evidence.

Reading books of contemporary authors and seeing films made at the time are helpful. After all, the writers and directors shared the experiences of their contemporaries and had to appeal to them by speaking their language and addressing their concerns. Even when they expressed ideas that they had to express, and even if they did so in the stilted language that was required, their works are revealing. These works both expressed and contributed to forming the spirit of the age.

From the point of view of the historian, movies provide better raw material than novels. First of all, the popularity of the new art form was great even in prerevolutionary Russia; films therefore reached a larger audience than literature. Also, during the worst period of Stalinist terror the Soviet people were not deprived completely of the possibility of turning to nineteenth-century classics in lieu of contemporary literature. As far as movies were concerned, however, there was no comparable escape. The movie houses showed what the regime wanted them to show. Second, the leaders of the regime even at the time of the Revolution saw clearly the propaganda potential of the cinema and were determined to use it. As a result, films even in the liberal 1920s were more ideological and less heterogeneous in their content than novels. Because filmmaking by its very nature is an expensive undertaking, the state had no trouble in enforcing its monopoly. Third, relatively few movies were made. (In the 1920s approximately one hundred a year; in the 1930s the output diminished to approximately forty annually. The industry reached its nadir in the early 1950s, when it produced no more than six or seven films yearly.) For these reasons the sociopolitical dimension of film culture submits more readily to generalization than the same domain of contemporary literature.

Films convey both conscious and unconscious messages, and through the pictures past ages speak to us. Because the Bolsheviks had a firm belief in the power of cinema to influence the thinking of audiences, they supported filmmakers and invested scarce resources. As a consequence, the history of Soviet cinema well reflects the changing political ideas that the Bolsheviks wished films to transmit. Eisenstein's great films in the 1920s, for example, celebrated the masses as heroes of history; his equally impressive films made fifteen to twenty years later concentrated on the role of the individual. In the early part of the 1930s many films were made about saboteurs, but at the end of the decade the favorite villains were foreign spies. Mapping these changes, some obvious and some not so obvious, helps us to understand the Soviet system.

The unconscious messages are even more interesting. Directors take the values of their society so much for granted that they can be unaware of what they are conveying. But we who are removed in time and space are often able to glean valuable information. We see, for example, how men and women related to one another. Films made about foreigners, capitalists, and "the enemy" are particularly interesting, for in them filmmakers revealed their fears, sometimes projecting the ills of their own society onto others. Clearly, they did this unconsciously. Films also provide us with priceless visual material: We gain a sense of daily life by seeing the bustling streets of Moscow and Leningrad in the 1920s, the inside of apartments, dusty villages, and so on.

It would be naïve to think that the worldview expressed in films ever directly represented the thinking of the citizens of any society. Cinema, even in the best case, is only a distorting mirror. Audiences go to movies in order to be entertained rather than to see the "truth" about themselves. Few movies ever made in any society have attempted an honest description of the everyday world of the simple citizen. In "real life" the young women are not as beautiful and the young men are not as handsome as actors and actresses. The adventures of detectives are more interesting than the lives of steelworkers; possibly Hollywood made more movies about detectives than there ever were private investigators. Dreams and preoccupations, however, can also be revealing. The abundant meals served in the collective-farm films of the 1930s, 1940s, and 1950s gave peasant audiences a vicarious satisfaction, even when the viewers knew full well that the peasant diet was by no means as rich and attractive as it was depicted.

Cinema reflects on itself. Films follow conventions and the audiences expect them to do so. Directors consciously or unconsciously, directly or obliquely, frequently refer to each other's work. In the 1930s, for example, two prominent directors, Leonid Trauberg and Grigorii Kozintsev, made a series of films about an imagined revolutionary hero, Maxim. He became well known and "real" to audiences. In World War II agitational films, this Maxim, along with living figures, appealed to audiences with a patriotic message.

Censorship also distorts. Soviet Russia was neither the only nor the first country to censor. Because of its powerful mimicry of reality, and its enormous mass appeal, cinema has always been considered dangerous by people in positions of authority. Within a short time the Bolsheviks pushed censorship to further extremes than any ruling group had ever tried. Their censorship became not only proscriptive, but also prescriptive. Soviet films in the 1930s and after came to depict a world almost entirely devoid of reality. In spite of its surface realism, a Soviet film depicting heroic workers whose chief aim in life is the building of socialism was every bit as fantastic as a Busby Berkeley spectacular. Yet, I would argue, a construction drama, a *kolkhoz* musical, or a film about catching saboteurs is revealing as a dream or a nightmare is revealing.

Films were important in the history of Soviet society as an instrument for spreading an approved message. Although it is to Lenin that the famous statement is attributed that film is the most important of all arts, it was Stalin who was preoccupied with cinema to an extraordinary extent. As he became an all-powerful dictator in the late 1930s, he came to be increasingly cut off from the real world around him. Today more and more evidence appears to show how Stalin became the first and most prominent victim of a propaganda campaign for which he was primarily responsible. Films allowed him to create an "alternative" reality, a "reality" that was a great deal easier to manipulate and transform than obstinate Russian society. The ordinary peasants and workers knew full well that collective farms and factories did not in the least look like those depicted by the directors, but Stalin did not know and did not want to know. The primary social role of films in the age of Stalin was not to portray reality but to help to deny it.

Writing a book on the history of Soviet film, from whatever vantage point, necessitates difficult choices. An author cannot take for granted that his readers will be familiar with the films about which he generalizes. A brief summary of many films, however, will not convey the special flavor of those works. On the other hand, an extensive discussion of a few works might give a misleading impression of the bulk of the films that Soviet viewers actually saw. In order to illustrate my points at times I merely count the number of films made on a certain topic, at other times summarize films briefly, and, on occasion, I describe a few in detail. I am aware that my choices might seem idiosyncratic to some. I made my choices not on the basis of artistic merit but in order to illustrate my arguments concerning the ever-changing ideological content of movies. These films, I believe, are representatives of their genres. Although aesthetics is not my primary concern, I cannot avoid making some admittedly subjective judgments. The reader may disregard these, but I see no reason why I should not make these explicit.

I am above all interested in the films of the Stalinist era, and therefore devote more space to them than to the works of the golden age of the late 1920s. I do so partly because we know much more of the earlier period and partly because Stalinist films were more uniquely Soviet and, therefore, in need of elucidation.[2] Stalinist cinema was an exotic flower of an extraordinary age. The death of Stalin in 1953 was a great turning point in all aspects of Soviet life, and therefore also in the history of Soviet film. Following the death of the tyrant, cinema, as other arts, revived and became much more heterogeneous. Indeed, the revival, following the Stalinist devastation, was well-nigh miraculous. The artists, many of them veterans of the great age of Soviet film, succeeded in reviving the traditions and excitement of an earlier age. Films made after 1953 are, of course, also revealing of the society in which they were made; however, analysis of these works requires a different approach and the subject deserves a book of its own.

Notes

1 *The Birth of the Propaganda State: Soviet Methods of Mass Mobilization, 1917–1929*, Cambridge University Press, 1985.

2 I have benefited from the recent work of Richard Taylor, *The Politics of the Soviet Cinema, 1917–1929*, Cambridge University Press, 1979, and in particular, Denise Youngblood, *Soviet Cinema in the Silent Era 1918–1935*, Ann Arbor, Mich., UMI Press, 1985.

PART I

The golden age

CHAPTER I

Cinema before October

The great Soviet directors did not start their work in a void. Indeed, they were very young and passionately rejected the old order and its aesthetics. At the same time the world against which they were rebelling was significantly influencing their work. Although Soviet scholars for a long time were hesitant to acknowledge it, and although the surviving films are only now becoming known in the West, it is obvious that Imperial Russia possessed a vibrant film industry and could boast of talented actors and directors whose artistry could stand comparison with anything that was happening abroad. The roots of Soviet film reached back to the prerevolutionary period to a greater extent perhaps than even the artists of the 1920s realized.

The first years

In the 1880s and 1890s about a dozen people in England, Germany, the United States, and France were close to solving the technological problems of projecting animated photographic images. No major scientific breakthrough was necessary; the solutions proposed by the different men were, in fact, quite similar. What distinguished the Lumière brothers, who, in December 1895, projected moving images in the Paris Grand Café before a paying audience, was not their brilliant inventiveness, but their combination of technological talent, entrepreneurial skill, and adequate capital.[1]

From its earliest infancy many characteristics of the cinema were already in evidence. First of all, it was an enormously popular medium. It was as if people were standing in line to go to the movies even before the technology of projection was developed. Cinema caught the eye of the public faster than the two other new forms of mass entertainment media of the twentieth century: radio and television. Unlike those, movies did not require heavy investment by either the producers or the consumers of entertainment. The source of the appeal has changed, but it has always remained powerful. First people were satisfied merely by witnessing the illusion of reality: a moving train, a running horse, two people fighting, and so on. Then audiences were attracted by seeing the familiar and the exotic (pictures from all over the

world). Only in the final stage did people expect that their films would tell
a story. Within two decades of cinema's appearance, hundreds of millions
of people had paid money to see a film.

Second, cinema has always been international. It is true that the French
at first enjoyed an advantage: During the first dozen years or so they dominated the market. Louis Lumière, Georges Méliès and, especially, Charles
Pathé were the first great figures of the industry. But these people always
searched for an audience beyond the borders of France. French companies,
for example, came to Russia and employed Russians to make films for the
international market on Russian topics. This success encouraged them to do
the same in Japan.[2] By 1907 Pathé had offices in fifteen cities, including
such unlikely ones as Calcutta and Singapore and by the time of World War
I the number had grown to forty-one.[3]

The community of filmmakers who developed the language of the cinema
was also international. National borders were no obstacle to the changing
interests and fashions in filmmaking. The first great stars, such as the French
comedian Max Linder and the Danish actress Asta Nielsen, were known the
world over; their faces were recognized by many more people than the portraits of statesmen of the age. The directors were keenly aware of each other's work; they learned from one another, and this learning largely explains
why the medium developed as rapidly as it did. When narrative film appeared, so did national styles. But these were different from one another
only in that they expressed different sensibilities, not in the techniques of
storytelling.

Third, cinema was a democratic medium. Its appearance coincided with
the vast changes brought about by industrialization and urbanization. The
downtrodden, exploited new workers could find cheap entertainment – a
diversion from their bleak lives. But the urban poor were not the only ones
attracted; unlike other forms of entertainment, the appeal of movies cut
across classes. Movies were made to entertain people and to make money
for enterprising businessmen. The idea that cinema was also a form of art
arose late, and even then it influenced only some of the directors. Only a
small minority of the audience has ever gone to the cinema in search of an
artistic experience.

The history of early Russian cinema closely parallels developments elsewhere. Remarkably, in May 1896 – only four months after the first exhibition in Paris – the Lumières' invention was shown both in St. Petersburg
and in Moscow.[4] During the summer of the same year at the Nizhnii-
Novgorod fair, one of the attractions was the showing of moving pictures.
M. Gorky was in the audience and described his impressions. His fresh
and unmediated description is remarkable.

Yesterday I was in the kingdom of shadows. How frightening it is to be there, if you
only knew! ... a railway train appears on the screen. It darts like an arrow straight
towards you – look out! It seems as if it is about to rush into the darkness where

you are sitting and reduce you to a mangled sack of skin, full of crumpled flesh and splintered bones, and destroy this hall and this building, so full of wine, women, music and vice, and transform it into fragments and into dust. But this, too, is merely a train of shadows.[5]

He conveys well the sense of excitement, a sense of witnessing a miracle. In the following decades everywhere in the world, millions of people of all social classes must have had similar experiences seeing their first moving pictures.[6]

Interestingly, showing and making films in Russia started at exactly the same time. People were fascinated by the exotic, and cinema was able to bring them impressions from far away and from strange lands such as Russia. The Lumière brothers sent a cameraman, Camille Cerf, to Moscow to photograph the coronation ceremonies of Nicholas II. The sequence taken in the Kremlin on this occasion is one of the first newsreels and documentary records of an important historical event.[7]

There was money to be made. At first the French entirely controlled the market. The Lumière brothers, and then Pathé, to whom the Lumières sold the patent, and Gaumont made their profit by selling projectors and also films. During the first years a Russian entrepreneur had to travel to France to buy his film. In 1904 Pathé, and in 1905 Gaumont, established offices in Russia itself. The entrepreneur still bought the film and traveled with it from city to city, from country fair to country fair. When audiences tired of his material, he would resell his films to someone else.[8] During the first decade an average program included four or five very short films. These consisted of short "dramas" – really a series of tableaux – and newsreels from different parts of the world, dealing with extraordinary events and strange people; cinema and circus still had a great deal in common. The entire program lasted between thirty minutes and an hour, and the theaters changed their programs at least weekly. The appetite of the audiences for new films was voracious; for the successful people in the industry it was not quality, but quantity that mattered.

The great bulk of movie theaters was in the cities; cinema was associated with urban life. Those among the intellectuals who professed to disdain the new form of entertainment saw it as one of the unattractive consequences of concentrating people in large cities. In 1913 the Russian Empire had 1,452 movie theaters: 134 in St. Petersburg, 107 in Moscow, 25 in Odessa, 21 in Riga, and the rest scattered among smaller towns.[9] In working-class districts where there was no electricity, ether–oxygen lamps were used, which created an unpleasant odor and, more important, a constant danger of fire. The Moscow city *duma* was compelled to take measures, such as requiring that movie houses be separated from living quarters by brick walls. It also forbade opening them next to apothecaries, for these were likely to have flammable material, and required cinemas to install artificial ventilation.[10] Although cinema was and remained for a long time an urban entertainment, some businessmen experimented with bringing films to the peasants. In 1906 on the Volga a barge carried a projector and a small generator and stopped at towns and villages in order to show films to the presumably amazed audiences.[11] This method of bringing films to the public was a forerunner of the Bolshevik agitational ship.

By 1907–8 the modern concept of rental had developed. Of all aspects of the film business, this was the most profitable. In some instances the rental business and ownership of theater chains were concentrated in the same hands, and some enterprising capitalists succeeded in making a great deal of money.[12] The accumulated capital – and the constant demand for films – created the basis for the birth of the Russian film industry, but it was difficult to compete with the foreigners. Foreign, mostly French companies, producing for an international market, had a network of distribution that allowed them to undersell domestic businessmen. Films were sold by the meter, and the large foreign companies charged only a fraction more for the finished product than the cost of the raw film. There was, however, one thing that domestic filmmakers could do better than the foreign competition. Because people liked to see familiar surroundings on the screen, the first indigenous efforts were concentrated on the production of documentary material. The production of newsreels took place first on a regional basis and then expanded on a national scale.[13]

French businessmen were well aware of the Russian desire to see Russian subjects and were determined not to lose their share of the market. In 1908 Pathé sent a French crew to Russia to make a film, *The Cossacks of the Don,* which, purely in terms of the size of its audience, became the most successful product of the prerevolutionary era. This brief film, lasting only a few minutes, showed Cossack horsemanship and camp life. There were 219 copies made of it, at a time when an average film was distributed in only 10 or 20 copies.[14]

The success of *The Cossacks of the Don* immediately inspired a Russian entrepreneur, Aleksandr Drankov, to produce the first Russian narrative film, *Stenka Razin.*[15] It was not really a film, but a collection of tableaux, depicting events of a well-known Russian folk song: In a fit of jealousy the drunken leader kills his beloved captive, a Persian princess. This film, which lasted only for seven and a half minutes, was, by common consent, a clumsy product. The actors grimaced dreadfully, were poorly made up, and made overly broad gestures. The camera hardly moved, the filming took place entirely outdoors and, because the camera was placed rather far from the actors, it was even difficult to tell who was playing whom. In this film the modern viewer can enjoy only pictures of the countryside, and perhaps be moved by watching a significant moment in film history.[16]

The years from the making of *Stenka Razin* to the outbreak of World War I constituted the formative period of Russian film. There was a vast expansion of movie theaters in the empire, and a great variety of films available from various parts of the world. By 1909 there were already twelve hundred theaters in the empire and 108 million viewers.[17] Although most of these theaters were quite small, accommodating perhaps one or two hundred people, the number was impressive. The industry was largely concentrated in Moscow, and the studios, the rental offices, the major directors, the best actors and actresses, and the best cameramen were all working in the old capital; Moscow was Russia's Hollywood.[18]

The British, the Italians, the Germans, the Americans, and the Danes joined the French in supplying the ever-growing Russian market. It was during this time that people gradually ceased to regard cinema as a technological novelty, at least in the cities, and came to expect a more sophisticated form of entertainment. The studios, in order to retain their audience, were compelled to give more than shorts showing circuslike attractions. The *film d'art* movement was a response to the changing needs of the market. It started in France, where, in 1908, a special company was formed under this name, but it quickly influenced filmmakers everywhere. In order to attract audiences to the cinemas, the studios commissioned scenarios from famous authors. They also aimed at enhancing the prestige of cinema by hiring well-known actors from the theater. The movement, especially in Russia, turned to the classics of literature for scenarios. Other frequent topics for films came from history. Beautiful costumes greatly appealed to audiences everywhere. This was an appeal that cinema would continue to exploit. The directors wanted to break the association in the public's mind between cinema and fairground entertainment; they were particularly anxious to bring middle-class people into the movie houses.[19]

The number of domestically made films between the first effort in 1908 and the outbreak of the war vastly expanded. In 1913 the fledgling industry produced 129 films. (Most of these were very short.) Even so, Russians controlled only 10 percent of the market;[20] the rest was in the hands of foreigners, largely French.

More impressive than the quantitative growth was the increased sophistication of Russian filmmakers. The difference between *Stenka Razin* and *The Defense of Sevastopol*, which was made only three years later, is extraordinary. *The Defense of Sevastopol* was an enormously more ambitious product. The film is more than two thousand meters long, the length of a modern film. Made in the Khanzhonkov studios and directed by Goncharov, this film used hundreds of extras in order to recreate the scenes of famous battles. The tsar himself gave his sponsorship and the local authorities in the Crimea gave all possible help; making the film became a patriotic undertaking. It was extraordinarily expensive, costing forty thousand rubles to make, far more than any other Russian film up to this time.[21] Napoleon III was played by Ivan Mozzhukhin, who was soon to become the most famous male film star of the prerevolutionary period. Although the camera remained stationary, the director handled the crowd scenes competently. He

Figure 1.   Veterans of the Crimean war in 1911: *The Defense of Sevastopol* (1911).

also well conveyed the excitement of the battle in some scenes. On the other hand, we see a great deal of marching in the film, which is rather repetitious. The film does not really have a story: It is a series of illustrations of the historical event. Because there is no central hero, it is difficult for the audience to find someone with whom to identify. The most remarkable part of this film is a kind of an epilogue. The director had assembled the surviving French, British, and Russian soldiers of the Crimean war, by this time extremely old men, who look into the camera smiling or shy (Figs. 1 and 2). It is a genuinely moving moment; the modern viewer gets a sense of closeness to a historical event that occurred 130 years ago. The film was both a commercial and a critical success and was widely and quickly distributed in the entire country. It was also widely imitated. Next year, on the occasion of the centennial of Napoleon's invasion of Russia, Khanzhonkov joined Pathé to make *1812;* and in 1913 several historical spectacles were made for the occasion of the tricentennial of the Romanov dynasty.

In 1912 the studios of Thiemann and Reinhardt made one of the most unusual films of the prerevolutionary period. *Departure of the Grand Old Man* was one of the first independent works of a director who would go on to make films for another thirty years, Iakov Protazanov. It was about the family life and death of Lev Tolstoy, depicting the relationship of Tolstoy

Figure 2.   Veterans of the Crimean war in 1911: *Defense of Sevastopol* (1911).

Figure 3.   A picture of L. N. Tolstoy in *Departure of the Grand Old Man* (1912).

and his wife entirely from the point of view of Lev Nikolaevich. We see the old sage attempting to help peasants, while his wife, Sofia Andreevna, is counting money and quarreling. His fear of his shrewish wife drives him to the edge of suicide. When the Great Man dies, he meets Jesus in heaven. The film could not be shown in Imperial Russia, because of the protest of the widow, who threatened to sue the filmmakers for libel. The film, however, was distributed elsewhere in Europe, and advertised as having been banned in tsarist Russia. This advertisement greatly contributed to its success. The most remarkable and valuable part of the film is the beginning, where genuine documentary footage of the old writer, made by A. Drankov, was well integrated (Fig. 3). In the rest of the film Tolstoy was played by an actor, V. Shaternikov.[22]

Before 1914 the government paid little attention to the film industry. Most histories of prerevolutionary cinema quote these sentences scribbled by Nicholas II on the margin of a police report in 1913:

I consider that cinematography is an empty matter, which no one needs. It is even something harmful. Only an abnormal person could place this farcical business on the level of art. This is silliness and we should not attribute any significance to such trifles.[23]

It would be hasty to conclude from these sentences that the tsar did not like movies. He was, in fact, a passionate photographer and was fascinated by the new technology. He created the title "court cinematographer" and awarded it to at least five people: B. Matuszewski, K. von Hahn, A. Drankov, V. Bulla, and A. Khanzhonkov. These people and others created a cinematographic record of the Romanov family that was second to none among royalty.[24] But Nicholas was not interested only in seeing himself and his family. Already in 1897 a special showing of films was organized for him in Livadia.[25] During the difficult days of the war, which he spent at the headquarters at Mogilev, he often found relaxation and entertainment in watching movies.[26]

Given the fact that the tsar obviously enjoyed films – and undoubtedly saw many more of them than Vladimir Illich Lenin, whose appreciation of the new medium is well known – how are we to explain his singularly unperceptive comments on the margin of the police report? Perhaps it was partly snobbery. Among many educated and half-educated people at the time it was customary to talk about the new form of entertainment with a condescension bordering on disdain.[27] Some saw in the cinema a danger to a legitimate form of art, the theater; others worried about the possible harmful effect of the cinema as a purveyor of pornography; and most people associated it with the unwashed masses who, in fact, did make up the bulk of the audience at this time.

Partly the tsar's comments can be explained by his failure to appreciate the significance of public opinion in the modern world. Nicholas's attitude was best expressed in his often quoted exchange with the British ambassador, Sir George Buchanan. The ambassador described his last audience with the tsar in January 1917.

"Your majesty, if I may be permitted to say so, has but one safe course open to you – namely, to break down the barrier that separates you from your people and to regain their confidence." Drawing himself up and looking hard at me, the Emperor asked: "Do you mean that I am to regain the confidence of my people, or that they are to regain my confidence?"[28]

Most people in his surroundings showed no better understanding of the nature of modern politics. It was not cinema alone that the government neglected; other methods of shaping public opinion were also ignored. The defenders of the monarchy did not consider it their task to convince people; they naïvely believed that it was the responsibility of the people to obey and follow.

However, the tsar was not entirely blind. He supported Khanzhonkov's ambitious venture, the making of *The Defense of Sevastopol,* and twice personally awarded a medal to the filmmaker.[29] He obviously encouraged filmmakers to mark the tricentennial of the rule of the Romanovs by making celebrity films. But such efforts pale into insignificance when we compare them to what the masters of modern politics, the Bolsheviks, would do within a few years.

Apart from *The Defense of Sevastopol* and a few other patriotic films that received support, the government made no positive intervention in the business of making films, for it did not consider the film industry worthy of support. Intervention in the form of censorship was entirely negative but haphazard. Some quirky prohibitions existed: Films could not depict members of the tsarist family and they could not show executions of crowned persons. The church also intervened: It protested some films made on biblical topics and approved others. But these were minor matters. It was the taste of the audience, or at least what the owners of studios thought the audience wanted, that determined the character of films on the screens. Filmmakers made melodramas and detective films because they were the ones the audiences wanted to see. The censors, correctly, did not perceive in them a threat to the existing political and social order. Sometimes local authorities forbade showing a film, which could then be exhibited in other provinces. In one district of the Don, for example, a local *ataman* (Cossack leader) forbade the showing of films that concluded with the death of the hero.[30]

Censorship made a greater difference in the production of newsreels. Newsreel makers, for example, could not show harsh conditions of labor.[31] Censors forbade the filming of strikes and other antigovernment disturbances in 1905. As a result, the historical record that is available today in Russian film archives is spotty. We have pictures of the tsar meeting foreign dignitaries but almost nothing on the crucial events of the Revolution of 1905.

World War I

The outbreak of the war brought major changes. Although imports were not forbidden, difficulties of transport and export restrictions imposed on the industry in many countries greatly reduced the supply of films. For a while enterprising importers even continued to bring in German films, pretending they were Danish. On the one hand filmmaking suffered because of the shortage of raw film, cameras, and other equipment. From this point on for many decades Russian filmmakers would complain bitterly of technological backwardness and poverty. On the other hand, at this time the Russian market was freed from cheap foreign competition, and this greatly accelerated the growth of the industry. The demand for films was extraordinary. In spite of the difficulties in the daily life, or perhaps because of them, people searched for entertainment, and the cinema was the most popular form. The number of movie tickets sold and the number of theaters in the empire greatly increased during the war. In 1916 alone 150 million movie tickets were sold.[32]

How to satisfy the demand? Most likely a domestic industry would have developed in the long run in any case; the market had been growing fast and Russian factories catering to Russian tastes would have found a niche. But cutting down foreign competition gave the Russian film industry a powerful and immediate boost. Now domestic filmmakers could charge more for their product, and films that no one had wanted to see before the war now produced a profit for their owners. The number of films produced vastly increased: 129 were made in 1913, and 499 in 1916. Even this number does not give an idea of the magnitude of the change. The years preceding the war were a period in which the audiences increasingly demanded feature-length films. While most of the prewar films were shorts, the films made later were full-length. The proportion of foreign films on Russian screens fell to 20 percent.[33]

Only during the last months of the existence of the imperial regime did the collapse of the economy reach such proportions that some movie houses had to be confiscated and turned into field hospitals. Also, the lack of heating material and the shortage of electricity made it necessary to limit the hours of those movie houses still operating. The film industry was beginning to suffer just like the rest of the economy.[34]

The outbreak of the war made a difference in the character of the Russian feature film not as a result of the purposeful intervention of the government, but because the filmmakers shared the momentary enthusiasm for the war, and because they believed that their audiences would pay money to see patriotic films. For a while the studios churned out an extraordinary number of films, sometimes completing them in a couple of days. The writer of the scenario sat in the studio and did his work while the shooting was already progressing. A partial listing of titles will give the idea of their character: *Glory to Us – Death to the Enemy; The Secret of the German Embassy; King, Law, Freedom; Tears of Destroyed Poland; In the Fire of the Storm; Among the Bullets of German Barbarians; Civilized Barbarians; For Tsar and Fatherland; Down with the German Yoke;* and *How a German General Signed a Pact with the Devil.*[35]

As it became clear that the war was not going to be a short and glorious campaign, people lost their taste for patriotic war films.[36] In this respect, as in so many others, developments in Russia closely paralleled developments in the other belligerent countries. What people wanted now, more than ever, was diversion and entertainment. As at other times and places, people were attracted to movies showing beautiful gardens and well-appointed apartments and depicting exaggerated sentiment. There was also a constant demand for stories of crime. As a result, the great bulk of the films exhibited were melodramas of questionable taste and extremely repetitious detective stories. When the great Soviet directors of the next decade, such as Sergei Eisenstein, Vsevolod Pudovkin, Dziga Vertov, would passionately and repeatedly reject "bourgeois" art as distasteful, they had these films in mind. They were determined to make films that were completely different. They were, however, rebelling against a cinema that had served mass audiences, rather than a narrowly bourgeois clientele.

As its output grew, cinema became more heterogeneous than ever before. Some works produced in Russia were on as high an artistic level as anywhere in the world. Russian filmmakers quickly learned from directors such as D. W. Griffith and Cecil B. DeMille, but at the same time, the Russian "psychological" film influenced American directors and audiences. Let us discuss briefly some of the films of the two best prerevolutionary directors, Evgenii Bauer and Iakov Protazanov.

Bauer had been a painter before he became a director. He continued to pay great attention to the physical beauty of the environment he filmed. He preferred to show beautifully appointed apartments and people. His work at the Khanzhonkov studios contributed to the fame of the two greatest stars of the period, Ivan Mozzhukhin and Vera Kholodnaia.[37] Bauer made an astonishing number of films (about eighty between 1913 and 1917) in which he usually served as scriptwriter, set designer, and director. (He died an untimely death in 1917 as a result of an accidental fall.)[38] A film he made in 1914, *Child of the Big City,* is a rather sophisticated psychological drama. The story at first seems conventional: It is about the seduction of a factory girl by two young men-about-town. But the film concludes with a twist. Under the corrupting influence of one of these men, the girl achieves success as a courtesan, while the other young man, who wishes to marry her, is psychologically and financially destroyed trying to win her love. In the last scene we see her leave a fashionable establishment and step over his body in the gutter (Fig. 4).

The Dying Swan, made in 1916, is an even more striking illustration of decadent themes common then in literature. Bauer, as many intellectuals of his and of the previous generations, was preoccupied with "the search for beauty," "the beauty of death and dying," and melancholy. Several Bauer films dealt with the topic of the beauty of death. In one of them, *Life in Death,* the scenario of which was written by V. Ia. Briusov, the artist kills his beloved and embalms her in order to preserve her beauty.[39] *The Dying Swan* impresses the modern viewer with the director's skill and the opulent staging, but it also seems almost a caricature of the decadent theme. The story is melodramatic. We meet an unfortunate, beautiful young woman, who is without speech, but an able dancer. Her lover betrays her, and her death is foretold. A painter wants to paint perfect beauty in attempting to capture death. After many unsuccessful efforts he finds his inspiration in the dance of the dying swan, performed by a young ballerina, our heroine. (The role of the ballerina was played by a star of ballet and film, Vera Koralli.) The painter takes home his model, but his work still does not satisfy him. Finally, having fallen in love with her, he chokes the young woman, who then becomes the perfect model for death. At the end of the film we see the painter for what he is, a crazed man, surrounded by skulls and bones.

Bauer made films almost exclusively on contemporary, psychological themes. His rival Protazanov, who worked for the Ermolev studios, made films in every genre. He, too, did not escape the influence of decadence. He made a film *Nishchaia (Podaite, Khrista radi, ei),* in which the poet – played by the omnipresent Mozzhukhin – kills himself because his beloved was losing her beauty.[40] Another film of his, *Satan Triumphant,* is a confused story about the power of evil. The film teaches us that evil is ever present, even in the most puritanical households; the devil succeeds in seducing even a pastor. Protazanov was particularly adept in making film versions of literary masterpieces. He used Pushkin, Chekhov, and, above all, Tolstoy, as a source for his scenarios. His most successful wartime film was *The Queen of Spades,* a straightforward version of Pushkin's story. Although the film lacked the subtlety of *Father Sergius,* which was made a couple of years later, Protazanov's skill is evident and Mozzhukhin gave one of his best performances here as Herman. Protazanov went on making films until 1945, ultimately producing an oeuvre larger than that of any other director.[41]

Considering the tendentious quality of Soviet films, it is striking that these early Russian films were free from cheap moralizing. Unlike the outcomes depicted in Soviet films, or, for that matter American films of the time, in the works of Bauer and Protazanov evil rarely got punished. There was a great deal of suffering in them, but it was usually the innocent victim who suffered rather than the wicked person. Most Russian films did not conclude happily. The directors, of course, were well aware that in this respect their

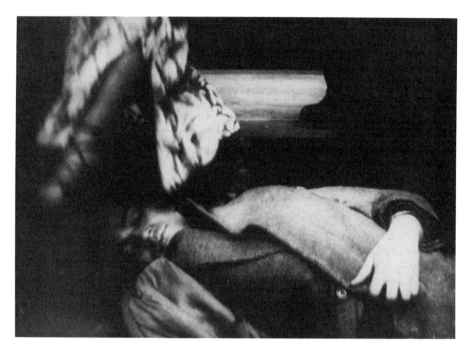

Figure 4.   The courtesan steps over the body of her ex-lover in *Child of the Big City* (1914).

films differed from Western ones. In order to penetrate Western markets, on occasion they prepared two endings for a film, a tragic one for domestic audiences and a happy ending for export. Iurii Tsivian, the Soviet film historian, speculated that the audiences, brought up on nineteenth-century melodrama, expected a tragic conclusion. The psychological interests of Russian directors also demanded a different tempo. Russian films were slower and few of them included chase scenes.[42]

Russian feature films made during World War I were similar in subject matter, though not in spirit, to those made elsewhere. But in the utilization of newsreels as an agent of mass mobilization, Russia was hopelessly backward. This is not at all surprising: Drawing the masses into politics with the aid of yellow journalism and other means of propaganda had progressed much further in Western Europe than in Russia. The West possessed the technological means and the distribution networks that made propaganda powerful. Western politicians also had a clearer understanding of the significance of the stability of the home front at a time of modern war; they went to great lengths in order to influence the thinking of their citizens. The war occasioned a hitherto unparalleled outpouring of propaganda. Most such efforts were simple and crude deceptions aimed at creating hatred of the enemy. The future leaders of the Soviet regime, of course, saw what was happening around them. These wartime lies may have contributed to their profound distrust of the "bourgeois" government, and their deep faith in the power of propaganda.

Immediately after the outbreak of hostilities, private Russian films on the basis of a happy mixture of commercial and patriotic motives put together a number of documentaries supporting the war effort. Films, precisely because they can give the impression of reality, have an extraordinary ability to create false impressions. Filmmakers discovered the opportunities for deception almost simultaneously with the birth of the industry. For example, when a French company was not allowed to film battles of the Russo–Japanese war, it manufactured such scenes in Paris. Audiences could not see through the deception.[43] During the first weeks of World War I such cheating reached extraordinary proportions. The market demanded a quick response, and the managers of studios satisfied the viewers by attaching phony titles to old pictures. Pictures of a German cruiser, for example, taken from old newsreels, were now shown with the intertitle: "German cruiser, sunk by our British Allies." At a moment of patriotic enthusiasm, Russian audiences were plied with such "documentaries." However, the period of enthusiasm was short-lived, and reworked old material could be exhibited only for a limited period. Filmmakers were not in a position to provide interesting footage from the front, because the government instituted a monopoly: Until December 1916, private firms were forbidden to send their cameramen to the front.[44] The monopoly turned out to be an extremely ill-conceived idea. An already-existing committee was charged, oddly enough, with carrying out both philanthropy and propaganda. The committee, which was nominally independent but in fact acted under the supervision of the government, was named after the famous nineteenth-century Russian general, Skobelev.[45] The source of the problem was that the committee was ludicrously ill-equipped. On the entire eastern front only five cameramen were working, two of whom were foreigners. Needless to say, they could hardly be expected to provide the country with a visual record of the war.[46] The ironic consequence of such a situation was that Russian moviegoers had a far better visual sense of the war on the western front than on the eastern; British and French newsreels kept on coming.

The government handling of newsreel making and propaganda during the war was an excellent example of its incompetence. The absurd decision to give a monopoly of newsreel making to an almost nonexistent body was determined by the fearfulness with which the tsar and the tsarist bureaucrats looked upon the whole world of ideas. The monarchists did not possess an ideology with which to mobilize; nor were they aware of the need to have one.

There were, however, some politicians, mostly out of government, who had a good understanding of the role of propaganda in the modern world.

A most remarkable set of suggestions came from V. M. Dement'ev, an extremely reactionary politician. In *Cinematography as Government Regalia*, a pamphlet published in 1915, he argued that cinema should be nationalized and used by the government as a monopoly, similar to the vodka monopoly. (Interestingly, the very same comparison would be used again and again by Bolshevik publicists in the following decades.) The purpose of the monopoly was to exclude foreign influences and to educate the workers and peasants in the spirit of monarchism. Dement'ev was ahead of his time in his awareness of the propaganda potential of cinema, in his willingness to suppress competing views, and in his desire to establish government control over the thinking of citizens. What made his ideas different from contemporary Western European practice was Dement'ev's desire to make propaganda speak with one voice. In Europe, after all, the newspapers and film studios remained in private hands, even if they served the interests of the government. No one had ever proposed such an ambitious program before, but in the future there would be many people, and not only in Russia, who would express similar thoughts. Dement'ev's project shows that Russia in its years of disintegration contained within itself not only the germs of leftist but also of rightist totalitarianism.[47]

Nothing came of Dement'ev's scheme, and he was not even taken seriously: The means and the will to carry out such a program were missing. A somewhat similar project, however, introduced at the end of 1916 by A. Protopopov, the semidemented minister of the interior, had a much better chance of being realized. He set up an interdepartmental commission, headed by the chief censor of newspapers, Udintsev, that had the task of developing legislation concerning the supervision of making and importing films.[48] The minister of education, Count P. Ignat'ev, the most liberal member of the cabinet, opposed the idea and prepared a counterproject, which called for the establishment of a Special Cinema Committee within his own ministry. The task of this committee would have been to encourage the making of films that had educational value. Ignat'ev and other opponents of Protopopov's scheme opposed the idea of government monopoly, pointing out that the example of the Skobelev Committee was hardly encouraging. Soon the February revolution made the issue moot.

That revolution brought neither major changes in the organization of the industry nor in the character of films; cinema did not become a major instrument of mass mobilization in democratic Russia. The government took charge of the Skobelev Committee, but administrative confusion was so great that the committee came under the authority of three different ministries during the next eight months. It finally functioned as a part of the Ministry of War.[49] The committee was led by moderate socialists, and the commentaries that accompanied the newsreels, of course, reflected their point of view; the government saw no need to interfere in the day-to-day affairs of the committee. The issues of the internecine struggles, however, were complex, and newsreels of the time did not turn out to be very effective in supporting one position against another.

In the immediate postrevolutionary days the studios attempted to take advantage of antimonarchist, anti-Romanov sentiment and in a short time issued a number of sensational films of questionable taste, aimed at unmasking the overthrown dynasty. The titles give an idea of the character of these films: *Dark Forces: Grigorii Rasputin and His Associates; In the Clutches of Judas; Governmental Deception; Mysterious Murder in Petrograd on December 16* (referring to the murder of Rasputin); and *The Trading House of Romanov, Rasputin, Sukhomlinov, Miasoedov, Protopopov, and Company.* (V. A. Sukhomlinov had been minister of war and charged with treason; Miasoedov, an officer, was hanged for treason.)[50] Interestingly, some figures of the left protested against the showing of such films, arguing that they demeaned the October Revolution. The government, however, declined to interfere. Soon the attraction of novelty diminished, and these films disappeared from the screens.

Censorship was abolished, but because censors had had only a marginal role, this step made little difference in the film industry. As before, studios made the kind of films which the audiences wanted to see: melodramas and crime stories. In fact, the more unsettled the political situation became, and the more the economy deteriorated, the more people wanted to escape from their daily problems. The appetite for new films remained voracious, and the industry, in spite of increasing difficulties, continued to produce an amazingly large number. Russian studios produced 245 feature films between February and October.[51]

Under the circumstances it is not surprising that few of these possessed artistic value. All the more striking, then, is *Father Sergius*, the crowning achievement of Russian prerevolutionary cinema and one of the finest silent films ever made anywhere. Protazanov's masterpiece was made in the Ermolev studios in 1917. Unlike many of its predecessors, which had merely illustrated literary texts, *Father Sergius* is an independent work of art. At the beginning of the film we see a young, vain officer, Prince Kasatkii, who comes to repudiate the social world as empty and corrupt and seeks salvation in religion (Fig. 5). The rest of the film traces the torments, temptations, and spiritual evolution of a saintly man, who comes inevitably into conflict with the authorities. Protazanov treats the religious issues respectfully and avoids the temptation of turning life at court into a caricature. The success of the film, aside from Protazanov's talent, attention to detail, and devotion to the Tolstoyan message, largely depended on the performance of Mozzhukhin. Tolstoy's character, Father Sergius, emerges in his grand portrayal in all his torment, yet there is none of the excessive theatricality characteristic of early films.

Because of the unsettled circumstances in which it was made, the film was first shown only in the spring of 1918. Thus, ironically, it was under Bolshevik rule that this superb Russian religious film reached its public. It

Отец Сергий

Figure 5. The ballroom scene in *Father Sergius* (1917).

was a bridge between the early days of the Russian film and the golden age
of the Soviet cinema.

The avant-garde Soviet directors aimed to make a complete break with the
past; they disdained the tastes of the petite bourgeoisie and most of them
preferred the fast, "American" style to the slower, Russian psychological
approach. They aimed to and, indeed, did start a new era. At the same time,
however, in the history of art – as in history – there is no such thing as
tabula rasa. Rebels are always influenced by those against whom they are
rebelling. The young filmmakers noisily repudiated features of cinema art
that they associated with their elders but at the same time, mostly unconsciously, quietly appropriated other features. Prerevolutionary cinema is a
worthy part of the history of Russian filmmaking.

Notes

1 Alan Williams, "The Lumière Organization and 'Documentary Realism,'"
in John L. Fell, *Film before Griffith*, University of California Press, Berkeley, 1983,
p. 154.

2 Jay Leyda, *Kino: A History of Russian and Soviet Film,* Collier Books, New York, 1960, pp. 37–8.

3 Robin Buss, *The French through Their Films,* Ungar, New York, 1988, p. 13.

4 S. S. Ginzburg, *Kinematografia dorevoliutsionnoi Rossii,* Iskusstvo, Moscow, 1963, p. 23. Ginzburg's excellent book is the definitive study of prerevolutionary Russian film.

5 M. Gorky, "The Lumière Cinematograph," in Ian Christie and Richard Taylor (eds.), *The Film Factory: Russian and Soviet Cinema Documents, 1896–1939,* Harvard University Press, Cambridge, 1988, pp. 25–6. I have made slight changes in the translation.

6 N. M. Zorkaia, *Na rubezhe stoletii. U istokov massovogo iskusstva v Rossii 1900–1910 godov,* Nauka, Moscow, 1976, pp. 52–3.

7 L. M. Budiak and V. P. Mikhailov, *Adresa Moskovskogo kino,* Moskovskii rabochii, Moscow, 1987, pp. 4–5.

8 Leyda, pp. 23–5; Ginzburg, 37–9; Budiak and Mikhailov, pp. 10–13; Richard Taylor, *The Politics of the Soviet Cinema, 1917–1929,* Cambridge University Press, 1979, pp. 1–5; A. A. Khanzhonkov, *Pervye gody russkoi kinematografii,* Iskusstvo, Moscow, 1937, pp. 11–17.

9 Budiak and Mikhailov, pp. 19–20.

10 Ibid., p. 17.

11 Khanzhonkov, pp. 11–12.

12 Ginzburg, p. 41.

13 Ibid., p. 47.

14 Ibid.

15 Whether *Stenka Razin* was in fact the first Russian feature film is a disputed matter. Drankov had started to make a film about Boris Godunov before *Stenka Razin,* but that film remained unfinished. At the end of 1908 several films were made by directors Drankov, Vasilii Goncharov, and Vladimir Siversen. See Paolo Cherchi et al. (eds.), *Silent Witnesses: Russian Films, 1908–1919,* BFI, 1989, pp. 46–60.

16 I saw this film at the Hungarian Film Archives in Budapest. I also saw the following prerevolutionary films there: *The Defense of Sevastopol, Departure of the Grand Old Man, Child of the Big City, The Dying Swan, Satan Triumphant,* and short animated films made by Starewicz. Starewicz' work was extremely skillful, witty, and original. A short film, *The Revenge of the Cameraman,* in which the roles played by insects, is especially amusing. Starewicz was the first or among the first artists in the world to make animated films. A. A. Khanzhonkov, "Pervyi mul'tiplikator," *Iz istorii kino* 7:200–3.

17 Budiak and Mikhailov, p. 65. The authors took their figures from a contemporary journal, *Sine-fono.*

18 Ibid., p. 53. Of the twenty-two firms that existed in the empire in 1915, eighteen were in Moscow.

19 David Robinson, *The History of World Cinema,* Stein and Day, New York, pp. 50–5.

20 Ginzburg, pp. 155–7.

21 Khanzhonkov, *Pervye gody,* pp. 47–56.

22 M. Arlazorov, *Protazanov,* Iskusstvo, Moscow, 1973, pp. 37–9.

23 A Soviet scholar, A. Zil'bershtein, found this comment of the tsar scribbled on a police report concerning the correspondence of a Duma deputy and an Ameri-

can moviemaking firm. N. A. Lebedev, *Ocherki istorii kino SSSR. Vol. 1: Nemoe kino, 1917–1934*, Iskusstvo, Moscow, 1965, pp. 43–4. Also, Leyda, pp. 68–9.

24 Ginzburg, pp. 33–5.

25 Leyda, p. 22.

26 Ibid., pp. 90–1.

27 On the attitude of intellectuals to film, see Zorkaia, pp. 47–92.

28 George Buchanan, *My Mission to Russia and Other Diplomatic Memories*, Little, Brown and Co., Boston, 1923, 2:46.

29 Khanzhonkov, *Pervye gody*, p. 7.

30 B. S. Likhachev, "Materialy k istorii kino v Rossii, 1914–1918," *Iz istorii kino*, vol. 3, Akademiia Nauk, Moscow, 1960, p. 40.

31 Khanzhonkov, *Pervye gody*, p. 76.

32 Ginzburg, p. 11.

33 Ibid., pp. 156–9. In 1913 eighteen firms made films, in 1916, forty-seven.

34 Ibid., pp. 175–6.

35 Likhachev, pp. 45–6.

36 Ibid., p. 54.

37 On Bauer, see E. Gromov, *L. V. Kuleshov*, Iskusstvo, Moscow, 1984, pp. 21–41. Bauer was Kuleshov's teacher and mentor. Also see, Ginzburg, pp. 310–16.

38 Khanzhonkov, *Pervye gody*, p. 110.

39 Ginzburg, p. 312.

40 Ibid.

41 On Protazanov, see Arlazorov.

42 See the introductory essay by Iurii Tsivian in *Silent Witnesses*, pp. 24–6.

43 Ginzburg, p. 38.

44 Likhachev, p. 47.

45 The committee was formed in November 1904 by the sister of General Skobelev, Princess N. D. Belosel'skaia-Belozerskaia, in order to help the victims of the Russo–Japanese war. At the conclusion of the war the committee aided veterans. In March 1914 this committee established a film section. The committee during the war had not only monopoly of newsreel production on the front but also engaged in the rental of feature films. It was nationalized in March 1918 and became the basis of Bolshevik filmmaking. Khanzhonkov, *Pervye gody*, p. 137.

46 Ginzburg, pp. 180–3.

47 Likhachev, pp. 88–9, and Ginzburg, pp. 170–2.

48 Ginzburg, pp. 172–3.

49 Lebedev, *Ocherki istorii kino v SSSR, Vol. 1: Nemoe kino, 1917–1934*, pp. 43–4, and Ginzburg, p. 333.

50 Ginzburg, pp. 352–3.

51 Ibid., p. 364.

CHAPTER 2

The birth of the Soviet film industry

The Bolsheviks and cinema

The Bolsheviks came to power with a breathtakingly ambitious program. They did not merely want to control the government, right wrongs, and eliminate abuses; they aimed to build a new society on the basis of rational principles, and in the process transform human nature and create the new socialist human being. Bolshevik radicalism was powerful in an age when it seemed that it would be impossible simply to return to prewar normality; the mad destruction of World War I compromised the nineteenth-century social and political order and undermined the faith of people in the smug values of the bourgeoisie. The Bolsheviks were not alone in believing that now a new era would begin.

The Bolsheviks not only took for granted that there could be no return to the old; they also thought that they knew what lay ahead. They profoundly believed that Marxism was a science that enabled them to interpret the past and predict the future. To be sure, the Revolution was victorious in circumstances quite different from what Marx had envisaged, and the problems the new rulers faced in staying in power were ones that the great nineteenth-century thinker had never considered. As the revolutionaries contemplated their victory, the world seemed full of exhilarating promise, but also dangers and disappointments.

The Mensheviks, every bit as good Marxists as the Leninists, argued that Russia was not ready for the socialist revolution. Indeed, the Bolsheviks themselves could not but see that their country was desperately backward, the European proletariat was not carrying out its assigned task, and even the Russian people, the workers and peasants, did not rally around the red flag. What was there to do? For Lenin and his comrades the answer was obvious: While fighting the "counterrevolutionaries" – that is, anyone who opposed them – the revolutionaries had to accomplish what capitalism had failed to do: Raise the cultural level of the people to rival that of Western Europeans.

At the heart of Leninist thought was the notion that the workers – and by extension, the common people – left to their own devices would never understand their self-interest and therefore would not develop revolutionary consciousness. It was the task of the revolutionaries, armed with Marxist knowledge acquired through thorough study, to bring the fruits of their own enlightenment to the people. The Leninists in their long years of underground work regarded themselves as and in fact were primarily propagandists. In this work, as they saw it, they had to confront their enemies, the agents of the bourgeoisie. Bourgeois propaganda was a pack of lies aimed at misleading the common people about the real causes of their misery. During the war the lies of bourgeois, patriotic propagandists became increasingly brazen. For the Bolsheviks now it was clearer than ever: The representatives of every social class used propaganda, the only difference being that the revolutionaries were in the position to tell the truth because history was on their side.

The revolutionary background of the Bolsheviks served them well in the Civil War. They brought to their new and difficult tasks a mode of thinking that was highly relevant and years of hard-won experience as propagandists. Their instinctive understanding of the significance of taking their message to the common people made them pathfinders of modern politics. More than any of their predecessors they experimented with new and sometimes imaginative ways of reaching the common people. They sent thousands of agitators to the villages in order to explain their program to the peasants; they took control of the press and made sure that it was only their interpretation of events that could be publicly circulated; they destroyed autonomous social organizations and established others, firmly under control.[1]

In their large propaganda arsenal, of course, cinema played only a modest role. Yet, there was something particularly attractive to the Bolsheviks in this new medium. If we are to believe A. Lunacharskii, who was not always a reliable witness, Lenin in February 1922 told him: "In our country you have the reputation of being a protector of the arts. So, you must firmly remember, that for us the most important of all arts is the cinema."[2] This purported statement of Lenin has been quoted so often that it has become a cliché. Even if Lenin did not in fact utter these very words, he could have. They were consistent with his thinking and actions. He spoke of cinema as the "most important of all arts" not because he understood the artistic potential of the medium. He obviously did not foresee the emergence within a few years of a group of first-rate artists, such as Kuleshov, Eisenstein, Pudovkin, and Vertov. Given his conservative tastes, it is unlikely that he believed that cinema could ever compete with theater on an artistic plane. He attributed great significance to this medium because he believed in its potential as an educator and propagandist. He was a politician, and as such he was primarily interested in movies as an instrument of political education. But that was not the only kind of education he envisaged. He had great faith in the use of movies in spreading all sorts of information among the people, for example about science and agriculture. Leading Bolsheviks shared the views of their leader and it was this great, perhaps excessive, faith in the power of the cinema as an educator that soon would lead to disappointment and increasingly bitter attacks on filmmakers.

It is easy to see why the Bolsheviks were so attracted to the cinema. First of all, they saw the enormous popularity of the medium, especially among those they wanted to reach. A good propagandist, after all, goes where his audience is. The urban lower classes loved movies and there was reason to think that peasants, given a chance, would respond similarly. Cinema could be used in two different ways: It could itself serve as a vehicle for the revolutionary message and it could be a bait for attracting audiences. People would come to see this new wonder of technology, and before or after the performance they would be willing to listen to a lecture by an agitator.

Here was a medium that the illiterate could understand, and in Soviet Russia only two out of five adults could read in 1920.[3] Since revising intertitles was a relatively easy task, silent films could also be used for reaching a multinational audience. At a time when the Party desperately needed agitators, cinema extended the reach of the few who could be used. The propaganda content of the agitational film was frozen, and therefore the Party leaders in Moscow did not have to fear that agitators who had only a vague understanding of the Party program, to say nothing about Marxism, would inadvertently convey the wrong message.

Beyond the immediate and concrete propaganda use of films were other reasons for the Bolsheviks to be attracted to cinema. They thought of the new medium as the latest achievement of technology, and they passionately identified with modernity and wanted others to identify them with it. They wanted to destroy "Asiatic," backward, peasant Russia, and build in its place an industrial country that would surpass Western Europe in its modernity. What would be more appropriate than to convey the idea of the beginning of a new era with the aid of the most modern medium?

Instinctive propagandists as they were, the Bolsheviks understood that successful propaganda had to be simple and that images could simplify better than words. They knew that these images could affect emotions directly and immediately. A person sitting at home reading a book or pamphlet might get bored, argue in his head with the author, or receive the ideas with skepticism. But during a performance the very fact that people were brought together and formed an audience was an advantage. Being exposed to a propaganda message in a crowd was more effective; the visible positive response of the others reinforced the power of the propagandist.[4]

The Civil War

The Bolsheviks' great interest in films as a vehicle of knowledge and propaganda soon had practical consequences. The young Soviet state invested scarce resources in filmmaking, and the Soviet Union started to make shorts for the popularization of science at a remarkably early date.[5] For the moment, however, little could be done. In January 1918, a movie subsection was organized within the Extramural Education Department of the Commissariat of Education (Narkompros). This department was headed by Lenin's wife, N. Krupskaia. It was revealing that the Bolsheviks chose to place film matters at this particular spot within their bureaucratic hierarchy. The task of Krupskaia's department was to carry out propaganda among adults, and this propaganda was regarded as a part of education.

At this point it had not yet occurred to anyone that this organization might take charge of the film industry. The task of the subsection was simply to encourage the use of film in political education. At the time of its establishment, the subsection had in its possession a single projector, a few reels of educational films, and newsreels from the days of the Provisional Government. On occasion agitators used these materials to accompany their lectures.[6]

The attitude of the Bolshevik leadership to the question of freedom within the movie industry was the same as it was in publishing. On the one hand, there was to be only one interpretation of politics tolerated; on the other, at this time at least, the Bolshevik leaders did not perceive in cultural matters or in various forms of entertainment a source of danger.[7] The leaders drew a sharp line between newsreels, which dealt with political material, and other films, which had the purpose of entertainment. The Bolsheviks were determined not to allow the making and showing of newsreels that were hostile to them. The Skobelev Committee, for self-protection, once again detached itself from the government and formed a "cooperative." As a private organization it continued to make newsreels. These newsreels expressed Socialist Revolutionary and Menshevik points of view, and so the first newsreels made in Soviet Russia were anti-Bolshevik in spirit. When the government suppressed hostile newspapers following the dispersal of the Constituent Assembly, it also closed down the Skobelev Committee and confiscated its property.[8]

In May 1918, the Soviet government established a national film organization and named D. I. Leshchenko its director. This all-Russian film committee incorporated the film sections of both the Moscow Soviet and the Extramural Department of Narkompros. The new organization came under the nominal authority of Narkompros, but in fact it operated autonomously.[9]

Soviet historians at times describe 1918 and 1919 as a transitional period, in which the old gradually died and the new came into being. In terms of film history the transition meant the collapse of private filmmaking, and the first, tentative efforts to take charge of the film industry by the Soviet state. The regime did not hesitate to interfere in the industry. Already in December 1917 and January 1918, some local soviets confiscated cinemas for their own use. When the owners appealed to the government for protection, the Commissariat for Internal Affairs sustained the soviets.[10] In April 1918, the government introduced monopoly over foreign trade, which, of course, greatly affected the film industry. Because the government did not easily give permission to buy the necessary material and equipment abroad, individual entrepreneurs acquired them by circumventing the law. The foreign trade monopoly also affected the distribution of foreign films in Soviet Russia. Gradually, in the course of the Civil War the importation of films ceased.

A regulation issued by the Moscow Soviet on March 4, 1918, promised that film factories would not be nationalized; they would, however, like other factories, be subjected to workers' control. No one knew at the time what exactly workers' control meant. The same decree demanded from the owners of studios an inventory of their property and raw materials and forbade the selling of studios.[11]

It is evident from the decree of the Moscow Soviet that the new authorities were above all concerned with the functioning of the economy. At a time of great unemployment they feared the closing down of studios. The government did not want to nationalize the industry because it did not want to assume responsibility for running it under very difficult circumstances. Lunacharskii, in an article in *Vecherniaia zhizn'* in April 1918, attempted to allay the fear of studio owners concerning nationalization. He even promised that Russian factories would start producing raw film, thereby alleviating the crippling shortage.[12]

Censorship was by no means heavy-handed. The authorities only wanted to prevent the showings of explicitly anti-Soviet films and those that the puritanical regime considered pornographic. Both the film committee and the soviets had the right to suppress films.[13] Naturally, the decisions of the Moscow Soviet were particularly important, not only because it controlled the capital, the largest market, but also because these decisions served as examples for the rest of the country. Both the Moscow Soviet and the film committee periodically issued bulletins of proscribed films. In August 1918, the film committee, for example, forbade the showing of these films: *The Lady of the Summer Resort Fears Not Even the Devil* and *The Knights of the Dark Nights* for "pornography," and *Liberation of the Serfs* and *Flags Wave Triumphantly* for "distorting history."[14]

It is amazing that under the extraordinarily difficult conditions prevailing in 1918, the industry continued to function. In that year, in territories under Bolshevik control almost 150 films were made.[15] Although one assumes that many of these must have been shorts, a number of ambitious projects were also carried out. Remarkably, films made in 1918, at a time when the country was experiencing a serious crisis, did not at all reflect the environment. The directors did not know how to deal with the Revolution, and in any case, had little interest in it. Studios, of course, worked on capitalist principles, and made the films that the audiences wanted. At a time of privation, moviegoers above all wanted entertainment. Consequently the studios continued to produce detective films, romances, and many dramatizations of classics. For example in 1918 three dramatizations of the works of L. Tolstoy appeared: *Father Sergius, The Living Corpse,* and *The Power of Darkness.*[16]

Important figures of the future golden age of the Soviet silent era, such as Protazanov, Turkin, Razumnyi, Zheliabuzhskii, and Perestiani, worked in private studios in 1918. The seventeen-year-old Lev Kuleshov, the most underappreciated genius of Soviet film, made his first work, *Engineer Prite's Project,* at this time.[17] The ubiquitous Maiakovskii was extremely active in movies: He wrote scenarios and acted in several films. His best known work was in *The Young Lady and the Hooligan,* a scenario he wrote on the basis of an Italian story. Both the scenario and Maiakovskii's acting were undistinguished. The undoubted talent of the poet lay elsewhere.[18]

Private film production gradually came to a halt. The shortage of all necessary materials for filmmaking, the closing down of theaters for lack of fuel and electricity, and the general uncertainty that prevailed finally made moviemaking impossible. The major studios – Khanzhonkov, Kharitonov, and Ermolev – left Moscow for the South. Actors, directors, and technical personnel first moved to the Crimea, Odessa, and the Caucasus and lived for a while under White rule. The Soviet film industry lost its most prominent people. I. Mozzhukhin and V. Kholodnaia went South (Kholodnaia died shortly after). Among the best known directors, Bauer was dead, and Protazanov and Chardynin worked in the Crimea. Perhaps more significant, the Bolsheviks lost not only talented and experienced people, but also irreplaceable raw material. The directors took everything movable, including raw film and cameras, with them when they left, and it would take a long time for the young Soviet film industry to make up for the loss.

Later, the great majority of these people followed the defeated White armies and ended up in various European capitals, especially in Paris and Berlin.[19] In the age of the silent film talent was an easily exportable commodity, and proportionately more filmmakers decided to emigrate than did other artists. The artists assumed that they would be able to continue their work in Western Europe and in the United States and that there would be demand for their skills. Indeed, many of them succeeded: Mozzhukhin, for example, remained a star, the wonderfully individual artist W. Starewicz, the animator, continued his work in Paris, and Protazanov made some successful films. But others, such as A. Drankov, the maker of one of the first Russian feature films, and as much a businessman as an artist, never made it in Hollywood, and ended up destitute.

Because filmmaking in Soviet controlled territories almost ground to a halt, the nationalization of the industry came as an anticlimax: On August 27, 1919, Sovnarkom decided to eliminate private studios and film distribution networks. The decree had little practical significance.[20] The state took over empty buildings, stripped of machinery, raw materials, and instruments. In order to take charge of the film industry, the government upgraded the All-Russian Film Committee to All-Russian Photo-Movie Department (VFKO) of Narkompros. Naturally, a simple administrative reorganization could accomplish little.

The beginnings of Soviet filmmaking were slow indeed. The first products were, naturally, newsreels, made with the confiscated equipment of the dispersed Skobelev Committee. The technical quality of the work was poor. Even worse from the point of view of Party activists, so little raw film was available that newsreels had to be made in very small numbers, often no more than five to ten copies for the entire country.[21] Because the Russians had little tradition in making newsreels or documentaries, young people with very little background could quickly receive responsible assignments. Among the talented young artists were E. Tisse and D. Vertov, who did not achieve spectacular results during the Civil War but did gain valuable experience.

Although newsreels were technically poor and in short supply besides, they did have some propaganda significance. The agitational trains and ships carried them into the countryside and the Russian peasants for the first time were able to see their leaders; they also saw film reports on demonstrations in the cities and the accomplishments of the Red Army. These agitational trains and ships were a remarkable Bolshevik innovation. The new rulers faced the seemingly insurmountable problem that they had no organization in the countryside. They decided to bring the government, and also their political message, to the peasants by sending out a group of people who acted both as representatives of various governmental departments and also as agitators. The trains and ships possessed their own printing machines and also equipment for showing films. Party activists who traveled on *agit*-trains reported very favorably on the effect of the newsreels.[22] It is likely that at the end of the Civil War the number of peasants who recognized Lenin and Trotsky exceeded the number of those who had ever seen a picture of the deposed tsar.

Soviet newsreels were not particularly innovative. At this time, however, the infant Soviet film industry did make a type of film that had never existed before, the so-called *agitki*. These were short films, from five to thirty minutes long, with extremely didactic content, aimed at an uneducated audience. In order to convey the flavor of the first Soviet films it is necessary to describe the content of at least some of them in detail. The simplest of the *agitki* had no plot at all, but were called living posters. One, for example, was called *Proletarians of the World Unite!* (1919).[23] The opening titles told the audience about the French Revolution. These were followed by two or three animated scenes from that great event. A long intertitle then explained: "The French Revolution was defeated, because it had no leader and it had no concrete program around which the workers could have united. Only 50 years after the French Revolution did Karl Marx advance the slogan: 'Proletarians of the world, unite!' " Next the audience saw an actor playing the role of Marx, sitting in front of a desk, writing: "Proletarians of the world unite!" There were two or three more pictures showing the suffering of revolutionaries in Siberian exile. The film ended with this text on the screen: "Eternal glory to those who with their blood painted our flags red." Another *agitka* simply exhorted the audience to give warm clothes to the suffering soldiers of the Red Army. It consisted of nothing more than a couple of pictures of ill-dressed fighting men.

Most of these short films, however, did have simple stories. Some were humorous sketches, such as *The Frightened Burzhui* (1919).[24] (Burzhui is a Russian corruption of bourgeois.) As a result of the Revolution a capitalist lost his appetite and became an insomniac. Then he is ordered to appear in a work battalion. Honest labor cures him immediately. Others were melodramas. In *For the Red Flag* (1919), a father joins the Red Army in order to take the place of his not satisfactorily class-conscious son. The son, recognizing the error of his ways, goes to search for the father. He finds him at the most critical moment and saves the wounded old man. Then the son himself is wounded, but exhibits great courage and saves the flag from the enemy.[25] In the film *Father and Son* (1919)[26] it is the son who is the convinced communist. As a Red Army soldier, he is captured by the enemy. The guard turns out to be none other than his father, who had been drafted by the Whites. The son explains to his father the superiority of the Soviet system and then the newly enlightened father frees all the prisoners and escapes with them in order to join the Red Army. *Peace to the Shack and War to the Palace* (1919)[27] is also about joining the Red Army. A peasant lad comes home from the war to poverty and misery. He sees that the landlord still lives well. This contrast between poor and rich makes him understand the correctness of the Bolshevik position.

The Bolshevik notion of propaganda was broader than "political education." Even in these very hard times some of the *agitki* aimed at educating the people. A particularly naïve *agitka* was *Children – The Flower of Life* (1919),[28] written, directed, and photographed by Zheliabuzhskii. We meet two families. One is the family of the worker Kuleshov, who does not observe the rules of hygiene, and therefore his young child gets sick. (One assumes that the name is meant to be a joke on the young director.) Instead of taking him to a doctor, his parents take him to a sorcerer. The child dies, and the unhappy couple breaks up. By contrast, the other family, which observes the advice of the doctor and appreciates the importance of cleanliness, have a healthy child and the family lives happily ever after. Other *agitki* were devoted to the description of the struggle against diseases such as cholera and tuberculosis.[29]

Between the summer of 1918 and the end of the Civil War Soviet studios

made approximately sixty *agitki*.[30] This is an impressive number if we remember that work had to be carried out under the most difficult circumstances: The studios not only lacked raw material, but also trained people
of all kinds, and there were never enough good scenarios. The Film Committee and later VFKO experimented with competitions for scripts, but these
were not very successful. Such important luminaries of Soviet intellectual
life as Lunacharskii, Aleksandr Serafimovich (the future author of *The Iron
Flood*), and Maiakovskii tried their hands at working for movies, but they
had little experience and understanding of the special needs of the cinema.
Most often the director worked without a script and improvised. The well-
known directors and actors stayed with the private studios as long as possible, and few of them wanted to identify themselves with the Soviet regime.
Communists, on the other hand, knew little about filmmaking. The directors who did work in the nationalized sector did what they were told, but
their work showed that their heart was not in it. Actors had so little experience in playing workers and knew so little about working-class life, that
they struck unnatural poses, which often caused hilarity in a working-class
audience.[31]

Yet, in spite of their primitive execution and simple message, the *agitki*
played an important propaganda role. From the reports of agitators it is
evident that audiences enjoyed the films; the agitators constantly asked for
more. The *agitki* could not by themselves do much for communist education. What they could do was to attract an audience. Then, if an agitator
was able enough, he could take over and explain to his listeners the message
of the film, connecting that message with the policies of the Soviet regime.
After the Civil War the *agitki* gradually disappeared. But at the time of
World War II, when the regime once again felt itself to be endangered, they
were revived with success.

The revival of the film industry

Both World War I and the Civil War devastated Russia. It was evident to
contemporaries, and is indisputable in retrospect, that extraordinary efforts
had to be made to rebuild the national economy. The Party could not avoid
giving concessions to the peasants and to the bourgeoisie in order to rekin-
dle private initiative, however intolerable private enterprise was to the Bolsheviks on ideological grounds. But they hated to watch their enemies grow
stronger.

Party activists believed that at a time when they had to give their enemies
free rein, it was especially important to strengthen propaganda work, but
they failed in this effort. Propaganda required money, and an essential feature of the new economic order was the return to financial orthodoxy, which
called for conservation of resoures. The Party had to cut back on propaganda work when it was most needed. The film industry was not alone in

suffering reduced support: The literacy drive, which was an essential element in the propaganda drive of the Bolsheviks during the Civil War, was
cut back; the circulation of newspapers was greatly reduced; and the agitation network was, at least temporarily, weakened. But the Party's dilemma
was particularly evident in the case of the film industry. The regime had to
tolerate questionable activities in the hope of making a profit. Soviet history
had many moments of great danger, and the early period of the New Economic Policy (NEP) was one of them.

The Civil War destroyed the film industry: Studios were idle, the distribution system stopped functioning, and the film theaters shut down. Moscow, for example, had 143 theaters operating before World War I, but in
the fall of 1921 not a single one remained in operation.[32] During the worst
period in 1921 film showings in Soviet Russia were limited to the exhibition
of *agitki* at agitational stations (*agitpunkty*) and infrequent and haphazard
showings of *agitki* at public places in the open air, such as railroad stations.
Some of the agitational trains continued to operate, carrying with them few
outdated *agitki* and showing them often in remote villages with the aid of
old projectors, which frequently broke down.

Commercial theaters could not reopen because the supply of electricity.
was unreliable and the halls could not be heated. The cinemas were taken
over by workers' clubs and by other organizations and used as offices. The
British journalist, Huntly Carter, who visited Soviet Russia several times in
the 1920s, described Moscow movie houses as poorly lit, lice infested, and
equipped with wooden benches in place of the previously comfortable seats.
He found the situation in Moscow far worse than in Petrograd where the
damage was more quickly repaired.[33] It testifies to the power of the cinema
that in these miserable times the Russian audiences had a pent-up hunger
for it. In late 1921 the first commercial movie house opened in Moscow on
the Tverskaia. It operated from eight o'clock in the morning until midnight
and exhibited prerevolutionary and foreign films, the first one being, *Quiet,
My Sorrow, Quiet*. The performances lasted only for an hour and yet people
waited in long lines for admission.[34]

Both private entrepreneurs and Soviet organizations quickly realized that
there was money to be made. Especially in Moscow and in Petrograd, but
also in the provincial cities, the revival of film life in the course of 1922 was
astoundingly rapid. In early 1923 in Moscow there were ninety functioning
movie theaters, and in Petrograd forty-nine. In Moscow thirty-five were pri-
vately owned, forty-five were leased from the government by private entrepreneurs, and the others were operated by government organizations.[35]

Cinema managers did not always acquire their films legally. In 1919 the
Soviet state nationalized and attempted to confiscate all of the films in the
country. The government had no means to enforce this measure, and like so
many other acts of this time, it remained an empty gesture. In fact, the new
economic policies superseded the nationalization edict. As a result, film after

film reappeared rather mysteriously. In the early days, the theaters' program was made up almost exclusively of prerevolutionary films and foreign imports. It is striking how quickly and how many foreign films came to Soviet Russia. Distributors had a large number of foreign films that had been shown profitably in Western Europe and in the United States and had never appeared on the Russian screens. It was a situation in which many people could quickly make a lot of money.

Soviet film historians like to stress how bad these films were, and they quote with relish from contemporary newspapers. *Daughter of the Night* was advertised in this way: "Grand American picture. Full of head-turning tricks." The advertisement for *Cagliostro* said: "Rendition of the life of the world's greatest adventurer. Based on historical facts as collected by Robert Liebman. Colossal mass scenes. Accurate description of the style of the epoch. This film was shot in the royal palace of Schoenbrunn. The furniture, carriages and other props were taken from the collection of the Austrian Imperial Family." Other titles were *Skull of the Pharaoh's Daughter* and *King of the Beasts*.[36] There is no question that the Russians were able to see and were attracted to all sorts of cheap second-rate foreign films. But it would be wrong to conclude that only such films appeared. Russian audiences could also see the best films produced abroad: *Dr. Mabuse, the Gambler* and *The Cabinet of Doctor Caligari* came to Russia soon after they were made.[37]

Why did the Party allow the importation of foreign films and the showing of prerevolutionary ones, which brought no ideological benefits? The answer is clear. The leaders deeply desired the revival of Russian filmmaking, but did not want to spend the necessary money. The regime hoped to benefit from the people's addiction to poor films, but this was a risky game. Non-Soviet films, from the point of view of the Bolsheviks, almost invariably included at least a bit of ideological poison, and these movies influenced people's tastes. Indeed, all through the 1920s, even when Soviet industry was able to produce first-rate films, Russian audiences remained enamored of foreign products.

The Bolsheviks were overly ambitious, and in the process they almost killed the goose that was to lay the golden egg. The government squeezed the industry too hard. In 1922 and in 1923, it set such high rental charges on films, and such high taxes on tickets, that moviegoing became almost impossibly expensive. At a time of great economic hardship, people who loved movies could not afford to go to see them. As a result, attendance started to fall, and theaters that had just opened were forced to close. The number of functioning movie theaters diminished all over the country, and many cities were left without movie houses altogether. Despite the high taxes, government revenues started to fall.[38]

Huntly Carter, who examined the movie situation at the time, wrote:

The managers all had the same story, they were glad to be in business again. But what a time they were having. No money for new films. Not allowed to show what they liked. Rents and taxes running into milliards of rubles. Their houses were falling to pieces, with no hope of repairing them at present. Prices? Well, they tried to make ends meet by putting up prices. At the Palace seats cost two million, 800,000 and 600,000 rubles. At the Art Kino 1,100,000, 700,000 and 600,000 rubles. At the Mirror 2,000,000, 900,000, 700,000 rubles. One film a night was shown, a serial, or four act drama, comedy or farce. There were four houses of one hour each. 5 p.m., 7:30, 9:00 and 10:00. And notwithstanding the prices, the brevity, the proletarians rolled up.[39]

Bolshevik thinking on movies can be clearly seen in a letter which Lenin wrote in early 1922 to E. A. Litkens, Lunacharskii's deputy in Narkompros.[40]

Narkompros should organize supervision of all (movie) exhibitions and systemize the matter. All films exhibited in the RSFSR should be registered and numbered by Narkompros.

All movie exhibition programs should include a certain percentage [of these]: (a) films of amusement, especially for advertisement (attracting an audience) and for profit (naturally without obscenity and counterrevolution); and (b) under the heading "from the lives of all people," pictures of especially propaganda character, such as the colonial policy of England in India, the work of the League of Nations, starving in Berlin, etc., etc.

It is necessary to show not only films, but also photographs which are interesting from the point of view of propaganda, with appropriate subtitles. Movie houses which are in private hands should give sufficient income to the government in forms of rent. We must give the right to entrepreneurs to increase the number of films and to bring in new films, but always under the condition of maintaining the proper proportion of films of amusement and films of propaganda character, under the heading "from the lives of all people." This should be done in such a way that the entrepreneurs would be interested in the creation and making of new films. They should have, within these limitations, broad initiative.

Films of propaganda character should be given for evaluation to old Marxist and literary people in order to make sure that such unfortunate events in which propaganda has backfired are not repeated.

Special attention should be given to the organization of movies in villages and in the East where this matter is a novelty, and therefore our propaganda should be especially successful.

Lenin's letter was deeply revealing of the mentality of the great leader. The letter shows first of all his remarkable practicality. He was interested in making money. He wanted to allow managers to show the films of Charlie Chaplin, Mary Pickford, Douglas Fairbanks, and other Western stars, in order to enrich themselves and in the process enrich the government. He saw that it was necessary to attract audiences to the movies not only in order to make money, but also to show them propaganda. He never believed that the people, after having listened to several points of view, would be able to decide correctly for themselves: Experienced people, such as old Marxists, had to decide for them. Censorship and propaganda were related, and Lenin attributed the greatest significance to them. It is interesting that when Lenin looked for examples of propaganda, he chose only foreign ones. In January 1922, at the height of famine, Lenin wanted to show the Russians that people were starving – in Berlin.

As on so many other occasions, most of the ideas of Lenin's fertile mind remained unrealized. The government did not have the means to set up a network in the villages or in the East. Government control was so weak that it could not compel the showing of propaganda films. Indeed, at that time such films hardly existed. The government could not even carry out successful censorship. Weakness and confusion protected liberty. When the local organs prohibited the exhibition of one film or another, the private distributor simply sent the film to some faraway place where it was likely to escape the attention of the authorities. In 1922, for example, a certain private distributor, Poliakov, attempted to show a film in Ekaterinburg entitled *The Fall of Nations*. When the local Narkompros office forbade the showing, he exhibited the film in outlying districts of Siberia.[41]

Naturally, the Bolshevik leaders understood that things were not going well on the cinema front. Because they had neither the money nor the personnel to bring about real change, they were reduced to tinkering with the existing system. In the early 1920s, there were constant discussions on the proper organization of film matters, and the regime changed the institutions in a dizzying fashion.

The Soviet movie industry and distribution system came under the authority of Narkompros. Following the nationalization of the industry in August 1919, the government set up the VFKO within Narkompros, responsible for the production and distribution of films, and a year or two later, similar departments were established within the commissariats of enlightenment of the future constituent republics of the Soviet Union.[42] Although the VFKO accomplished little, it would be unfair to blame it. The studios lay in ruins and there was no film stock.

The situation changed with the introduction of NEP. Now that there was money to be made, private, governmental, and semigovernmental agencies scrambled for the business. To the great dismay of Soviet leaders, it even happened that Russian film organizations competed against one another in getting rights for showing foreign films, and thereby bid up the cost. For a while Soviet Russia operated almost like a capitalist country.

In 1921 and 1922, P. Voevodin, head of VFKO, constantly petitioned the Sovnarkom for money. The filmmakers especially desired convertible currency in order to buy film and equipment from abroad. Without such purchases, the studios could not operate. The Sovnarkom refused to make the investment, still hoping that the film industry itself would generate the necessary capital. How this should be accomplished was discussed by a committee headed by Voevodin. On the basis of the committee's report, in December 1922, the Sovnarkom abolished the VFKO and in its place set up the Central State Photographic and Cinematic Enterprise (Goskino).[43] Goskino, like its predecessor, was located within the Narkompros. Its first director was L. A. Liberman, who had considerable independence from Narkompros supervision.

The work began under inauspicious circumstances.[44] Goskino's tasks included the importation of films, the organization of the revival of film studios, and the enforcement of the monopoly of rentals. Once again, the imposition of central control was difficult – indeed, impossible. In the previous months a number of film organizations had come into being, many with strong protectors in the Soviet hierarchy. Goskino had no authority outside of the Russian republic, while the revival of filmmaking in Georgia and especially in the Ukraine was faster than within Russia itself. The strongest film organization in Russia was Sevzapkino, which had the best studio and also the largest distribution network. Although Sevzapkino was based in Petrograd, its Moscow office controlled a larger network of theaters than Goskino itself. The educational department of the Moscow Soviet also had a film office, Kino-Moskva, which wanted to defend its autonomy. The Petrograd Soviet protected Kino-sever. The Red Army's political education department, PUR, supported the film organization, Krasnaia zvezda, and the trade unions maintained Proletkino primarily to supply workers' clubs.[45]

In addition, the NEP allowed the formation of the private joint-stock companies. Of these, the two most important were Rus and Mezhrabpom, which were later to form Mezhrabpom–Rus. Mezhrabpom was a remarkable organization, something that could exist only in the confused, ambiguous world of the early 1920s. Mezhrabpom was an acronym for International Workers' Aid, an organization that was established in Germany in 1921 by pro-Soviet and pro-Communist elements. Its original task was to help Soviet Russia fight famine. Once the initial emergency passed, the accumulated capital was used to help the nascent Soviet film industry.[46] This capital was an essential source for buying the necessary equipment and film abroad. Although the Mezhrabpom was reorganized and its German ties became less significant, all through the 1920s it remained a useful link between Russia and Western Europe. Mezhrabpom–Rus made a great contribution to making the work of Soviet directors known first in Germany, and later in the rest of Europe. The studios of Mezhrabpom–Rus also turned out some of the most interesting films produced in the Soviet Union. After 1923, all private film companies with the exception of Mezhrabpom–Rus were closed down.

Because Goskino had a monopoly on film rentals, other film organizations had to enter into contractual relations with it. This setup was such that conflicts could hardly be avoided. Goskino demanded 50 percent of the profits. Its leaders realized that it was essential to revive Russian filmmaking, and since the government was unwilling to contribute, it had to squeeze rental organizations. On the other hand, the army, the trade unions, and even Sevzapkino, were strong enough to resist. They each wanted more money. Goskino, in order to lessen the competition, wanted to close the Moscow offices of Sevzapkino; however, the government refused, and Sevzapkino remained a thorn in the side of the Goskino.[47]

Goskino was unable to generate the capital, and Sovnarkom repeatedly refused to help, so the film industry could be revived only with private capital, domestic or foreign.[48] At the recommendation of the government, Goskino entered into negotiations with a number of firms. Discussions with the American Fox and German Springer were fruitless. Negotiations went furthest with the domestic private company of L. Azarkh, and an agreement was even signed, with the approval of Narkompros. In this contract, Azarkh promised

a. to put up the capital of half a million gold rubles;
b. to give Goskino 53 percent of the shares;
c. to produce a yearly profit of fifty thousand gold rubles; and
d. to make at least twenty feature films yearly.

In exchange, Goskino agreed to allow Azarkh to use the only functioning Moscow studio, the ex-Khanzhonkov studio. Perhaps more important, by implication, Azarkh was able to take advantage of the monopoly enjoyed by Goskino. The agreement, however, remained only on paper. The government soon accused Azarkh of not observing its share of the bargain, and repudiated the deal. From the available sources, it is impossible to establish whether Azarkh was in fact at fault, but it is clear that the government officials had second thoughts.[49] Giving up the Khanzhonkov studios meant that the government, at least for the time being, could not even hope to make the kind of films it wanted to have. The Communist leaders feared losing control over the final product. Filmmaking was obviously a sensitive matter; the role and function of private capital was more complicated than in the case of other industries.

Within a few months of its establishment, it was already evident that Goskino could cope with its problems no better that its predecessor. In April 1923, Lieberman was replaced by E. S. Kadomtsev as head of the organization, but a mere change in leadership did not make much difference.

The leaders of Goskino considered the very high taxes on cinema one of the greatest problems of the industry. They believed that without alleviating that burden, filmmaking could not revive, and therefore turned to Sovnarkom for help. Evidently the government had little confidence in the judgment of the Goskino leaders, because instead of granting this reasonable request, it set up a commission to study the problem.[50]

In the next two years, two major commissions dealt with the problems of the industry; these problems were discussed at the Thirteenth Party Congress in May 1924; and Sovnarkom also devoted considerable time and attention to them. The first commission, which worked from April to September 1923, was headed by N. N. Adveev and representatives from Narkomfin, Narkompros, and Rabkrin participated in it. These people acknowledged that the situation was deteriorating. They noted that aside from the government, local organizations, constantly in need of money, levied taxes on cinema tickets. The Moscow Soviet, for example, levied a 30 percent tax; in the Ukraine, theatergoers paid republic and local taxes and 10 percent extra to allow Red Army soldiers to go for free.[51] Adveev's commission recommended lowering taxes.

In September 1923, Sovnarkom appointed another commission; this one headed by A. V. Mantsev. Reporting to Sovnarkom in November, it went much further than the previous group, recommending lowering ticket prices, eliminating taxes, and establishing a new organization to start work with a substantial government loan. It took, however, another year and long discussions before the recommendations were realized.

Sovnarkom set up Sovkino in December 1924, and the new organization began its work in January 1925. It was a joint-stock company in which all shares were held by governmental organizations: VSNKh got 15 percent, the Narkompros, Petrograd, and Moscow soviets together got 55 percent, and Narkomvneshtorg got 30 percent.[52] That the largest single bloc of shares was given to the foreign trade agency, shows the decisive importance of imports at the time. The establishment of Sovkino did not mean the immediate dissolution of Goskino. That organization survived as a production unit until 1926. The new arrangements finally brought stability into the movie industry, which was a precondition for later accomplishments.

The constant reorganizations betrayed an impatience and concern on the part of Bolshevik leaders about how the cinema was fulfilling its educational and propaganda roles. The leaders had reasons for dissatisfaction.

The first Soviet feature films

Between the introduction of NEP and the establishment of Sovkino, the most valuable products in respect to political education, and also perhaps artistically, were newsreels, and the regime concentrated its scarce resources on their production. Lebedev, a young Communist activist in the film industry, reported that in 1921 and early 1922 it was the newsreel section of the Moscow studios alone that showed any signs of life. In this section worked Edward Tisse (the future collaborator of Eisenstein), G. Giber, A. Levitskii, and, most important, Vertov.[53] Vertov had been making newsreels since the early days of the Civil War, but the first in his famous *Film-Truth* series appeared only in May 1922. Working conditions were extremely difficult. Cameramen had to work with outdated and inadequate equipment. Worst of all, in the middle of the winter, they had to do their cutting and editing in totally unheated studios, working in their overcoats.[54]

According to Lebedev, the artistic quality of the early newsreels was low. Action was photographed from a single point of view. The cameramen did not know how to find significant detail that would have emotionally involved the viewer. The newsreels constantly compared the "terrible past" with the "hopeful present." Lebedev observed that this particular characteristic of early propaganda newsreels came to be an important influence on Vertov's and Eisenstein's ideas about clashing montage, a montage of opposites.[55]

Aside from the newsreels, the studios made *agitki*. In artistic conception, length, and style, these were closely related to the newsreels. The main difference was that in the *agitki,* actors (and not always professional ones) assumed roles. In 1921, which was the worst year, only four *agitki* were made in Moscow, two in Petrograd, three in the Ukraine, and one in Georgia.[56]

The most ambitious of these films was the *The Sickle and the Hammer,* directed by Vladimir Gardin, a prominent director from the prerevolutionary era, and photographed by Tisse.[57] V. Pudovkin played the main role. The film's misfortune was that its main agitational point became irrelevant before it was first shown. The film attempted to justify forced collection of food from the peasants by showing starving workers and by showing how peasants and workers fought together against the oppressors. The NEP, however, repudiated forced collection of food, so the film was never widely distributed. In one respect the film contained a characteristic of many later products: The wicked *kulak* wanted to take advantage of the virtuous wife of a worker. As in other Soviet films of the future, the enemy was more highly sexed.[58]

A shorter, but more successful work was *Hunger . . . Hunger . . . Hunger,* also directed by Gardin and shot by Tisse.[59] The film was largely assembled from documentary footage taken by Tisse in the famine-devastated Volga region. It was widely used abroad for soliciting famine relief. The appeal of the film comes from the inherent strength of the material. In the most easily measurable terms of money collected, this film was surely one of the most effective propaganda works ever made for foreign consumption.

The first film that can be more or less described as entertainment was *The Miracle Worker,* made in 1922 by Aleksandr Panteleev. This was a historical antireligious film that contained some of the features of the *agitki.* Watching Panteleev's work today we get a good idea of the nature of the antireligious compaign of the early 1920s. That campaign was determined and rather naïve in its effort to unmask the church, but it was not yet vicious. At the time of Nicholas I a young serf, a troublemaker, is given by his master to serve in the army. The young soldier steals a diamond from an icon and then pretends that the Virgin Mary gave it to him. The authorities are put in a quandary when the news of the "miracle" spreads all over St. Petersburg. Should they undermine the faith of the simpleminded by revealing that the "miracle" was phony, or should they let the scoundrel get away with his crime? The film has a happy ending: Boy gets girl, and the sly peasant lad has outwitted the authorities. The story is presented in an overly theatrical fashion and there is little pretense of portraying reality, but the film is not without simple charm. The life of the soldiers and even of the serfs is not depicted in a somber fashion.

A film similar in its level of sophistication and propaganda is *Brigade Commander Ivanov*, made in Moscow in 1923.[60] The movie tells the story of a Communist officer, Ivanov, falling in love with the daughter of a priest, and after some difficulties, persuading her to dispense with a church wedding. The criticism of the church is not particularly harsh: The priest is an obsequious fool, but not really wicked. The Communist is not really a positive hero: He boasts, falls in love, and enjoys luxury. The film is silly and primitively made; the heroine flutters her eyelids excessively, and the intertitles are interminably long and boring.

In 1923 and 1924, Soviet film finally surpassed the level of *agitki*. One of the most successful films of the 1920s in terms of audience appeal was made by Perestiani in 1923, *The Little Red Devils*, which continued to draw audiences for at least twenty years. This film, like many others before and since, manages at the same time to parody and exploit the adventure genre. It is about three adolescents during the Ukrainian Civil War. One of them, rather incongruously, is an American black. The movie anticipated others in its most cavalier disregard of historical facts. In the course of their adventures, the children capture anarchist chief Makhno and hand him over to the Red troops of Budenyi. This incident was a figment of the imagination of the scenarist, for Makhno in fact died of tuberculosis in his bed many years later in Paris. The director also made the Ukraine mountainous in order to make it more picturesque. Once again, the wickedness of the villain is shown by the fact that he lusts after women. Among the many crimes of Makhno, this was the one which struck the imagination of filmmakers. The audience enjoyed the fast-moving action and the good performance of the young actors, and the critics approved of selecting the Civil War as background for fabulous adventures.

Another important film of 1923 was not nearly as successful. This movie, *Locksmith and Chancellor*, directed by Gardin, was based on a Lunacharskii play. Although the action takes place in a mythical country during World War I, the story is a transparent allegory of the Russian Revolution. The ire of the filmmakers is concentrated not so much on the representatives of the old regime as, in proper Bolshevik fashion, on the Kerensky figure, who "betrays the revolution." Once again, the wickedness is conveyed by his seduction of women. The story is confused, the characters are stereotyped, and the film is clumsily directed. *Locksmith and Chancellor* received uni-

Figure 6.   Aleksandra Khokhlova in *Extraordinary Adventures of Mr. West in the Land of the Bolsheviks* (1924).

versally bad reviews in the press. Writing in *Pravda*, Lebedev went so far as to express concern that such a bad film made out of a decent play might set back the cause of filmmaking.[61]

Aelita, made by Protazanov, was incomparably more interesting. One of the two great figures of prerevolutionary cinema, Protazanov emigrated after the Revolution, and was in the process of establishing for himself a reputation in France, when he was persuaded to return. In the 1920s he became the most commercially successful Soviet director. *Aelita* was his first Soviet film. The film was based on Aleksei Tolstoy's story. In it, a Soviet engineer dreams of a trip to Mars, at least partially to escape his earthly problems. He arrives on Mars just in time to witness the revolution of the exploited. Although the constructivist sets for the action on the alien planet are striking, the action in NEP Russia is more interesting, at least in retrospect. The film was praised by critics for its technical accomplishments, but was attacked for showing the young Soviet Union in an overly critical fashion.[62] One was not supposed to wish to escape from Communist Russia – even as a joke.

The finest comedy of the decade was made by Lev Kuleshov in 1924,

Extraordinary Adventures of Mr. West in the Land of the Bolsheviks (Fig. 6). Boris Barnet and Pudovkin, who were both to become great directors, played major roles in it. The film was made to ridicule Western rumors about Bolshevik Russia. Mr. West, a rich American, comes to Moscow on business. Because he had heard many fantastic tales about life in the Soviet Union, he decides to bring a bodyguard – a cowboy. Despite his precautions, he falls into the hands of a group of bandits who take advantage of his naïveté. Naturally, the film ends happily: The authorities destroy the bandit group, and Mr. West can now become acquainted with the happy and civilized life of the Russian people.

The satire is double-edged. Although it is true that the rumors are exaggerated, the Soviet Union is still depicted as a country in which a group of bandits can take on the regime, more or less as equals. The film parodies the conventions of the American Western; however, much of the excitement and its appeal to the audience is based on the exploitation of the very same conventions. It is a loving satire of the genre.

Protazanov's *Aelita* and Kuleshov's experimental and highly imaginative work already belong to the golden age of the Soviet film, for the difference between them and the rather primitive works that preceded them is vast.

The historian is interested in changes and continuities, and therefore the question necessarily arises: To what extent can we see the later characteristics of Soviet cinema at the earliest stages? The continuities are striking. The leaders of the regime had a deep-seated belief in the malleability of human nature and were convinced of the great power of the cinema. They believed that it was their duty to use this power for the creation of a new socialist humanity. Under extraordinarily difficult circumstances, they spared neither effort nor scarce resources. The dizzying and confusing reorganizations of the industry were a consequence at this time – as they would be in the future – of the conviction that film was not living up to its potential. New ways had to be found.

It is fair to say that Soviet cinema grew out of its first original product, the *agitka*. Whatever we think of the artistic quality of these films, they do have a charming naïveté. Politicians and many of the artists at that point still believed that the task of propaganda was easy and straightforward.

Notes

1 On Bolshevik propaganda during the Civil War and after, see Peter Kenez, *The Birth of the Propaganda State: Soviet Methods of Mass Mobilization, 1917–1929*, Cambridge University Press, 1985.

2 *Samoe vazhnoe iz vsekh iskusstv. Lenin o kino*, Iskusstvo, Moscow, 1963, p. 124.

3 Kenez, p. 73.

4 That the Bolsheviks appreciated this point can be seen in a speech given by

N. I. Bukharin to the Fifth Congress of the Komsomol, *Piatyi vserossiskii s"ezd RKSM. 11–19 Okt. 1922 goda*, Politizdat, Moscow, 1927.

5 N. A. Lebedev, *Ocherk istorii kino SSSR*, Iskusstvo, Moscow, 1947, pp. 64–6.

6 Akselrod, "Dokumenty po istorii natsionlizatsii russkoi kinematografi," *Iz istorii kino* 1: 25–6, 1958.

7 The Bolshevik leaders differed from one another on the issue of freedom of thought. Some of the revolutionaries were more liberal than others. Lenin, however, prevailed on a crucial meeting of the Executive Committee of the Congress of Soviets that took place on November 4. His colleagues accepted that there could be only one permissible interpretation of political events. Kenez, pp. 38–40.

8 Ibid., p. 29.

9 Lebedev, *Ocherk*, p. 68.

10 V. Listov, "U istokov sovetskogo kino," *Iskusstvo kino* 3: 3–4, 1969.

11 Akselrod, p. 27.

12 Listov, pp. 8–9.

13 S. Bratoliubov, *Na zare Sovetskoi kinematografii*, Iskusstvo, Leningrad, 1976, p. 24.

14 Listov, p. 12, and V. T. Ermakov, "Ideinaia bor'ba na kul'turnom fronte v pervom gode sovetskoi vlasti," *Voprosy istorii*, Nov. 1971, p. 19.

15 Lebedev, *Ocherk*, p. 68. Our basic source of knowledge about Soviet films is the massive four-volume catalog: *Sovetskie khudozhestvennye fil'my. Annotirovan-nyi katalog* (hereafter referred to as *S. kh. f.*), 4 vols., Iskusstvo, Moscow, 1961–8. All page references are to vol. 1. This catalog does not include films that were made during the Civil War by private companies.

16 Jay Leyda, *Kino: A History of the Russian and Soviet Film*, Collier Books, New York, 1960, pp. 423–4.

17 Ibid., and Lebedev, *Ocherk*, pp. 68–71. I saw this film at the Hungarian Film Archives in Budapest.

18 This film is available at the Pacific Film Archive in Berkeley, California.

19 Leyda, pp. 111–20.

20 Akselrod, p. 34.

21 Lebedev, *Ocherk*, pp. 76–9.

22 N. A. Lebedev, *Ocherki istorii kino SSSR, Vol. 1: Nemoe kino 1917–1934*, Iskusstvo, Moscow, 1965, pp. 108–16. On *agit*-trains, see Kenez, pp. 58–63.

23 Lebedev, *Ocherk*, esp. p. 15. I saw this film at the Hungarian Film Archives in Budapest.

24 Ibid., p. 11.

25 Ibid.

26 Ibid., p. 14.

27 Ibid., p. 13, and Lebedev, *Ocherki*, p. 133.

28 *S.kh.f.*, p. 10.

29 Ibid., pp. 5–19.

30 Ibid.

31 Lebedev, *Ocherk*, pp. 79–83.

32 Huntly Carter, *The New Theater and Cinema of Soviet Russia*, Chapman and Dodd, London, 1924, p. 238, and Lebedev, *Ocherk*, p. 87.

33 Carter, pp. 238–9.

34 Lebedev, *Ocherk*, p. 87.

35 Carter, p. 238.

36 N. A. Lebedev, "Boevye dvadtsatye gody," *Iskusstvo kino* 12: 88, 1968. *Skull of the Pharaoh's Daughter* was a mistranslation. The German title was *Skull of the Pharaoh's Wife*. But such minor inaccuracies did not matter to the audience.

37 Carter, p. 250.

38 A. Gak, "K istorii sozdaniia Sovkino," *Iz istorii kino* 5: 136, 1962.

39 Carter, p. 241. It is impossible to give the value of a million rubles at the time. Inflation was extremely rapid.

40 V. I. Lenin, *Polnoe sobranie sochinenii*, vol. 44, Politizdat, Moscow, 1964, pp. 360–1.

41 Gak, p. 133.

42 Lebedev, *Ocherk*, p. 72.

43 Gak, p. 131. The establishment of Goskino is also discussed in detail in Richard Taylor, *The Politics of the Soviet Cinema, 1917–1929*, Cambridge University Press, 1979, pp. 71–2.

44 Gak, pp. 132–3.

45 Ibid., p. 133.

46 Iu. A. Fridman, "Dvizhenie pomoshchi mezhdunarodnogo proletariata Sovetskoi Rossii v 1921–1922 godakh," *Voprosy istorii* 1: 100, 1958. Also in Taylor, p. 73.

47 Gak, pp. 133–4.

48 Ibid., p. 134.

49 Ibid., pp. 134–5.

50 Ibid., p. 139.

51 Ibid.

52 Ibid., pp. 141–4.

53 Lebedev, "Boevye," p. 95.

54 Leyda, pp. 161–2.

55 Lebedev, *Ocherk*, pp. 104–5.

56 *S.kh.f.*, pp. 27–31.

57 Most of the films that I mention in this chapter I saw at the Pacific Film Archives, Berkeley, California. I saw *Brigade Commander Ivanov* at the Hoover Institution Archives, Stanford, California. For the films I could not see, I base myself on the descriptions given in *S.kh.f.* I shall footnote only those for which my source was the Soviet catalog.

58 *S.kh.f.*, p. 30.

59 Ibid., p. 29.

60 This film was sanitized before its U.S. release to make it acceptable for American audiences.

61 *Pravda*, Dec. 13, 1923.

62 Ibid., Oct. 1, 1924.

CHAPTER 3

The films of the golden age, 1925–1929

The Western European public quickly came to appreciate the avant-garde Soviet filmmakers of the silent era. Film, especially the silent film, is an international medium, and the works of Vertov, Pudovkin, Dovzhenko, and, above all, Eisenstein, therefore attracted the interest of contemporaries. As time went on this interest not only did not decline, but increase; an ever larger segment of Western opinion came to regard cinema as a major form of art and a medium that had a special significance in shaping the twentieth-century mind. The film and the study of film became fashionable, and in the mushrooming film histories the great Soviet figures usually received their due.

The ostensible communist ideology of the artists and the fact that they served the Soviet regime did not at all harm their reputation. Indeed, in the 1930s and once again since the 1960s the adjective "revolutionary" had a positive connotation among Western intellectuals. They looked on the Soviet directors as creators of the "revolutionary cinema."

Revolutionary cinema is an ambiguous phrase; different people at different times have attributed different meanings to it. Often it refers to innovative filmmaking. Eisenstein and his colleagues, of course, made great contributions to the development of the special language of the cinema and therefore they were revolutionary in this sense, but so are all other great artists at all times and everywhere. In a trivial sense revolutionary cinema means nothing more than choosing revolutions as subject matter. Soviet directors in the 1920s often selected their topics from the history of the revolutionary movement, and, naturally, invariably depicted revolutionaries in a favorable light.

In the most meaningful sense revolutionary films are those that are subversive to the values of the society in which they are created. Contrary to what some enthusiasts believe, movies are rarely revolutionary. In capitalist societies the studios to remain in business have to cater to the taste of their audiences. Very rarely could they afford – even if they wanted to, which is dubious – the luxury of making an ideological statement that was not in line with the opinions, prejudices, and convictions of their viewers. In non-democratic societies, fascist or communist, naturally the state has been unwilling to finance its own subversion. (One counterexample is the situation in Eastern Europe in the 1960s, 1970s, and 1980s, when fine Hungarian, Czech, Polish, and, on occasion, Soviet directors were able to make films that in thinly veiled form undermined the basic ideological assumptions of the regime. However, when we speak of "revolutionary" films, we rarely think of these.)

The Soviet directors of the golden age were hardly revolutionary. They accepted with seeming enthusiasm the values of the state and were content to propagate such values. The Soviet state described itself as revolutionary, and to its tremendous advantage succeeded in persuading both friends and enemies to accept its self-definition. However, such manipulation of words should not prevent us from seeing that what was remarkable about Soviet directors was not that they were "revolutionary" but, on the contrary, that they were willing to serve the state and a prescribed ideology to a hitherto unparalleled extent. How successful they were as propagandists is another matter. The difference between the Soviet directors and directors working elsewhere was only that the Soviets were both more self-aware and more obedient.[1]

It is not surprising that the Soviet state was the first to embark on the organization of a large-scale indoctrination network that included the film in its arsenal. The Soviet leaders, instinctive propagandists as they were, had a prescient and impressively clear appreciation of the possibilities inherent in the medium. Lenin, Trotsky, and Stalin, among others, repeatedly expressed their faith in the future of film as a propaganda weapon. Party congresses one after another paid lip service to the necessity of using film for the purposes of indictrination. A wide gap remained, however, between intentions and reality.

Films

The great reputation of Soviet film was based on the work of a handful of directors. It could hardly have been otherwise; many directors were talented craftsmen who produced interesting work, but only a few could be considered to have made a contribution to the development of world cinema. The line between talent and genius is obviously thin; however, there is general agreement that the works of Eisenstein, Kuleshov, Vertov, Pudovkin, A. Dovzhenko, and at least one film made by Kozintsev and Trauberg, *The New Babylon*, achieved the status of classics. This remarkable flourishing of many talents took place within a very short period. We may date the beginning of the golden age with the appearance of Kuleshov's comedy, *Extraordinary Adventures of Mr. West in the Land of the Bolsheviks*, in 1924, and the last fine film of this era was Dovzhenko's *Earth* made in 1930. When foreign critics wrote about Soviet films they usually had in mind only the works of a handful of artists.

Although here we cannot give a full description of the artistic achievements of the Soviet artists, a few generalizations are in order. The great Soviet directors worked at the twilight of the silent era, at a time when the medium was fully mature. Dovzhenko, for example, made his most admired work *Earth,* when in the United States only sound films were made. Therefore the Soviet artists, more than any other group, were able to take advantage of all the possibilities offered by the medium, and could learn from the experiments of others; their work was the culmination of a great age.

Second, the great Soviet directors, but especially Kuleshov, Eisenstein, Vertov, and Pudovkin, were cerebral artists; they were theoreticians. They wrote with intelligence and insight on issues such as the nature of cinema, the political significance of the medium, montage, the work of actors, and the composition of individual frames. Griffith, for example, may have used the "Kuleshov effect" in his work, but it was the Russian who made us understand exactly what the artist was doing. (In one interesting experiment among many, Kuleshov spliced the face of the famous actor Mozzhukhin after a picture of a bowl of soup, a smiling child, and a dead body, creating the impression that the impassive face actually changed. In another, he created a nonexistent person by splicing together different body parts.) The literature these directors produced, partly as a consequence of polemicizing against one another, possesses lasting value.[2] Even after the passage of sixty years the students of cinema can still profit from reading the works of Eisenstein, Kuleshov, and Pudovkin on the art of filmmaking.

There is another reason for reading the works of Vertov: His writings allow us to recapture the utopian spirit that was powerful at the time. He was a true radical, who believed that the Russian Revolution was merely an aspect of the renewal of everything in human life. He rejected literature, plays, and acting. As he put it: "Movie drama – this is the opium for the people. Movie drama and religion are the most deadly weapons in the hands of the capitalists." Elsewhere he said: "The very term art is in essence counterrevolutionary."[3] Vertov made documentaries because he believed that this was the only acceptable form of filmmaking in the proletarian era. Vertov did not like Eisenstein's work, because Eisenstein used scenarios and did tell something of a story. The two articulate avant-garde artists polemicized against one another. Eisenstein denied that he was influenced by Vertov, and indeed, it is self-evident that the two directors had different artistic credos. Nevertheless, it was at least partially because of Vertov that in the mid-1920s films without a particularly interesting story line, without actors, without individuals, somehow seemed particularly "revolutionary" and "antibourgeois."

Third, the great Russian artists were the most daring innovators. In both style and content they consciously strove to achieve something new. This was so partially because they were very young. In the circumstances that prevailed in revolutionary Russia, boys in their late teens and early twenties were able to make films. They wanted to be different from the previous generation whose work they passionately rejected. More important, they could be wildly innovative, because the Soviet regime, in the hope that they would produce politically useful propaganda, in part freed them from commercial considerations. Their work, especially Vertov's, has enormous vibrancy; at times the viewer becomes dizzy because of the abundance of images, ideas, camera angles. Above all, it is this extraordinary vitality that gives Soviet films of the late 1920s enduring appeal.

The relatively free artistic discussions and the competing talents produced an impressive film industry. The question arises whether the artistic innovations were at all connected with the political innovations taking place at the same time. Russia had a great revolution, and a short time later enjoyed the flourishing of a new art. Were these two facts connected? It certainly never occurred to anyone to give credit for the great talents of Tolstoy, Dostoevsky, Turgenev, and Chekhov to the particular tsarist social and political system in which the artists worked. The issue, however, may be more complicated with the film industry. Bolshevism cannot claim credit for the almost-mysterious convergence of so many first-rate artists in such a short time; on the other hand, the Bolshevik regime, by setting political goals, did at least partially free some of the directors from commercial considerations. It is unlikely that a capitalist studio would have financed Eisenstein's first artistic experiments because his work could not possibly appeal to a large audience. Further, the regime and the artists tacitly cooperated: The regime provided the myths and the artists the iconography. Each benefited.

Contemporary Soviet audiences, unlike foreign critics, judged Soviet film not on the basis of the work of a few outstanding directors but on the basis of the films of dozens of others, many of whom were talented and able people, but less ambitious and innovative than the best known. The films of, for example, Eggert, Protazanov, and Ermler, who aimed to entertain audiences, were seen by many more people than the works of Vertov or Eisenstein.

One might assume that people who came to maturity more or less at the same time, who worked under similarly difficult material conditions, who at least ostensibly shared the same political ideology, would develop similar styles. This was not the case; a multiplicity of styles flourished. Soviet directors influenced one another not so much by imitating each other's techniques, though that happened, but, more important, by providing negative models for each other. Artists found their individuality in juxtaposition to the work of their contemporaries. The Bolsheviks, who were great centralizers, paradoxically built no Hollywood, and the country had many film centers. Leningrad competed with Moscow; the Georgians and the Ukrainians, who were the first among the national minorities to establish film industries, fairly soon developed different and characteristic styles. For example, the greatest of the Ukrainian directors, Dovzhenko, was a nationalist and a true original. Obviously, people operating in the very different cultural milieu of the Caucasian republics or in Central Asia made very different films.

Among the famous Russian directors, there was a gap between those who came to maturity before the establishment of Soviet power and those who started their work only in the 1920s. There were directors, such as Vladimir Gardin, Iakov Protazanov, and Iurii Zheliabuzhskii, who were willing to use technical innovations developed by others but were not particularly experimental themselves, and men such as Vertov, Kuleshov, Eisenstein, and Pudovkin, who were natural innovators. Even the camp of the innovators was deeply divided. They disagreed with one another on issues such as whether a film should tell a story, whether there should be professional actors, how the actors should be used, and what was the proper use of montage.

Between 1925 and 1929, the studios made 514 films.[4] These differed so much in subject matter and style that it is difficult to make generalizations. A few observations, however, can be made. First of all, with only a few exceptions, the films were made in order to serve the interests of the state. Some were made to popularize sports or the state lottery, or to help the fight against venereal disease, but the great majority were political. Even in these relatively liberal days, the Soviet regime rarely and barely tolerated a film that was made either "only" to entertain or to give nothing but aesthetic pleasure.

Artists dealt with the pressures differently. Some convinced Bolsheviks naturally made the type of film that was expected of them. Others cared little about ideologies and were perfectly happy to serve any master that allowed them to make films. Nikolai Lebedev, a film theorist, historian, and scenarist who worked in the early 1920s, talked to cameramen who made newsreels. He found that they were professionals who saw little ideological significance in their work. One of them said to him: "Our task is small: We just turn the handle. Where and what to photograph are matters which will be decided by the bosses."[5] Many of the directors compromised. They made the films they wanted to make, and appended the necessary political message as a price to be allowed to do their work. There were few Soviet films from this period that were completely without political propaganda.

One outstanding example is Kuleshov's *By the Law* made in 1926 (Fig. 7). Since the studio did not approve the script, it was made as an "experiment" and it had to be done on a shoestring.[6] There were only five actors and one interior set, a ramshackle cabin. The script was based on a Jack London story ("The Unexpected"), of gold prospectors in the Yukon territory. One of them goes berserk and starts to shoot his comrades in order to acquire more gold; however, a married couple manages to restrain him. Since the husband and wife believe that it is their duty to hand him over to the authorities, they keep him as a prisoner through the long winter

Figure 7. Poster for *By the Law* (1926).

Figure 8.   Michael, the prisoner, played by V. Fogel, in *By the Law* (1926).

(Fig. 8). The bulk of the film deals with the evolving relationship of the three people. Like very few artists of that era working anywhere, Kuleshov here presents subtle psychological studies of three characters. He was fortunate to have the help of first-rate actors. The simplicity of means actually adds to the power of the film. The miserable little cabin where much of the action takes place creates a claustrophobic atmosphere (Fig. 9). Many of the frames are spectacularly composed and make an indelible impression (Fig. 10). In order to make the film palatable, some of Kuleshov's friends argued that it was about capitalist greed. Kuleshov, in fact, was heavily attacked for his apoliticism. He never again made a film that reached the artistic standard of this magnificent work.[7]

Figure 9.   Edith, played by Khokhlova, in *By the Law* (1926).

Figure 10.   The hanging scene in *By the Law* (1926).

Figure 11.   Liudmilla, the heroine of *Third Meshchanskaia Street* (1927).

Although Soviet directors – as directors elsewhere – rarely attempted to give a realistic description of life, they could still, unlike in the following decade, deal with real issues that interested people. However, the approach was almost invariably stylized: Films had a fairy-tale quality, the wicked being very wicked, and the good a little too good. There was one outstanding exception, *Third Meshchanskaia Street* (known abroad as *Bed and Sofa*), made by Abram Room in 1927.

Figure 12.   Liudmilla departs in *Third Meshchanskaia Street* (1927).

This film is a modest slice-of-life drama. A working-class couple lives in a small, one-room apartment. The husband is a construction worker and the wife, steeped in petit-bourgeois mentality, stays home (Fig. 11). The construction worker's friend, a printer, comes to town and finds a job; but because of a severe apartment shortage, he is forced to move in with the couple. When the construction worker goes out of town on assignment, the wife, who is bored and has been neglected, easily enters into a relationship with the tenant. When the husband returns, it is he who has to sleep on the sofa. The woman becomes pregnant, and she herself does not know who the father is. The two men together try to persuade her to have an abortion. At this point she repudiates both her previous petit-bourgeois existence, and the two men, and decides to start a new life for herself with her baby (Fig. 12).

Many other contemporary and later films depicted triangles So basic a human situation is the triangle that even Soviet directors during the most repressive times could not always avoid it. Also, although Soviet films often depicted strong women, *Third Meshchanskaia Street* is rightly regarded today as one of the earliest feminist films. What was remarkable about Room's work is that he portrayed the wife as a victim because she was a woman. At the end, of course, she emerges as the strongest, the one who overcomes her oppression.[8]

Room's film is noteworthy because of its honesty. There were no films made in the Soviet Union until the late 1950s in which average people were depicted in such nonjudgmental fashion. There were certainly no Soviet films in which sex was treated so matter-of-factly. The film was greeted with a storm of abuse. Soviet critics did not want to see films about life as it was.[9] Room's talent was in his minute observation of little people and of revealing details.

Soviet film was still defining itself; directors were still searching for the limits of the permissible. Directors continued to make dramatizations from classics, historical costume dramas, and films that escape categorization, but the majority of films dealt with the history of the revolutionary movement or with current, NEP Russia. Out of the 514 films, the history of the revolutionary movement was the subject matter of 144.[10] If we consider only full-length films, the proportion would certainly reach at least one-third. Admittedly, at times it is hard to put movies into one group or another. In some cases the revolution is there only as a distant background; in others, movies that purported to depict the hard life of the workers in the past could easily be placed among the revolutionary films. Exact numbers, however, do not matter: It is indisputable that a very large proportion of Soviet films of the time dealt with this subject.

Among the revolutionary films, we might establish a subcategory that, in the absence of a better term, might be called "revolutionary spectacle." Prime examples of the revolutionary spectacle are the first three films of Eisenstein (*Strike, Battleship Potemkin,* and *October*), Pudovkin's *The End of St. Petersburg,* and Dovzhenko's *Arsenal.* What these movies and other similar ones have in common is a lack of interest in story and in character – in fact, the absence of recognizable human beings. What we have instead are types, symbols, and gestures.

Although only a few of the revolutionary films fall into this subcategory, they are important. Indeed, in the West, and even in Russia, when one talks about Soviet political cinema, these are the films one thinks of first. It was here that Soviet cinema was most original and innovative. No one had made revolutionary spectacles before Eisenstein, and not many have made them since. These films impressed some segments of the Western public so much that many unconsciously came to believe that all Soviet films were like *Battleship Potemkin.*

Eisenstein was the decisive figure in the development of the genre. His films are perhaps the most frequently analyzed ones in the history of world cinema. He combined a daring imagination and intuition with extraordinarily careful planning. His strength did not lay in dealing with the minutiae of everyday life. His style was operatic: He favored large gestures and symbols. As a young man he particularly admired Japanese Kabuki theater and it may be that he learned from it a technique of building effects and the notion of attraction of opposites, which came to be the most significant aspect of his montage.[11] But most important, he learned from the Japanese the importance of gestures and stylization.

The intellectual content of his early films was profoundly influenced by his earlier association with Proletkul't, a complex politicocultural movement that reached the height of its influence during the revolutionary period.[12] It organized associations for cultural and educational activities among workers. Some of the intellectual leaders of the movement, who were only tenuously connected with the indigenous working-class activities, worked out far-reaching theories about the nature of culture. They argued that the new, socialist culture would be profoundly different from what it replaced. In their view there could be no accommodation with the old world; the proletariat on the basis of its experience would create a new culture that would reflect the spirit of the collective. The theorists were convinced that in history it was always the masses and not the individual heroes who mattered. It followed that the new art had to emphasize not the accomplishments of individuals but those of the workers and peasants. Eisenstein was attracted to this movement, because it justified the necessity of a complete break with the art of the "bourgeois" world. All of his early films expressed, though in his own idiom, the ideology of the Proletkul't.

Eisenstein's first film, *Strike,* made in 1925, already contained all the important characteristics of his later works. The film tells the story of a strike. The workers are oppressed, take heroic and collective action, and are defeated. Eisenstein's "intellectual" montage was already in evidence here. As the soldiers put down the workers, the capitalist squeezes a lemon. As the soldiers fire on the workers, Eisenstein cuts to a scene in which bulls are slaughtered. He acquired his world reputation through the success of his second film, *Battleship Potemkin,* which was first shown in 1926, and which came to be perhaps the most frequently analyzed work in the history of cinema. The film is based on the story of a mutiny on a tsarist ship in 1905 and the street demonstrations that followed in Odessa. In this film also there are no well-delineated characters: The hero of the film is the battleship.

When the director worked on his next film, *October,* made for the tenth anniversary of the revolution, he had a reputation to live up to. He did not resist the temptation of gigantomania, but made a sprawling film – unlike his previous ones – lacking in artistic unity. While Eisenstein's montage is always obtrusive, in this film it is particularly so.

Eisenstein's admirers often pointed out that *Battleship Potemkin* and especially *October* were taken by contemporaries and by later generations as documentary accounts. It is true that even historians have had trouble in escaping the impact of pictorial presentation of events. This result in itself, however, does not testify to the director's artistry. *October* gives the effect of a documentary because no real documentaries exist of the taking of the

Winter Palace, because the film has no actors, and because, with the lavish support of the Soviet state, Eisenstein used thousands of extras.

Although his montage, his individual frames, and some of his ideas for expressing preconceived messages were indeed strikingly original, Eisenstein, of course, did not attempt an independent interpretation of the revolution. He was content to act as a well-paid servant of an increasingly repressive state. The authorities provided him with everything he asked for, including thousands of extras and the use of buildings and battleships. The price he had to pay for this patronage was to paint a picture of the revolution as the current leadership of the Party wanted to remember it. This most ambitious film about the October Revolution was ready to be shown in time for the celebration of the tenth anniversary, when Trotsky's final defeat in the internecine struggle necessitated far-reaching changes. Aleksandrov in his memoirs, published in 1976, tells us that after Stalin saw the finished work he directed the film to be recut and some scenes reshot.[13] There is no evidence that either Eisenstein or Aleksandrov then or later saw anything unusual and unacceptable at this type of intervention. These fine artists saw no distinction between serving the lofty aims of communism and the far less lofty purposes of Stalin.

Eisenstein's film shows how the bourgeoisie "stole" the revolution of the workers and peasants, that Kerensky was nothing but a poseur, that the Bolsheviks stopped the reactionary coup d'état of Kornilov, and that, above all, the October Revolution was a mass rising against the Provisional Government. In Eisenstein's version of history the storming of the Winter Palace was a major and majestic event appropriate for the great turning point in human history. *October* is a remarkable film for it contains most of the myths concerning the revolution from which the Soviet regime derived its legitimacy for many decades to come. In this sense perhaps it is the most important Soviet film.

Pudovkin, Eisenstein's not always friendly rival, was ready for his anniversary offering. His *The End of St. Petersburg* was one of the most impressive films of the 1927 season. Pudovkin, unlike Eisenstein, was interested in individuals. At the center of the film there is a story of a peasant lad becoming a worker and then, finally, a conscious revolutionary. It is characteristic of the genre, however, that we never learn his name. He is always referred to in the titles as "lad"; clearly, here we are dealing with a case of symbolism.

Aleksandr Dovzhenko was much more drawn to symbols than Pudovkin. His fine revolutionary spectacle, *Arsenal,* made in 1929, was steeped in symbolism. The film was loosely built on a small-scale but bloody strike in Kiev in 1918. However, the uninitiated viewer can follow the story line only with the greatest difficulty. Dovzhenko wanted to present images and did so in a balladic fashion. These images are haunting, and they remain with the viewer (Figs. 13 and 14). Whereas *Potemkin*'s hero was the battleship, Pudovkin

Figure 13.   A crazed soldier in *Arsenal* (1929).

chose Everyman, the little person who sided with the revolution; *Arsenal's* hero is the unconquerable Ukrainian worker, whose strength reaches mythic proportions. In the famous ending of this film, Timosh, the central character, bares his breast in front of the firing squad, but bullets cannot kill him (Fig. 15).

That artists as different in temperament and style as Eisenstein, Pudovkin, and Dovzhenko made films that shared so much shows that the appearance of the revolutionary spectacle in the late 1920s was not the consequence of the individual director's predeliction. The period shaped this genre.

What ideological message did the Soviet people get from these revolutionary spectacles? The films mentioned here all legitimized the revolution and thereby the child of the revolution, the regime. The films portrayed the revolution not as a series of contingent events but as something predetermined. Good and evil clashed, and good inevitably won. In the film version of the events, political issues were not decided by the behavior of ordinary mortals, full of foibles, prejudices, and self-interest. The films removed the revolution from the realm of the ordinary.

These films were a step toward socialist realism. They pointed to the future by repudiating realism and in its stead assuming a heroic, romantic stance. They showed a contempt for events as they really happened, and for human beings as they really were. To be sure, before reaching socialist realism several important steps still had to be taken. The notion of the nameless hero, the collective, the little man as a decisive force had to be abandoned in the age of Stalinism. More important, artistic experimentation, which makes these films impressive at a distance of six decades, was not to be tolerated in the new age.

Most people did not want their revolutionary heroics straight. There are few audience statistics available, but the evidence suggests that films such as *Battleship Potemkin* and *Arsenal,* however much they impressed foreign critics, did not appeal to Russian audiences, and that is not at all surprising. Most people wanted to be entertained: They wanted a story, and they wanted characters with whom they could identify. The great bulk of the revolutionary films at least attempted to entertain while instructing.

Revolutionary movies can be placed on a continuum. At one end the revolutionary message was central to the film, whereas on the other, the revolution was there in order to make the film modish or to provide an interesting background for romantic and other adventures. In Pudovkin's two great films, made at the end of the 1920s, *Mother* and *The Heir of Genghis Khan,* the revolutionary message was central. Both films, as well as *The End of St. Petersburg,* were about the development of class and revolutionary consciousness. *Mother,* made in 1926, and based on Maxim Gorky's book, was Pudovkin's first great success. In the film, as in Gorky's book, a mother decides to follow her son's footsteps and joins the revolutionaries in their struggle (Fig. 16). *The Heir of Genghis Khan* (released abroad as *Storm over Asia*), is one of the best films of the decade. In an exotic locale, a young Mongolian, reputed to be a descendant of the great conqueror, is picked by the British to play the role of the puppet (Fig. 17). The young man, however, when he learns about the nefarious dealings of the imperialists and their cruelty, decides to lead his people against the exploiters.

The theme of *Mother* was that in the new world it is the old who must learn from the young. This theme came to be very popular among Soviet directors. A Ukrainian film, *Two Days,* made by G. Stabovoi in 1927, makes the same point. During the Civil War when members of the upper classes escape from Bolshevik rule, an old servant hides the young son of his mas-

Figure 14.   Soldiers returning from the front in *Arsenal* (1929).

ter, who was left behind by accident. The old man does not even tell his Bolshevik son what he is doing. When the Whites return, the young upper-class boy, a little snake, informs on the servant's Bolshevik son, who is then killed. Now the old man finally understands that in the struggle of classes any feeling of pity for the enemy is misplaced. The enemy is merciless and so it must be fought mercilessly. The old man takes it on himself to burn down the manor house and in it the White officers and his treacherous young master.

The argument that class interest supersedes other causes and other human feelings was also expressed in one of the most popular revolutionary

Figure 15.   Timosh, the Ukrainian revolutionary, faces his enemies in *Arsenal* (1929).

Figure 16 (*facing, above*).   *Mother* (1926).

Figure 17 (*facing, below*).   *The Heir of Genghis Khan* (1928).

films, Protazanov's *The Forty-First*, made in 1927. This is a Civil War love story with fabular qualities. A Bolshevik woman soldier and a White officer are stranded on a desert island. They fall in love. When an enemy ship appears on the horizon, the class-conscious woman realizes that the ship will rescue the officer, and to avoid helping the enemy, she shoots her man. He is her forty-first kill. What makes the film better than Stabovoi's is that Protazanov at least hints at a moral complexity. The woman, without doubt, does the "right thing," but the viewer is not absolutely sure that Protazanov approves.

Many directors chose foreign and therefore exotic locales for their revolutionary stories. Room's *The Ghost That Will Not Return* was set in a Latin American country. Kozintsev's and Trauberg's *The New Babylon* dealt with the Paris commune. What these films had in common was a totally unrealistic portrayal of a non-Russian environment. Dovzhenko's first full-length film, *The Diplomatic Pouch*, made in 1927, was almost comic in this respect. The British "political police" behave very much like Russians. All British workers and sailors are class-conscious proletarians, who happily risk their lives in the service of the Soviet cause. The enemy is decadent and

corrupt. We can tell that the representatives of the enemy are decadent because they dance with scantily dressed women. Class conscious proletarians, on the other hand, are able to resist the allure of such females. There is very little in this film that would betray Dovzhenko's considerable talent.

In many a "revolutionary" film, the revolution was there only for decoration. Kozintsev's and Trauberg's visually interesting, but confused film, *S.V.D. – Union of the Great Cause,* is one example. The directors did not seem to be interested in the history of the Decembrist rising, which is the ostensible topic of the movie, nor did they care much about such abstract subjects as the nature of injustice or why people become revolutionaries. The film is full of unusual angle shots, lights photographed through night fog, and interesting reflections. The story is built on fantastic, overdrawn characters, who are not placed in any definite period of history (Figs. 18 and 19). Films such as this one hardly strengthened anyone's revolutionary consciousness.

Films dealing with the contemporary world usually had a more complex message and expressed a more complex worldview than the "revolutionary" films. Directors who distinguished themselves in making revolutionary spectacles were not particularly adept in dealing with the contemporary scene. The most interesting films about NEP Russia were made not by the famous directors Eisenstein, Pudovkin, or Dovzhenko, but by Room, Protazanov, and Ermler. These men shared an interest in real people and in their foibles. It was their ability to bring human beings to the screen that attracted the audience.

Their films, with the exception of Room's *Third Meshchanskaia Street,* were not true-to-life dramas. Silent filmmakers even outside Russia rarely attempted unvarnished realism. Soviet directors mercilessly caricatured – and often in the process unwittingly glamorized – wicked NEP men. They attacked bureaucracy. They warned their viewers against the evils of bourgeois decadence. Nevertheless, the problems that the directors discussed and the characters they caricatured were exaggerated and distorted versions of something real. On rare occasions, the Soviet people had the pleasure of getting glimpses of people like themselves. In the usual contemporary film, first some wrong or injustice was presented, which at the end was righted: The police arrived just in time, the Party understood the problem, the Komsomol intervened. Before reaching the end of the film, the director delivered some stinging observations about his society. The happy ending was always the least believable part.

Protazanov, the most senior, versatile, and one of the most prolific of the Soviet directors, was primarily the portraitist of the village and little town. Since he left Russia at the end of the Civil War in 1920 and returned only in 1923, there is no reason to believe in his original commitment to communism.[14] He was not a deeply political person, and not particularly interested in technical innovations. He had a remarkable ability to adjust to the

Figure 18. *S.V.D.* –
*Union of the Great
Cause* (1927).

Figure 19. Gerasimov
in *S.V.D. – Union of
the Great Cause* (1927).

ever-changing circumstances and sense the mood of his audiences; he was the consummate survivor. He was perfectly happy to adopt techniques developed by others. His strength was his ability to observe the minutiae of life, his interest in character, and in telling a story.

After the rather hostile reception of *Aelita*, Protazanov made *His Call* in 1925. In *Aelita* the recently returned emigrant showed Mars to be a more interesting place than Soviet Russia and in general depicted Soviet reality in somber colors. By contrast, *His Call* was, from a political point of view, much more acceptable. The story concerns a vicious emigrant who returns to Russia incognito to look for his hidden jewels. In order to accomplish this nefarious purpose, he pretends to fall in love with a young textile worker who is living in the place where the valuables were hidden. The plot enabled the director to show what was called at the time "new Soviet life" – the introduction of electricity, the kindergarten, the workers' club, and the library.[15] The young man soon exhibits his wickedness, and he is, of course, unmasked. The last reel of the film is in no obvious way connected with the rest of the story. Into this little town comes the sad news that the leader of the world proletariat, Lenin, has died. This is the time for the workers to show their redoubled commitment to the Leninist cause and join the Party. The young woman who fell for the capitalist rat feels herself unworthy of such an honor. Nevertheless, the Party is forgiving and she is redeemed. This film was a step in the development of the Lenin cult, and in this respect, if in no other, it was ahead of its time.

Protazanov's next film, much less ambitious, was far more attractive. *The Tailor from Torzhok,* made in 1925, is about a lost and regained lottery ticket. The central character is an archetypical little man, who, when he wins a lot of money, can dream only a very bourgeois dream of owning his own elegant tailor shop. The film is without true villains. Protazanov gently warns his peasant viewers that they must watch out for the sharp dealings of the city folk.[16]

Aside from Protazanov, Fridrich Ermler was the most successful portrayer of contemporary life. His film, *Katka's Reinette Apples,* made in 1926, is a most interesting and critical portrayal of early NEP urban society. Katka, a young peasant girl, comes to Petrograd to earn enough money to buy a cow, but she cannot find a job at a factory and is forced to sell apples on the street. Private trade is the first step toward degeneracy and criminal life. She gets mixed up with a wicked villain, Semka, and she becomes pregnant. However, she is still basically good and therefore realizes the wickedness of the man and breaks with him.

The film acquaints us with the society of street vendors (Fig. 20). In Ermler's scheme of values, Katka is preferable to Semka's new girlfriend, Verka, because Katka trades in apples, and Verka in foreign goods. The street vendors, illegal little business people, also have their sense of community. They hire someone, Vadka, an unemployed intellectual, to look out for the police.

Figure 20.   Market in Leningrad in *Katka's Reinette Apples* (1926).

We learn how loathsome Verka really is when she refuses to contribute to Vadka's meager compensation. In this bustling, exciting, but very poor world, Soviet power seems very remote. There is no mention of Lenin, of the Party, or of the noble goals of communism. The authorities exist only in the form of the police, who seem none too capable.

The most remarkable character in the movie is not the grotesquely over-drawn Semka, or even the prototype of the strong Soviet woman figure, Katka, but the unemployed intellectual, Vadka, a man who is incapable of taking care of himself in the new circumstances. He cannot even properly kill himself: He jumps into shallow water. He returns to the bridge to find that his only jacket has been stolen. Katka saves the unfortunate fellow several times. She takes him in and she gives him something to do – the job of taking care of her new baby while she is out working. Vadka is a thoroughly decent man. In the climactic scene of the movie, he confronts, fights, and defeats Semka. The happy ending is inevitable, although Katka's sudden transformation is unmotivated. She gives up her shady job and becomes a worker. She marries the deserving and loving Vadka, and the alliance of working classes and honest intelligentsia is reaffirmed. In depicting Katka as a breadwinner, and much the stronger character, the film has a feminist message.

Ermler's other film on a contemporary topic, *The Parisian Cobbler*, takes place in a village, but presents an equally dark view of Soviet reality. The subject matter of the film is the loose sexual mores among village Komsomol youth. The pregnant heroine, once again named Katia, is abandoned by her lover, Andrei, a member of the Komsomol. The Komsomol cell does not take the side of the unfortunate girl. Andrei joins the local hooligans in their attack on Katia, who is defended by an unlikely hero, a deaf and mute Kirik – the "Parisian Cobbler" of the title.[17]

The films of Ermler and Protazanov, and other directors who attempted to portray contemporary life, were often attacked by critics. Party activists hardly wanted moviemakers to hold up a mirror for their society. It was this genre that suffered the most, indeed, disappeared in the 1930s when the political climate changed.

Foreign films

Party activists may have found the message in some Soviet films not to their liking, but in their view the popularity of foreign films posed a much greater danger. The evidence was overwhelming that, if given a chance, the Soviet people preferred foreign products. *The Mark of Zorro, Robin Hood,* and *The Thief of Baghdad,* all starring Douglas Fairbanks, played in the best and largest theaters in the capital with full houses, and were seen by many more people than *Battleship Potemkin*. These were the most popular films that played in the Soviet Union in the 1920s (Fig. 21). Even opponents of the policy of imports had to admit that on the average foreign films produced ten times as much profit as domestic ones.[18]

In the early 1920s German films dominated the market. As late as 1924 80 percent of the foreign films playing in the Soviet Unon were made in Germany.[19] A Leningrad Komsomol paper, *Smena,* carried out a survey in the midtwenties that showed that the most popular actor was the German comedian, Harry Piel. The popularity of this actor was so great that the Soviet authorities were concerned. Factories and Komsomol cells organized discussions how Communists should fight "Harry Pielism" ("*garripilevsh-china*").[20]

At first, however, it was not Soviet films that replaced German ones, but the products of Hollywood; in the middle of the decade the Americans succeeded in conquering the world market, and the changes that took place in the Soviet Union were part of a worldwide phenomenon. The invasion of American films started in 1923 and quickly accelerated. The finest American film, D. W. Griffith's *Intolerance* – which had the greatest influence on Eisenstein – had already been shown in 1921. Soviet audiences had not liked the film. In Soviet distribution the entire sequence dealing with Jesus Christ had been cut and the montage changed to such an extent that the viewers had had trouble understanding what was happening.[21]

Figure 21.   Poster for 1929 screening of [*Don Q,*] *Son of Zorro* (1925).

Taking liberties with foreign works was frequent. The studios regarded them as raw material and considered that they had the right to do anything with them. Although in the era of the silent films idiosyncratic intertitles and recutting was widespread everywhere, the Russians went furthest. They changed the intent of the director purposefully and openly. One critic, V. Zhemchuzhnyi, went so far as to advocate that the intertitles should turn the film into a parody of itself and thereby reduce the love of Soviet people for foreign works.[22] More often, however, the intertitles were simply clumsy, and there was no obvious connection between what the picture showed and the text that followed. It would happen that the same foreign film playing in the Russian Republic and in the Ukraine had altogether different intertitles; in effect, the audiences saw different films. Not surprisingly, the Soviet authorities chose titles that stressed the social content of the film, however little that may have had to do with the original intent of the filmmaker.[23] For economic reasons the Soviet Union could not buy the newest and best films. Some of the films reached Soviet audiences many years after they were made. Chaplin's *The Kid,* for example, made in 1921, was not shown in the Soviet Union until 1929 and *The Gold Rush* never reached Soviet screens.[24] Also, Soviet representatives usually bought copies of American films from European distributors, after those films had their European runs.[25] Yet, in spite of the confusing cuts and titles, in spite of the poor quality of the copy, no Soviet artist could match the popularity of the American films and stars.

Russian love for Hollywood needs no special explanation. People all over the world enjoyed the adventures, the glamorous stars, and the spectacles that Hollywood alone was able to manufacture. Hollywood found the recipe: The hero in search of fortune visits locales, goes through extraordinary adventures, and achieves love and fortune. People did not get tired of the same formula. It made no difference that intellectuals all over the world deplored the effects of American films on the audiences, often in terms similar to Bolshevik critics. The difference was, of course, that the Bolsheviks did not have to stop at criticism; they were in the position to do something about it. For some time it was impossible to do without exports; Soviet studios produced too few films. As a result the Soviet people enjoyed the luxury of seeing what in fact they wanted to see, because their state was still too poor to provide them with what they should have wanted to see. The authorities had to limit themselves to combating foreign, and especially American influences by education.[26] Publicists wrote articles deploring the influence of foreign, subversive influences; Party and Komsomol cells held meetings to discuss the danger. Russian studios made several films that satirized the mania for foreign products. In 1926 a studio (Goskino) made a parody of *The Thief of Baghdad* (*The Thief, but Not from Baghdad*), and next S. Komarov at Mezhrabpom made *The Kiss of Mary Pickford,* a popular and witty film, which gently ridiculed the hero worship of foreign stars. Not surprisingly, meetings and articles made little impact. The Soviet authorities, however, could control what entered the country, and the number of foreign films gradually diminished. In 1924 Soviet films made up only 8 percent of the works exhibited, in 1925 35 percent, and in 1927 65 percent.[27] As the number of Soviet films grew, the number of foreign titles diminished. By the end of the First Five-Year Plan, for all practical purposes, they disappeared altogether. This development had far-reaching consequences: The disappearance of foreign films not merely limited the choice available to the Soviet people, but also saved Soviet directors from the need to compete with attractive foreign products.

Historians agree that Stalin's "cultural revolution" transformed Russian culture to a greater extent than the Bolsheviks' conquest of power in 1917. In the history of Soviet cinema also, the ending of the relative pluralism of the NEP was a major turning point. History, however, knows no tabula rasa: As the infant Soviet film industry was not free from the influence of prerevolutionary movies, the Stalinist, "socialist realist" cinema to a great extent was founded on the achievements of the golden age. Some of the preparatory work of the 1920s is obvious: Already at that time directors accepted and, indeed, took it for granted that they were working for the interests of the state and that political authorities had the right to interfere even in the most minute aspects of the creative process.

As we shall see in later chapters, during the "cultural revolution" the avant-garde directors were attacked most viciously and the slogan of the day, "films for the millions," was a euphemism for the repudiation of innovative filmmaking. One is, therefore, tempted to say that the directors who worked for mass audiences won out and that their work was to be the basis of the future. Such an evaluation, however, would not be entirely accurate. The makers of "socialist realist" art learned a great deal from the most innovative artists such as Eisenstein, Dovzhenko, and Pudovkin. "Socialist realist" films, like the great avant-garde works of the golden age, depicted conflicts not as struggles between complex human beings but between good and evil. The positive hero, an essential ingredient of the new art, was partially based on the highly stylized, larger-than-life characters of the great artists of an earlier age.

Notes

1 I am, of course, aware that here I am contradicting widely accepted ideas about the "revolutionary" character of cinema. The talk about "revolutionary" film seems to me a facile generalization; when this generalization is applied to Soviet cinema, it is simply incorrect.

2 Many of these works are available in English. Sergei Eisenstein, *The Film Form and the Film Sense,* Meridian, New York, 1957, and *Notes of a Film Director,* Dover, New York, 1970; Lev Kuleshov, *Kuleshov on Film,* Berkeley, University of California Press, 1974; Vsevolod Pudovkin, *Film Technique and Film Acting,* Lear,

New York, 1948; Dziga Vertov, *Kino-eye*, University of California Press, Berkeley, 1984; and Aleksandr Dovzhenko, *The Poet as Film Maker*, MIT Press, Cambridge, 1973.

3 N. A. Lebedev, *Ocherk istorii kino SSSR*, Iskusstvo, Moscow, 1947, p. 106.

4 *Sovetskie khudozhestvennye fil'my. Annotirovannyi katalog* (hereafter, *S.kh.f*), vol. 1, Iskusstvo, Moscow, 1961.

5 N. Lebedev, "Boevye dradtsatye gody," *Iskusstvo kino* 12: 95, 1968.

6 Jay Leyda, *Kino: A History of Russian and Soviet Film*, Collier Books, New York, 1960, p. 213, and E. Gromov, *L. V. Kuleshov*, Iskusstvo, Moscow, 1984, pp. 185–205.

7 See, for example, the review in *Pravda*, Dec. 4, 1926.

8 Judith Mayne, *Kino and the Woman Question: Feminism and Soviet Silent Film*, Ohio State University Press, Columbus, 1989, pp. 110–29. Mayne argues that this film did not have a feminist message.

9 Denise Youngblood, *Soviet Cinema in the Silent Era, 1918–1935*, UMI Press, Ann Arbor, Mich., 1985, pp. 119–21.

10 *S.kh.f.*

11 Marie Seton, *Sergei M. Eisenstein*, A. A. Wyn, New York, 1952, p. 38.

12 On the Proletkul't, see Lynn Mally, *Culture of the Future: The Prolet-kult Movement in Revolutionary Russia*, University of California Press, Berkeley, 1990.

13 G. Aleksandrov, *Epokha i kino*, Politizdat, Moscow, 1983.

14 N. M. Zorkaia, "Iakov Protazanov i Sovetskoe kinoiskusstvo 20-kh godov," *Voprosy kinoiskusstva*, Moscow, 6: 166, 1962.

15 *Izvestiia*, Feb. 19, 1925.

16 The film was heavily attacked for its apoliticism. See Youngblood, p. 105.

17 On the films of Ermler, see Denise Youngblood, "Cinema as Social Criticism: The Early Films of Fridrich Ermler," in Anna Lawton, (ed.), *The Red Screen: Image Making and Social Impact*, Harper Collins, New York, 1991.

18 K. Mal'tsev, "Sovetskoe kino na novykh putiakh," *Novyi mir*, May, 1929, pp. 243–8.

19 "Nemetskie fil'my v sovetskom prokate," *Kino i vremia*, Gosfil'mfond, Moscow, 1965, p. 380.

20 Ibid., p. 384.

21 "Amerikanskie fil'my v sovetskom prokate," *Kino i vremia*, Gosfil'mfond, Moscow, 1960, p. 193. Leyda maintains that *Intolerance* was first shown in 1919 and that it enjoyed a great popular success. He does not footnote his source, and therefore to me the version given by the Soviet scholar seems more convincing. Leyda, pp. 142–3. Artists may have been impressed, but contrary to Leyda, audiences were not attracted.

22 "Kak pokazat' zagranichnye kartiny?" *Sovetskii ekran*, June 26, 1928, p. 5.

23 "Frantsuzkie fil'my v sovetskom prokate," *Kino i vremia*, Gosfil'mfond, Moscow, 1965, p. 351.

24 *Kino i vremia*, 1960, pp. 197–200.

25 Only the Soviet foreign trade agency, Narkomtrog, was entitled to purchase films. Most of the trade was carried out in Paris and Berlin, but Latvia was also a source. First the Soviet representatives sent home a copy for the censor, and only if

permission came to purchase was the transaction carried out. *Kinospravochnik*, ed. G. M. Boltianskii, Kinoizdatel'stvo, Moscow, 1926, p. 37.

26 One of the most moderate and intelligent evaluations of the impact of foreign films came from A. V. Lunacharskii. See his *Kino na zapade i u nas*, Tea-kino pechat', Moscow, 1928.

27 Ibid., p. 210.

CHAPTER 4

Reaching the people, 1925–1929

The ideology of the New Economic Policy (NEP) was built on a contradiction: On the one hand the Bolsheviks had far-reaching ambitions in remaking society and man, and on the other they did not possess the means to assert their will in the existing society. Their reach exceeded their grasp. Bolshevik utopianism was born out of weakness: It made little sense to develop modest plans at a time when they lacked the tools for accomplishing even these; they felt free to allow their imagination to roam. As a result, they disliked gradualist, ameliorist methods, and instead were attracted to all sorts of ephemeral schemes. Many of the unusual features of Soviet life in the period can be explained by keeping in mind the contradiction between great ambitions and limited means.

The Bolsheviks were weakest in the countryside. They had not succeeded in transforming it; peasant life continued more or less undisturbed by the "greatest revolution in world history," as the Bolsheviks liked to describe their victory in 1917–21. It is not that Bolshevik rule was insecure: The peasants did not threaten the new order and were happy to be left alone. Had the Bolsheviks been like their tsarist predecessors, they might have been content to leave matters as they were. But this was unthinkable for them. In the 1920s they attempted to make their influence felt in the villages through a series of undertakings, and to instill in the peasantry a new way of thinking and a desire for a different way of life. The campaign to bring films to the peasants was an important part of this larger effort. The history of the campaign is interesting because it shows with exceptioinal clarity Bolshevik attitudes to politics and propaganda in the 1920s. Significantly, the Bolsheviks coined the term *kinofikatsiia*, "cinefication," to denote this campaign. The analogy with electrification (*elektrifikatsiia*), is obvious: As electrification was to create the material preconditions for a socialist society, so cinefication was to be an important element in preparing the mind of the peasantry for the new way of life.

The industry

The simultaneous appearance of many talented artists cannot easily be explained, but the expansion of the industry can be shown in numerical terms. The number of films registered in the Catalog of Soviet Feature Films indicates the magnitude of the growth.[1] In 1921, there were 9 titles, in 1922, there were 16 and in 1923, there were 26. The great jump took place in 1924, when 68 films were made; in 1926, 102; and in 1927, 119. The peak was reached in 1928, when the Soviet Union produced 123 films. In the following year, the number fell to 91. These numbers do not even show the full extent of the growth, for during the early years the studios made almost exclusively short *agitki*. Moviegoing in the Soviet Union was obviously popular. In 1928, 300 million tickets were sold. An average film was seen by 2.5 million people.[2]

Sovkino opened a new studio in Leningrad, Mezhrabpom started one in Moscow, and the Ukrainians built studios in Kiev, Odessa, and Yalta. In addition, the national minorities started to make films in Baku, Erevan, and Tashkent.[3] In 1928, the country had thirteen functioning studios. Four of these, Sovkino, VUFKU (the Ukrainian organization), Gruziafilm (the Georgian studio), and Mezhrabpom produced over 80 percent of the movies.[4]

From our present vantage point it is extraordinary that neither the Bolshevik leaders nor the critics were pleased with the achievement. Indeed, on the contrary: Contemporary literature was full of criticisms of the industry and there was constant talk about a state of crisis. In the second half of the 1920s there was still a cacophony of views; observers, politicians, and critics quarreled with one another. Most of the critics were dissatisfied, even if they disagreed with one another on the nature of the problem and on the proper solution. Ironically, at the time when the best directors were producing their masterpieces, the denunciation of the industry became increasingly bitter. There can be few examples of such disjunction of contemporary opinion and the evaluation of posterity.

The explanation of the seeming paradox, that great accomplishments and bitter disappointments coincided, is to be found in the impossible expectations of the Bolsheviks. The Bolsheviks were able propagandists and, as most people, tended to overestimate the power of that tool. In particular, they overestimated the ability of cinema under the prevailing circumstances to influence people. It turned out that while films did make an impression, their impact could not be measured, and most activists believed that the overall influence of cinema was not as favorable and as powerful as they had hoped.

While the late 1920s was a wonderful period in Soviet film both in terms of artistic achievement and in quantitative growth, the industry also had genuine problems. Some of these were a consequence of the poverty of the country and others followed from the nature of the Soviet regime. First of all, there were constant shortages of equipment and raw material. Directors bemoaned the continued poverty of the industry. They envied their Western colleagues who had incomparably superior equipment. Indeed, conditions were poor. Because the Soviet Union did not manufacture raw film, it had to be bought abroad with precious convertible currency.[5] Consequently, there was a shortage, and film directors often could not afford the luxury of shooting a scene over again. In addition, the film factories did not have proper lighting or good quality chemicals for developing the films.[6] The consequence of the poverty was that complaints about the technological backwardness of Soviet film poured in from every direction. Viewers complained that films were so dark that they could hardly make out the figures; they deplored the grainy, gray appearance of the pictures, lacking in sharpness. The comparison of typical Soviet films with the works of foreign studios was painful.[7]

Given the poverty and backwardness of the country, it was difficult to catch up with Western technology. Fortunately, however, beyond a certain minimum level the quality of the equipment had little to do with artistry. It is impressive that the great Russian directors achieved international recognition while working in studios that no Westerner would have tolerated. Indeed, some argued that the technical poverty compelled some of the Soviet directors, such as Kuleshov and Eisenstein, to be very conscious of what they were doing. These men worked out everything on paper first, because they could not afford to waste film. They were forced to become theoreticians of filmmaking.

The shortage of raw materials was largely inevitable; the scenario shortage, however, was a different matter. The lack of good scripts was a worldwide problem. The appetite of the audiences for novelties, for good and entertaining films grew faster than writers could satisfy. The writing of a scenario required special skills and knowledge, and given the youth of the medium, few people possessed these.[8] Many, if not most, writers had a condescending attitude to cinema, and therefore writing scripts did not promise much prestige.

The script shortage in the Soviet Union had somewhat different causes than elsewhere. The attitude of the Bolsheviks to cinema made the situation a great deal worse. The Bolsheviks believed that films had to educate; once again, there was a wide gap between ambitions and available means. During World War I Russian studios produced hundreds of films. The scenarist participated in the shooting process, making up the story as his fellow filmmakers went along doing their job. A large number of nonsensical films were made this way, and the audiences found these amusing; otherwise they would not have paid money to see them. Such frivolous entertainment, however, was not good enough for those who were responsible for Soviet film.

The Bolsheviks made every effort to raise the prestige of the writer at the expense of the director. Given the expectations of those responsible for Soviet film, this attitude was understandable. It was mainly the script that contained the ideological message. Furthermore, the script could be checked and evaluated much more easily than the director's work. In the Bolshevik scheme of things, it was the writer who was ultimately responsible and it was he who was to get most of the credit and financial rewards. It was expected that he would write an "iron scenario" and that the director would faithfully follow it. In the conditions prevailing in the 1920s, however, unlike in the following decade, first-rate directors were able to disregard instructions from above, and do their work as they saw fit. Eisenstein, for example, used only a couple of pages from a scenario written by N. Agadzhanova-Shutko in making *Battleship Potemkin*. It is clear that the completed film was entirely the director's, and the scenarist's contribution was exactly zero.[9] This ability of the director to disobey and retain his independence was a precondition for making masterpieces; when the "iron scenario" became a reality, the great age of Soviet film ended.

The shortage of suitable scripts was as old as Soviet film itself. To help matters, in 1924 Goskino held a contest for scenario writers, and the contest was followed by others.[10] However, neither the attempt to raise the prestige of the writer nor the contests to encourage amateurs helped much. There were plenty of enterprising amateurs, but their products were not found suitable by the studios. Most scripts submitted, whether in the course of a contest or independently, were rejected. From October 1923 to October 1924 Goskino accepted only 26 scripts out of 365. In future years the proportions did not change.[11] No doubt, not all scripts were rejected for political reasons. Many of them, one assumes, were simply poor and would not have been filmed in any country. But it is obvious that political considerations and the ever-present and complex censorship bodies made matters a great deal worse. During the period of the New Economic Policy, the regime still tolerated a variety of voices in the realm of arts. Trotsky best expressed the attitude of the leadership in his book, *Literature and Revolution*:

If the Revolution has the right to destroy bridges and art monuments whenever necessary, it will stop still less from laying its hand on any tendency in art, which, no matter how great its achievement in form, threatens to disintegrate the revolutionary environment or to arouse the internal forces of the Revolution, that is the proletariat, the peasantry and the intelligentsia, to a hostile opposition to one another. Our standard is, clearly, political, imperative and intolerant. But for this very reason it must define the limits of its activity clearly. For a more precise expression of my meaning, I will say: we ought to have a watchful revolutionary censorship, and a broad and flexible policy in the field of art, free from petty partisan maliciousness.[12]

Censorship was an obstacle to the further development of Soviet cinema not merely because it established political standards and forbade the expression of some views and the treatment of numerous topics. The censorship bureaucracy, overlapping jurisdictions, and competing bodies created confusion. The Main Committee on Repertory (Glavrepetkom) within Narkompros had censorship authority both over foreign and domestic film. This body was created by a decision of the Council of Commissars of the Russian Republic in November 1923. It prepared lists of permitted and forbidden films which were then sent to the provinces. In July 1924, however, another organization was created within Narkompros, the Art Council (Khudozhestvennyi sovet).[13] Its eleven members had to approve every scenario before filming could begin in any of the studios of the Russian Republic. During the first year of its existence it approved only 147 out of the 307 that were submitted. The studios themselves had "artistic bureaus," which first examined the submitted manuscripts. No wonder that many of the writers became frustrated. Vladimir Maiakovskii described his experience with the censorship organizations in an article he wrote in 1927. One group, which included Kuleshov, Victor Shklovskii, the famous literary theorist and scenarist, and P. Bliakhin, a critic, found his work wonderful, but another group, made up of bureaucrats, would not allow filming. Maiakovskii deplored the lack of artistic autonomy and ended his article with this pious hope: "There is one consolation for those who work in the cinema: 'Governing bodies come and go – but art remains.' "[14]

The bulk of the critical literature, however, dealt not with such real issues as the shortage of materials and scripts, but deplored real and imagined ideological weaknesses and the inability of Soviet film to reach and influence a target audience. It is something of an irony that Soviet film in the period of its greatest artistic achievements failed to please the political leadership of the country. The reason was clear enough: The Bolsheviks set impossible tasks for the Soviet film industry. They wanted the directors to make films that could be used for propaganda purposes, would be artistically satisfactory, and would attract an audience. Upon a moment's reflection it is obvious that satisfying each of these goals would have called for different policies. On occasion it was possible to satisfy two of the three goals, but never all three. Ideology blinded the Bolsheviks. They could not see the self-evident truth that Soviet audiences, especially workers and peasants, wanted above all to be entertained.

We have a rather clear idea about popular tastes in movies. Soviet people, as people elsewhere, went to movies to be entertained. They liked romance, adventure, and laughter. As discussed in the previous chapter, the films of Hollywood were as popular in the Soviet Union as they were everywhere else. Among domestic films the most popular ones were made by directors who had little interest in innovation and were content to follow foreign models. Although these directors may have contributed little to the cinema as an art form, they knew how to hold an audience and how to tell a story.

In 1926 and 1928 the authorities carried out surveys in Moscow film theaters, which were never published. From these it emerged that the bulk of the audience in Moscow was made up of white-collar workers and students. The audiences, then as today, were overwhelmingly young. The majority of them declared that they went to the movies to be entertained.[15] Some of the respondents went so far as to say that they wanted films without "excessive proletarian ideology."

Such attitudes were deeply disturbing to Party activists, who had always regarded political education as the primary task of the cinema. They dealt with this uncomfortable reality by denying it. They insisted that the workers demanded films with "proletarian ideology" and that the workers and peasants disapproved of foreign films and films that were meant only to entertain.[16] Soviet historians have repeated this nonsense endlessly until very recent times.[17] Needless to say, they never advanced any evidence to support this proposition. In fact the opposite was true: To the extent that the political films of an Eisentstein or a Pudovkin found an audience, it was among the "bourgeois" intelligentsia.

Cinefication

In the 1920s cinema remained largely an urban entertainment. (In January 1926 the Russian Federal Republic had 807 commercial movie houses and of these 51 were in Moscow and approximately the same number in Leningrad.)[18] In the middle of the decade movie life revived. The state lowered the rental charges and taxes on movie tickets and, as a consequence, between 1923 and 1925 the number of cinemas more than doubled, though still not reaching prerevolutionary levels.[19] In the cities, but especially in Moscow and Leningrad, a thriving film culture developed. Film magazines catered to movie lovers, and the newspapers carried film reviews and advertisements. These advertisements were very important in determining the popular success of a film.[20]

The movie houses were very different from one another. In Moscow out of fifty-one theaters seven were designated as first-run cinemas. These charged as much as a ruble or a ruble and a half for a ticket, as against 40–80 kopecks for the second- and third-run cinemas. The former, of course, were located in the center of the city and received films from the rental office several weeks (or, in the case of a very popular foreign film, several months) before the program reached the modest movie houses located in the proletarian outskirts. One may assume that the skill and taste of the pianists who accompanied the silent films were superior to what was available in the cheaper cinemas. Some of the expensive movie houses were rather elegant: Orchestras were playing in the foyers, and there were reading rooms and other forms of entertainment for the waiting public.[21] These differences were somewhat reduced at the end of the decade, when the theaters were gradually nationalized once again.

In this period of growth and artistic accomplishments, the Soviet leaders attempted to realize their long-standing intention to use the cinema for political education. They had in mind three special target audiences: soldiers, workers, and peasants. It was easiest to supply the Red Army, because the soldiers had few entertainments and they loved movies. The regime considered political education among soldiers a high priority and therefore supplied resources generously. There were no special organizational problems. At the end of the 1920s the average soldier saw three times as many films as other Soviet citizens.[22] Their fare was limited: The political leadership made certain that no heterodox ideas could undermine the ideology it was attempting to instill, and therefore it imposed strict limitations. After 1928 no foreign films were shown to soldiers, and even some of the Soviet films were considered inappropriate. The very successful and amusing *The Kiss of Mary Pickford*, for example, could not be shown.[23] However, the soldiers went to see whatever was shown.

The Red Army became an important helpmate in cinefication. Because there were not enough trained projectionists, the Army organized courses, lasting 350–400 hours, for film technicians. These courses, naturally, included political education, and the graduates, after they returned to civilian life, provided the villages with much-needed technicians.[24]

Most workers saw films in their clubs. These clubs were administered by the Cultural Department of the Trade Unions, which were entrusted with all educational activity among workers. Because the price of admission was much lower than in the commercial theaters (15–20 kopecks) clubs were enormously popular. Some of the clubs exhibited films almost every night. The great expansion in movie life in the clubs occurred between 1923 and 1926. In 1926 in the Russian Republic alone there were 1,413 projectors in workers' clubs.[25] Neither Sovkino nor the leaders entrusted with political education among workers were altogether satisfied. Because Sovkino charged low rental fees to clubs, those responsible for Soviet cinema were concerned that the clubs undermined the profitability of the industry. Sovkino drew up a contract with the trade unions in which the unions promised that only members of the unions and their families would be allowed to attend. On its part Sovkino promised that Soviet-made films would be made available to clubs no later than four weeks after their showing in first-run cinemas. Foreign films, interestingly, were explicitly excluded from this agreement. All through the 1920s Sovkino was attacked by its radical critics for its supposed failure to provide a sufficient number of ideologically correct films to the clubs.[26]

The leaders of the trade-union movement were concerned that cinema would squeeze out all other cultural activities. It was evident on the one hand that films were a wonderful magnet but, on the other, that communist educators could not regard watching films as a goal in itself. The task of the clubs, after all, was not merely to amuse and entertain. On January 1, 1926, Seniushkin, the head of the Cultural Department of the National Organization of Trade Unions (VTsSPS), wrote to all cultural sections about the proper role of films in clubs.[27] He recommended setting up film circles, which would be responsible for the selection of ideologically correct films and also for integrating them into the general cultural work. Furthermore, these circles would have the task of propagandizing Soviet films against ideologically dubious foreign ones and organizing discussion sessions after the performances, when the audience was to be encouraged to judge the political content and the behavior of the heroes of the films.

The secretary of the union of the workers of community enterprises (Soiuz Rabotnikov Kommunalnogo Khozaistva), Ratmanov, in a letter of August of the same year, spelled out in greater detail the role of films:

Showing films is often not connected with general cultural work and it is only for commercial purposes. Some clubs charge as much as 50 kopecks. In order to improve the situation, the Union recommends to the cultural department the following: 1. check on the work of clubs and make clear to them the role of movies. 2. Do not allow films to take up a larger role in the work of the club than other forms of mass work. No more than two evenings per week should be devoted to the showing of films. 3. The cultural sections should contact the film section of the Central trade union organization in order to receive proper films for the clubs. In the selection of the films the needs of the audience should be taken into account. 4. It is essential to organize film circles, and these, with the cooperation of the provincial organizations, should choose ideologically correct films. 5. The price of the ticket should only pay for the film and for incidental expenses. It should not be more than 20 kopecks. 6. In order to use the time properly, the clubs should organize orchestras, drama circles, etc. Organize work in the clubs in such a way that showing of films will not disturb the development of other forms of mass work.[28]

However annoying it may have been for the Soviet leaders to see the workers spending their time on "frivolous entertainments," on balance the clubs were useful in contributing to the political education of the working classes.

Bringing films to the peasants was vastly more difficult than supplying workers' clubs. Not only was the countryside backward, poor, and lacking electricity, but perhaps most important, the Party still had little organizational strength. In view of their later radical transformation of village life, it is difficult for us to recall how extremely weak the Bolsheviks were at one time. The Party had few peasant members, and the indigenous peasant commune, which often resisted government intervention, was a more powerful organization than the village soviet. It was a vicious circle: The Party did not have enough followers, and therefore it could not advertise its point of view and thereby win new converts.

The work began only in 1924; before that the Party had made only haphazard attempts.[29] The task was given to Glavpolitprosvet, an agency that was established in 1920 within the Commissariat of Enlightenment, and entrusted with the supervision of adult and political education. Glavpolitprosvet dealt with the issue by setting up a special section that was to get projectors and films suitable for peasants, propagandize cinema in the countryside, and make sure that the correct ideological message was transmitted.[30] Sovkino also established a special department in August 1925, which had the task of collecting films for peasant audiences and working out rental arrangements.[31]

According to Soviet views of the time it was not enough for the central authorities to set up some bureaucratic bodies; it was necessary to draw in the people. The very process of carrying out the work was to have propaganda significance. The Bolsheviks managed the drive for "cinefication" as they did campaigns concerning other important issues, such as those against illiteracy, alcoholism, and the church. They mobilized whatever organized strength was available. In this case, they sent out groups of agitators with mobile projectors, used the cooperative movement, and formed a "voluntary" society. Obshchestvo Druzei Sovetskogo Kino (ODSK, Society of Friends of Soviet Cinema) was established in 1925, and its first president was Felix Dzerzhinskii. The tasks of the organization were to carry out propaganda in favor of the cinema, to introduce films to audiences, and to report back on audience reactions. ODSK was the counterpart of such organizations as Society "Down with Illiteracy" or ODN (formed to combat illiteracy), the League of the Militant Godless, the Society of the Friends of the Red Fleet, and the Society of the Friends of the Red Air Fleet. ODSK published a journal, and from its meager financial resources it contributed to buying projectors. The problem of this society was the same as that of the other similar ones: There were not enough cadres in the villages. As a consequence, it was the same few people who participated in all government-inspired campaigns. The local cells in most instances existed only on paper.

The cooperative movement had a considerable role to play in bringing films to the countryside. The cooperatives were persuaded to buy portable or stationary projectors and organized film performances. Especially in the last two years of the NEP, the cooperatives had significant achievements.[32] In 1929 they owned approximately half of the projectors in the villages.[33]

The peculiar Soviet method of agitation, the so-called *shefstvo* system, was also exploited. *Shefstvo* meant that, say, a factory or a university "adopted" a village, provided whatever help it could, and assumed responsibility for propaganda work. Agitators from the city on occasion brought projectors and films for movie performances.[34]

The most important foundation of cinefication was the Party organization. It was the district Party committee that organized "film tours" in the countryside. A small group of agitators and mechanics traveled in the countryside for about a month at a time. On each trip they managed to visit ten to fifteen villages, where they showed a feature film and a collection of shorts. Since they could not visit every village, people often came from neighboring settlements to see the show. In fact, usually the problem was that the villages did not possess large enough halls to accommodate everyone who wanted to see the performance.[35] Traveling in the countryside with films required special talents. A. Katsigras, the chief activist in the "cinefication" campaign, described the requirements:

The circumstances in which the village film worker operates constantly change. As he travels from place to place, the people change, their requirements change, the circumstances of work change. The very nature of the work, constant movement from village to village, requires considerable physical and moral strength, a sociable and tactful nature.[36]

Katsigras went on to say that these people had to have a good knowledge of the village, be educated, understand the political situation as well as the domestic and foreign policies of the Bolshevik Party, be able to explain the films to the peasants, and be capable of organizing the available local pro-Soviet forces. At the same time, of course, they had to know how to operate and repair the projector. Given these requirements, no wonder that Katsigras complained that there were not enough such people and that their absence was the main stumbling block in the development of the "cinefication" campaign.[37]

By using all available methods, the achievements of the regime in cinefication were considerable. In October 1925 in the entire Soviet Union there were only 457 stationary projectors in villages and an approximately equal number of movable ones.[38] From this point on, the growth was impressive. In April 1929 there were 4,340 projectors.[39] During this period the intake for movie tickets increased from 400,000 to 3 million rubles. In 1927 approximately 20 million tickets were sold in the countryside, and at the end of the NEP period 80 million.[40] Because there were 300 million visitors to movie theaters in the entire country in 1929, that meant that the peasants, who made up more than 80 percent of the population, bought a little over a quarter of the movie tickets. To put it differently, an average peasant saw considerably less than one film a year. Such a growth of the village film network was a considerable accomplishment when one considers the obstacles the regime had to overcome. Aside from a shortage of cadres and a lack of organizational base, there had been major material problems. Most of these were the predictable consequences of the backwardness and poverty of the country. For cinefication to be a success, the countryside needed a minimum of sixty to seventy copies of the few films that were considered suitable for peasant audiences.

A second problem was the availability of projectors. Before the revolution Russian industry did not make projectors, and during the early years of the Soviet regime, all projectors were foreign made. As time went on, more and more of these broke down and there were no spare parts for repair. Finally, the Soviet regime was compelled to produce its own machines. The advanced industrial countries had no use any longer for projectors with built-in generators, which was the only kind that made sense in the Soviet countryside. In any case, foreign projectors were too delicate for the task.[41] Between 1925 and 1929 two Soviet factories, one in Leningrad and one in Odessa, produced nine thousand machines. (This figure included both stationary and portable ones.) Out of these less than half were operating in 1929.

Soviet-made machines were both expensive and unreliable. In 1929 each cost nine hundred rubles, which meant that two projectors cost as much as a tractor. Given the considerable expense, it is understandable that village authorities were reluctant to spend the money.[42] The unreliability of projectors was the bane of the village film network. It would often happen that the activists after considerable difficulties organized a village tour. They would get the necessary films and projectors and bring an audience together. They were then embarrassed to find that the projector either did not work at all, or broke down in the middle of the performance. It aggravated the problem that in the countryside there was a dearth of skilled mechanics. In one instance, at least, we have record of a mechanic who lubricated the projectors with tar, instead of oil.[43] As in so many other aspects of Soviet industry, then and later, low-quality products combined with untrained and uncaring maintenance led to waste. The poorly functioning projectors often damaged the film and its replacement was difficult. While in the cities the same film could be shown on the average eight thousand times, in the village its life expectancy was only two hundred showings.[44]

The cinefication campaign took place in the midst of extensive and increasingly bitter debates concerning the film industry. Radical publicists made unfair attacks on the policies of Sovkino. They criticized the ideological message of the most popular films, they criticized importing "ideological poison," and they expressed their dissatisfaction for not paying enough attention to the film fare offered by workers' clubs and, most insistently, for not paying enough attention to the task of cinefication. On the one hand the publicists wanted Sovkino to invest more in providing films for the villages and, on the other, wanted to deprive Sovkino of its best source of revenue, importing foreign hits.

The attacks on Sovkino's policies gathered momentum from the middle of the decade but were expressed most clearly at a national conference on film organized by the Party in March 1928. The resolution of the conference among other things said:

The film in the countryside should become a weapon of the proletariat in transforming the individualist views of the smallholder peasants, a weapon in the struggle for winning over the middle and poor peasants for the socialist reconstruction of the land of the Soviets. . . . At the same time, the countryside should become a large and profitable market for Soviet films, an economic basis for the cinefication of the entire country.[45]

It is clear now, as it should have been then, that the two goals were mutually exclusive, and that the directives were utopian and did not take account of the real world. The combination of money making and political education in the countryside was an impossible task and it was bound to fail.

The most controversial issue concerning cinefication was finance. All participants in the controversy assumed that the government would not and could not pay. Further, everyone took it for granted that in the long run the film industry was to be a major source of revenue. Trotsky wrote in a 1923 article that movies were to take the place of vodka in the villages.[46] What he had in mind was that on the one hand movies would provide a more cultured entertainment for the Russian people than alcohol and, on the other, that the government's revenue from the sale of vodka could be replaced by the sale of movie tickets. Stalin at the Fifteenth Party Congress in 1927 repeated Trotsky's expression almost verbatim; and ever since then the idea that cinema should take the place of vodka has been a cliché of Soviet publicists. After the passage of more than six decades, it is fair to say that the idea that somehow the cinema would lessen the Russian people's reliance on alcohol was wildly optimistic.

Whatever the distant future might bring, for practical people the significant question was where should the money for village cinema come from right now. Sovkino, which was responsible for distribution, was mercilessly attacked by its enemies, for "rightist deviation," that is, for not paying enough attention to the peasant viewer and for charging too high rental rates.[47] From the point of view of Sovkino, the heart of the matter was that, although by 1929 almost half of the film performances in the Soviet Union were held in villages, these performances yielded only 16 percent of all income.[48] In order to diminish losses from village film distribution, Sovkino would have to set ticket prices relatively high. Interestingly, everyone agreed that it would be wrong to allow unions and cooperatives to pay for the cost of the performance. The agitators believed that free movies would lower the prestige of films and therefore their agitational value. The peasants had to pay for the performance.[49]

The radical critics of Sovkino, most prominently A. Katsigras, who wrote countless articles and even a book on the subject, believed that charging more than ten kopecks for a ticket was "a socially incorrect" policy that favored *kulaks* and hurt the interests of the village poor. What could be done? Katsigras and his ideological colleagues argued that Sovkino erred in importing expensive foreign films and producing expensive films at home. Instead, in their view, Sovkino should have produced more politically educational films and newsreels.[50] Obviously the production of these films was many times cheaper. Such an argument, however, did not recognize that the peasant might not want to pay even ten kopecks for a "politicoeducational" film. The initial appeal of the medium would quickly wear off, and peasants, like everyone else, would pay only for films that they wanted to see. In these circumstances the losses of Sovkino would increase.

The representatives of Sovkino were unable to counter Katsigras's argument, because it was increasingly dangerous to do so. The debate was taking place at a time when ever more unrealistic plans for industrialization were being drawn up and when the country was experiencing the first series of show trials. The radicals' assault on Sovkino was a part of the resurgent radical attack on the entire political and social system of the NEP. Those who attacked the "incorrect" class policy of Sovkino were in fact also opposing the existing freedom of expression in Soviet cinema and the variety of artistic fare still available.

Films for the peasants

Condescension toward the Russian people, but especially toward the peasantry, was an integral part of the Bolshevik worldview. In this respect the Leninists were typical representatives of the nineteenth-century intelligentsia. Many of them assumed that there was nothing worthwhile in the peasant way of life and that their task was to persuade the peasants to change it. They wanted the peasants to live and think like cultured Europeans. From this attitude followed the Bolshevik strategy of using the cinema for "political education." All Bolsheviks took for granted that the cinema was an excellent instrument for this purpose. The very medium itself was education, for almost any film would show the peasants a life different from their own and thereby broaden their vision. The peasants were obviously interested in seeing pictures of cities and of the many strange things the outside world had to offer. Village agitators reported already at the time of the Civil War that merely showing moving images of the leaders, Lenin and Trotsky, and demonstrations in cities was effective for it made for the peasants the distant Bolsheviks somehow more real.[51]

Nevertheless the question remained, what kind of films would be most politically beneficial? This problem became part of the larger debate concerning the present and future of the film industry that took place in the late 1920s. No one suggested simply supplying the villages with the type of films that the peasants seemed to want. After all, the Bolsheviks believed that they knew better than the peasants what films were best for them.

Some protagonists in the debate advocated that given the low cultural level of the peasantry, the peasants should see only educational films. Others argued that, on the contrary, feature films were the most effective propaganda. Barshak, the official at Sovkino responsible for cinefication, inclined toward the second view. He wrote:

First of all, is our task only to amuse the peasant? Of course not. Our task is to bring the issues to the peasantry that are raised by socialist construction. Every film should strengthen the will of the peasantry in the struggle for the new Soviet village, for socialism in the countryside. And, of course, the more artistic, the more absorbing the film, the less it looks like naked agitation, the better it can reach the masses of the peasantry.[52]

What kind of feature films were effective among the peasants? All participants in the discussions agreed that the peasants needed different films from those that appealed to city people. The leaders of the film industry decided to approach the question scientifically. As early as in 1925 Glavpolitprosvet attempted a study of village viewers.[53] The study was based on several sources: Trained observers registered noises made by audiences during performances; village correspondents wrote on peasant preferences; and the organizers of the study handed out questionnaires to literate peasants. This study may have been the first such effort undertaken anywhere in the world.

The results were hardly surprising. The peasants liked amusing films. They liked to be entertained. They were interested both in life in the villages and in the cities. They did not care for artistic experimentation, such as quick cutting and unusual juxtapositions in montage. Films with long intertitles were also hardly suitable for a largely illiterate audience. Agitators often had to read the titles aloud to the peasants in order to help them to make sense out of what they saw. Films with few words and a great deal of action were popular.[54] From such observations it followed that the best Soviet films, including the works of Eisenstein and Dovzhenko, were incomprehensible and boring for the peasants.[55] Such incomprehension followed not so much from the ignorance of the peasant masses, but from the fact that the medium was new to them and therefore they had not had a chance to acquaint themselves with its conventions. A successful cinefication campaign might have eventually reduced the gap between the taste of city and village audiences.

Sovkino responded to the constant criticism of not having enough appropriate films for village audiences by an ingenious method. It reedited films in such a way as to make the montage even by reducing the number of changes of scenes, and to eliminate those elements that the peasants found unrealistic and therefore disturbing. Also, the intertitles were changed and simplified. Thus, in the Soviet Union in the late 1920s there were often two versions of the same film: a city version and a village version.[56] Some agitators even experimented with the rather strange idea of slowing down the speed of projection. We have no reports how the peasants responded to seeing their films in slow motion.[57]

As the enemies of Sovkino did not tire in emphasizing, there were not enough films for village audiences. The situation was very bad in the middle of the decade and it improved only a little in the last years of the 1920s. The problem had several sources. For political reasons, the leaders of the film establishment considered many of the most successful films of the decade unsuitable for peasants. The great box office hit in the cities, *The Bear's Wedding,* for example, whose scenario ironically was written by Commissar of Enlightenment Anatolii Lunacharskii on the basis of a Prosper Merimée story, was considered too risqué. This rather strange film showed the mad and murderous behavior of a nineteenth-century lord and included, for the

1920s, some sexually suggestive scenes. Furthermore, the mad nobleman was portrayed with a certain degree of sympathy. Protazanov's science-fiction film, *Aelita,* was not shown to peasants because it depicted aspects of Soviet life in a not altogether favorable light. The best and most realistic picture of daily life *(byt)* in the city was given by Abram Room in his *Third Meshchanskaia Street,* which in a matter-of-fact way portrayed a ménage à trois. It was considered too immoral to be shown to peasants.[58]

Another reason for the dearth of films was commercial. Sovkino, which was under constant pressure to make money, sent the copies of most popular films first to city theaters, where the profits were much greater and where the film was less likely to be damaged by improper handling. From a purely commercial point of view it made sense to show the films first to city audiences and only after a passage of some months send them to provincial cities, and even later to workers clubs and to the countryside. For this distribution policy, the leaders of Sovkino were bitterly attacked.

We have only scattered accounts, coming from reports of agitators and village correspondents, of what the peasants actually saw and liked. People in the cities, who in the 1920s enjoyed considerable choice, could express what they liked by buying tickets. We can tell, for example, that Douglas Fairbanks and Mary Pickford were the greatest box office hits because their films enjoyed the longest runs in the best and largest theaters in the cities. Peasants, like soldiers, had no comparable choice; they went to see the films offered to them. The fact that films were shown to them did not in itself testify to their popularity. One suspects that the peasants often begrudged the ten or fifteen kopecks they paid for a ticket.

The Little Red Devils, an adventure film made in 1923, was very popular among peasants, as it was among all Soviet people. This good-natured film showed fantastic adventures of three youths during the time of the Civil War. The peasants liked it so much that when they had a chance, they would see it more than once. Another extremely popular film was the first Soviet feature film, *Polikushka* (1919; first shown in 1922), based on a Lev Tolstoy story. The peasants loved this film even more than people in the cities did. They were moved by its sentiments and did not seem to mind that it was excessively theatrical.[59]

Some of the films shown in villages were ludicrously inappropriate. An agitator, for example, writing from Irkutsk province in 1926, complained that for their film tour through the villages the regional office of Sovkino sent them films such as *How Snooky Became a Capitalist* (Snooky was an ape) and "educational" films, such as *Cooperatives in Normandy,* which were outdated and boring and had absolutely nothing to do with the problems of the Russian village in the NEP period.[60] The three feature films shown on the same tour, *Evdokia Rozhnovskaia, Khveska,* and *The Wolf's Duty,* were five and six years old and had never enjoyed a successful run in the cities.

Only a few Soviet films dealt with contemporary life, and only a small minority of these took place in the villages. Most of the peasant films were poorly made. The journal *Sovetskii ekran* complained that directors knew more about jungles and about life in prehistoric times than they knew about peasant life. Consequently, in the view of the writer, they portrayed pseudopeasants with pseudoproblems. They put clothes on the actors and actresses that they thought the peasants wore and betrayed no knowledge of regional variations and local customs. All peasants looked and behaved the same way.[61] The journal's description of the characteristics of peasant films is worth quoting in its entirety:

Characters: priest, *kulak,* poor peasant, daughter of poor peasant, – more unusually: teacher, Komsomol member, and demobilized soldier. Situation: priest and *kulak* insult the poor peasant. The poor peasant wants to force his daughter to marry someone she does not love. The *kulak* burns down the cooperative. The *kulak* and the priest are portrayed never without a bottle of vodka in their hands. The teacher and the Komsomol member give speeches at meetings, but in fact they address the audience. As a result of their intervention everything ends as it should: the *kulak* is arrested, the priest is discredited, the poor peasant is satisfied and his daughter marries her beloved. Vice is punished and virtue triumphs. And all this is unconvincing, because the peasant knows that it is not only the *kulak* who drinks home brew. And the peasant knows much else that is different in real life from how it is portrayed in the film.[62]

Almost all peasant films reflected the intelligentsia's condescension toward the masses. The peasants usually needed the help of outsiders to right things. In *The Lucky Ten Ruble Piece*, for example, the peasant, Ershov, travels to the city to sell eggs and butter and there he meets a worker, Kuznetsov. Ershov tells Kuznetsov about the poor work of the village cooperative, who then suggests to his new peasant friend to come to a meeting of workers. There the peasant sees how the workers criticize one another, regardless of position. Ershov returns to the village and brings order into the collective.[63] One may surmise that the peasants resented such exhibitions of patronizing attitudes. According to the testimony of *Sovetskii ekran,* the peasants did not like *The Lucky Ten Ruble Piece*.

The world-famous Soviet directors succeeded neither in reaching a village audience nor in portraying contemporary peasant life. Vertov, for example, generally objected to films that told stories and had professional actors. Pudovkin did not make films about contemporary Soviet life. Kuleshov's *Your Acquaintance* and *Extraordinary Adventures of Mr. West in the Land of the Bolsheviks* took place in the city. Some of Dovzhenko's best works are placed in the Ukrainian countryside; however, this elliptic, experimental style could not possibly entertain an uneducated audience.

In his entire life Eisenstein made only one film about the contemporary world. (Not counting *Bezhin Meadow*, which he was not allowed to complete.) This was *The Old and the New*, undoubtedly his least successful film (shown abroad as *The General Line*). The director, who was attracted to the monumental and the dramatic, had developed a style that did not fit this topic. Stylistic devices that were appropriate when dealing, for example, with the heroism of revolutionary sailors appeared ludicrous in the depiction of a milk separator. During this period of his creativity, Eisenstein consciously avoided portraying characters but wanted to draw "types." In making *The Old and the New* he went to extraordinary trouble to find the "right faces" among the nonprofessionals.[64] Therefore, it is all the more remarkable – and at the same time revealing about his attitude to the countryside – that he chose his central figure to be a woman who was not only illiterate but, by all contemporary accounts, stupid looking and ugly. In general, his village was a rather deplorable and dark place. Nor was Eisenstein interested in telling a story. This film has no center and the various episodes do not add up to much. The most dramatic moment of the film depicts the arrival of a new milk separator. Will it work? The other famous episode concerns the marriage of cattle who are dressed up for the occasion. In this film one remembers the bull better than the human beings.[65]

There were other directors, of perhaps slightly lesser stature, who were interested in telling a story and who did want to portray contemporary reality. Some of their films depicted peasant life with an honesty that one would not again find in a Soviet film until the time of N. S. Khrushchev. One was Fridrich Ermler's *The Parisian Cobbler* (1927). It depicts the morality of village youth in unflattering terms, and it celebrates heroism and old-fashioned chivalry. Olga I. Preobrazhenskaia's *The Peasant Women of Riazan* (1927) told a melodramatic story of daughter-in-law rape and compared the old and new way of thinking in a convincing fashion. Preobrezhanskaia's work belongs among the small number of films that could be fairly described as feminist. The film was praised by critics for its warmth and realistic characters.[66]

Perhaps the best of the village films was Protazanov's *Don Diego and Pelagea* (1927). It was a "problem" film, and a biting satire on the heartlessness of Soviet bureaucracy. The film, unlike many others, is without condescension. Its story was based on a feuilleton that had appeared in *Pravda*. An old peasant woman is jailed for the ridiculously insignificant offense of crossing the railroad tracks at the wrong place. She is treated most uncaringly by domineering, stupid little men. Her husband turns to everyone for help. In the process we get a startlingly realistic depiction of some aspects of Soviet life. The representatives of the city, who lord it over the peasants, cannot tell a beet from a potato. The old peasant is befuddled not only by the problems but even by phrases that are incomprehensible to him. When someone suggests to him that he should apply for amnesty on international women's day, he answers: "Kakaia zhe mezhdunarodnaia – ona derevenskaia" ("What are you talking about 'international' – she is a village woman!"). The film was meant to be amusing but what one remembers is the genuine tragedy of simple people caught up in a machine that they do not understand. Finally, of course, there is a resolution. The Komsomol cell learns about the problem and the young people take it on themselves to help and intervene. When the old woman is freed, she joins the Komsomol.

The peasants enjoyed the films that showed their lives in a more or less realistic fashion, and the Soviet film industry in the 1920s gave them at least some products that were worth seeing. One might say, however, that there was an inverse relationship between the popularity of the film and its propaganda value from the point of view of the Communist authorities.

In evaluating Soviet accomplishments in cinefication, one must balance the achievements against the task still needed to be done. Clearly, at a considerable cost, and as a result of almost heroic efforts, the cinema did appear in the Soviet village and it did have some effect. On the other hand, one might also point out that the achievement was far too small to make a large impact, and that at the end of the NEP period, when moviegoing became a favorite pastime for city dwellers, film remained hardly more than a curiosity for the great bulk of the peasantry. As in so many other aspects of Soviet life, the gap between ambitious goals and stubborn reality remained wide.

Notes

1 *Sovetskie khudozhestvennye fil'my. Annotirovannyi katalog*, vol. 1, Iskusstvo, Moscow, 1961 (hereafter cited as *S.kh.f.*).

2 K. Mal'tsev, "Sovetskoe kino na novykh putiakh," *Novyi mir*, May 1929, p. 243. On the other hand *Zhizn' iskusstva* in Sept. 1927 wrote that 50–60 million tickets were sold a year. It is unlikely that from 1927 to 1928 the number increased sixfold. "K predstoiashchemu kino-soveshchaniiu," *Zhizn' iskusstva*, Sept. 27, 1927, p. 1.

3 N. A. Lebedev, *Ocherk istorii kino USSR*, Iskusstvo, Moscow, 1947, p. 144.

4 Mal'tsev, p. 244.

5 The best source of equipment and raw film remained Pathé of France. The other important supplier was Agfa of Germany. *Kinospravochnik*, ed. G. M. Boltianskii, Kinoizdatel'stvo, Moscow, 1926, p. 33.

6 Denise Youngblood, *Soviet Cinema in the Silent Era, 1918–1935*, UMI Research Press, Ann Arbor, 1985, p. 41.

7 See, for example, "Opyt izucheniia kino-zritelia," Rabochii klub 3–4: 45–6, 1927, and "Na kartinu strashno smotret'," *Sovetskii ekran*, Aug. 21, 1928, p. 4.

8 See an interesting article by T. Rokotov, "Itogi stsenarnogo soveshchaniia," *Sovetskii ekran*, Apr. 7, 1927.

9 Agadzhanova-Shutko, perhaps understandably, was upset by Eisenstein's cavalier attitude to her work. She never forgave the director. See, for example, Yon Barna, *Eisenstein*, Secker and Warburg, London, 1973, pp. 91–2, and N. Zorkaia,

Sovetskii istoricheskii fil'm, Akademii Nauk, Moscow, 1962, pp. 41–2. R. Iurenev, *Sergei Eisenshtein. Zamysly. Fil'my. Metod,* vol. 1, Iskusstvo, Moscow, 1985, pp. 108–67.

10 Youngblood, p. 13.

11 The script shortage is described in detail and well by Youngblood, pp. 68–73.

12 Leon Trotsky, *Literature and Revolution,* University of Michigan Press, Ann Arbor, 1960, pp. 220–1.

13 *Kinospravochnik,* pp. 25–9.

14 "Karaul," *Novyi lef,* no. 2, 1927. The article is translated in Ian Christie and Richard Taylor, *The Film Factory: Russian and Soviet Cinema Documents, 1896–1939,* Harvard University Press, Cambridge, 1988, pp. 160–61.

15 E. Gromov, *Lev Vladimirovich Kuleshov,* Iskusstvo, Moscow, 1984, pp. 220–2. Unfortunately Gromov does not say which institution carried out the surveys.

16 See for example the article of Mal'tsev, pp. 243–50, or A. Piotrovskii, "Ob ideologii i kommertsii," *Zhizn' iskusstva,* Dec. 27, 1927, p. 5. This article is translated in Christie and Taylor, pp. 188–90.

17 See, for example, L. M. Budiak and V. P. Mikhailov, *Adresa moskovskogo kino,* Moskovskii rabochii, Moscow, 1987, pp. 244–6.

18 *Kinospravochnik,* p. 164.

19 Ibid., p. 144.

20 Ibid., p. 174.

21 Budiak and Mikhailov, pp. 245–7.

22 M. Sychev and V. Perlin, *Kino v Krasnoi Armii,* Teakinopechat', Moscow, 1929, p. 20.

23 Ibid., p. 38.

24 Ibid., pp. 54–5.

25 *Kinospravochnik,* p. 161.

26 Ibid., p. 152.

27 Circular of Seniushkin, head of cultural department of VTsSPS to cultural sections of Unions, Jan. 1, 1926, L5451 o10 d476.

28 Ratmanov, Secretary of the Central Committee of Workers in Community Enterprises (Ts.K. SRKKh), to union locals, Aug. 26, 1926, L5451 o10 d476. The files are from Trade Union Archives from Central State Archive of the October Revolution. I have also used the same quotation in my previous book, *The Birth of the Propaganda State: Soviet Methods of Mass Mobilization, 1917–1929,* Cambridge University Press, 1985, pp. 136–7.

29 A. Katsigras, *Kinorabota v derevne,* Kinopechat', Moscow, 1926, p. 10.

30 Ibid., p. 11.

31 *Kinospravochnik,* p. 152.

32 G. Esikov, "Potrebitel'skaia kooperatsiia in kinofikatsiia SSSR," *Kino i kultura* 7–8: 28, 1929.

33 N. Karintsev, "Kino v derevniu cherez kooperatsiiu," *Sovetskii ekran,* June 16, 1929.

34 On *shefstvo,* see Kenez, pp. 143–4.

35 P. Rudenko, "Novyi derevenskii agitator," *Kommunisticheskaia revoliutsiia,* Mar. 1926, p. 44.

36 Katsigras, *Kino rabota,* pp. 54–5.

37 Ibid., pp. 57–61.

38 Figure for stationary projectors from O. Barshak, "Istochniki finansirovaniia kinofikatsii derevni," *Kino i kultura* 9–10: 4, 1929. Figure for movable projectors from "Kino dlia derevni," in *Izvestiia Tsentral'nogo Komiteta*. RKP 28: 4, 1925.

39 Barshak, p. 4.

40 A. I. Katsigras, "Eshche o politike Sovkino v derevne," *Kino i kultura* 9–10: 13, 1929.

41 Katsigras, *Kinorabota*, pp. 23–30.

42 Ibid., p. 14.

43 Richard Taylor, *The Politics of Soviet Cinema, 1917–1923*, Cambridge University Press, 1979, p. 89.

44 Katsigras, *Kinorabota*, p. 15.

45 *Sovetskii ekran*, Aug. 6. 1929, p. 1.

46 Leon Trotsky, "Vodka, Church and the Cinema," in *Problems of Everyday Life*, Monad Press, New York, 1973, p. 33.

47 The question of cinefication is discussed by Youngblood, pp. 47–55. She describes in detail the debates.

48 Katsigras, *Kinorabota*, p. 16.

49 See, for example, Barshak, p. 7, for the expression of this point of view.

50 Ibid., p. 17.

51 N. A. Lebedev, *Ocherki istorii kino SSSR. Vol 1: Nemoe kino, 1917–1934*, Iskusstvo, Moscow, 1965, pp. 108–16.

52 O. Barshak, "Kino v derevne," *Sovetskii ekran*, Oct. 22, 1929.

53 *Sovetskii ekran*, June 9, 1925.

54 See Katsigras's article in *Sovetskii ekran*, June 8, 1926, and Bliakhin, "Kakaia fil'ma nuzhna derevne," *Sovetskii ekran*, June 19, 1928.

55 *Sovetskii ekran*, "Derevnia zhdet," Aug. 6, 1929.

56 Barshak.

57 N. Khrenov, "K probleme sotsiologii i psikhologii kino 20kh godov," *Voprosy kinoiskusstva*, 1976, p. 171.

58 Katsigras in his appendix includes a complete list of films that were allowed to be shown as of September 1926. The list includes seventy-three Soviet dramas and seven comedies, eleven foreign dramas and fifteen comedies. The list does not include Kuleshov's comedy, *Extraordinary Adventures of Mr. West in the Land of the Bolsheviks*. The censors presumably thought that the peasants would take seriously a depiction of Moscow that was full of dangers and only incompletely controlled by the Bolshevik authorities. Katsigras, *Kinorabota*, pp. 120–5.

59 *Sovetskii ekran*, June 19, 1928.

60 Rudenko, p. 44.

61 "Psevdo-krestianskoe," *Sovetskii ekran*, Apr. 28, 1925.

62 "O fil'me dlia derevni," *Sovetskii ekran*, June 30, 1925.

63 *S.kh.f.*, 296–7.

64 Jay Leyda, *Kino: A History of the Russian and Soviet Film*, Collier Books, New York, 1960, pp. 262–9.

65 The title of the film, *The General Line*, is full of unintended irony. "The general line" referred to the party's policy toward the peasantry. Eisenstein started to make his film in 1926 but interrupted it in order to make *October*; unfortunately, for him, when he returned to his original project, "the general line" was about to

undergo an extraordinary change: The Stalinists were gathering forces for an all out attack on the peasantry. Eisenstein, of course, had no trouble at all changing the character of his film to fit the "general line," but however much he tried he was not to have the satisfaction of this rather pretentious title. After the leading figures of the Party, including Stalin, saw the film they were not very impressed. Although the film has most of the elements that we associate with Bolshevik propaganda slogans of the day (vicious *kulak* kills the bull of the collective, the priest misleads the poor peasants, the proletariat rushes to the aid of the peasants, the peasants recognize the superiority of the collective, etc.), the film still did not satisfy the Party leaders. In their view the *kulak* was not vicious enough and the role of the Party in the collectivization drive was not spelled out clearly enough. They allowed it to be shown, but only after the title was changed to *The Old and the New*. Contrary to the director's hopes, the film had little propaganda impact. The peasants found the film as boring as other audiences did.

66 For example, Alpers in "Novyi etap v sovetskom kino," *Novyi mir*, Dec. 1928, p. 240, and Bliakhin in "Kakaia fil'ma nuzhna derevne?" *Sovetskii ekran*, June 19, 1928.

PART II

The age of Stalin

CHAPTER 5

The cultural revolution in cinema

Cultural revolution

The program of New Economic Policy (NEP) was an inherently unstable social and political system: It contained within itself the seeds of its own destruction. The Bolsheviks carried out policies in which they did not fully believe, and whose implications worried them. Although the tenth Party Congress in 1921 forbade factions within the Party, the struggle for power during Lenin's final illness and after his death inevitably created factions. The struggle for power and the conflict between contrasting views concerning the future of society came to be intertwined. For the sake of economic reconstruction the Party had to allow the reemergence of private enterprise. As time went on, many Bolshevik leaders came to be convinced supporters of the mixed economic system, while others, on the basis of their reading of Marxist ideology, found such policies distasteful. Many Bolsheviks feared that the new economic policies would strengthen social forces that, in the long run, might endanger socialism. The Bolsheviks were particularly concerned about developments in the countryside. While in the cities their rule was firmly established, in the villages they did not possess the organizational strength to enforce their will. Under these circumstances the power of the *kulaks* seemed especially threatening. Ambivalence led to confused policies. The peasants were encouraged to produce because the government desperately needed their products, but at the same time the successful peasants faced the threat of being defined as *kulaks,* and therefore enemies.

Soviet cultural policies were equally ambivalent. The Bolsheviks considered enlightenment a helpmate in the struggle for socialism, and in their vocabulary "culture" was an unambiguously positive word. At the same time they jealously guarded their ideological hegemony. As time went on they discovered that cultural pluralism implied dangers. The ideas and values that some of the artists transmitted contradicted the world view in which the Bolsheviks deeply believed. This ambivalence explains the contradictions in Soviet policy toward intellectuals: Considerable freedom coexisted with areas of repression.

The NEP system ended in an explosion. Collectivization and forced industrialization ended the era of mixed economy with startling speed. Stalin's victory over his competitors meant repression, show trials, and suspension of more or less open discussion concerning the basic issues facing society. The "cultural revolution," a term frequently used at the time, was as much a part of the extraordinary Stalinist transformation of society as was collectivization. Furthermore, this upheaval in the cultural realm can only be understood in the context of these social and political events.

When Lenin spoke of the necessity of "cultural revolution," he had in mind the desperate need to catch up with the industrial and advanced West, and to overcome the dreadful weight of Russian backwardness. He considered such a cultural revolution a precondition for building socialism. The "enemy" in that revolution was backwardness. Now, in the politically charged atmosphere of the late 1920s, Lenin's successors meant something very different when they used this concept. In this period, "cultural revolution" represented a resurgence of utopian notions about the culture and politics and a demand for a complete break with the past. Most specifically, the cultural pluralism that had existed in the 1920s was to be rejected. Under these circumstances the "enemy" was no longer an abstraction, but flesh and blood: anyone who aimed at protecting the tiniest bit of autonomy of culture.

At a time of profound changes, those who had been uncomfortable in the relatively permissive age of the NEP could press their attack. In some ways the atmosphere resembled the utopian spirit of the age of the Revolution and the Civil War. Once again the energies of a determined minority were mobilized for great tasks, and once again the phrase that there were no bastions that the Bolsheviks could not storm was heard by everyone and believed by many. However, there was a significant difference. This time there was an undercurrent of threat and sinister warnings that had been missing in a more innocent, even though ultimately no less bloody, age. Now the Bolsheviks could have no doubt that the creation of the society for which they labored would not be easy and, above all, it would not be achieved without sacrifice of human beings.

The period of the First Five-Year Plan was a major turning point in the history of Russian culture, perhaps more important than the Revolution itself. An aspect of that great transformation was the destruction of the golden age of the Soviet film.[1]

The end of the golden age and the assault on film organizations

The beginning of the cultural revolution in cinema cannot be exactly dated. Soviet cinema was never free from government intervention, and it suffered much more than, for example, literature. Politicians had repeatedly expressed their fear of ideological contamination carried by foreign products.

The tone of criticism had always been sharp, and films that seem innocuous to us had been denounced violently by intolerant critics. Already in 1926, for example, a meeting of political education organizations *(politprosvet)* passed a resolution that called for the reduction of the share of foreign films in the market, deplored excessive concern with profits, and recommended that the scarce resources be used for making agitational films.[2] Next year the critics attacked two first-rate films, Protazanov's *Forty-first* and Room's *Third Meshchanskaia Street* for expressing a bourgeois point of view.

Although the criticisms did not change, the tone of the discussions and the relative weight of the critical comments did. As the industrialization drive was gathering force, and as the social and economic system of the NEP came unraveled, criticisms became ever more strident. As long as the political struggle in the country continued, those under attack at least could answer their critics, but after the Stalinists got rid of their competitors in the leadership struggle, the genuine artists were increasingly on the defensive.

The cultural revolution in cinema was born out of frustration among politicians. The cinema did not live up to their expectations: Directors wanted to please their audiences and produced romances and adventure stories with little ideological content. Great directors, like Eisenstein, Dovzhenko, Pudovkin, and Vertov, who were ideologically motivated and did produce films with "correct" messages, also could not serve the purposes of the agitators, because the experimental style of the finest directors alienated the audiences. It was above all against these directors that the critics directed their fire. The charge against them was "formalism." Formalism was an important movement among literary critics before and immediately after the revolution. The formalist critics stressed the autonomy of literature, and believed that all information for evaluating a literary text was contained within the text itself. In the polemics against "formalism" in cinema, however, the term came to describe any concern with the specifically aesthetic aspect of filmmaking, any deviation from a simple narrative line, and any artistic innovation.

From about the middle of the decade political activists, some of them professional film critics, started to attack directors and film institutions ever more emphatically. They criticized the industry for not producing enough films for worker and peasant audiences, for importing too many films, and for caring too much about making money. The critics also took on the film directors for not making ideologically correct films that were accessible to the simple workers and peasants.

The decisive event in the history of the film industry was a conference organized by the *agitprop* section of the Central Committee in March 1928. That such important figures as S. Kosior, A. Lunacharskii, and V. Meshcheriakov took prominent parts in the proceedings shows that the Party continued to attribute great significance to the propaganda use of film. The conference afforded Party leaders an opportunity to define the terms of the debate. Here, the Bolsheviks decided to end the heterogeneous character of

Soviet film and impose a "correct" line. Lunacharskii, though still commissar of enlightenment, was relentlessly attacked.[3] Approximately two hundred people participated in this gathering, representing Party, government, trade unions, and various film organizations. The conference was definitely not a gathering of filmmakers who got together to discuss technical aspects of their work.[4] Indeed, among the dozens of speakers only a single director, F. Ermler, addressed the assembled group. The meeting was essentially a gathering of people who were interested in the political use of film.

That the conference took place at all was a political defeat for the leadership of Sovkino, the organization responsible for film production, distribution, and import since 1924. Foreseeing that the conference would give a platform to their critics, the leaders of Sovkino had tried to prevent it.[5] Predictably, they were once again mercilessly attacked for ideological errors made in films and for being commercially minded. Their critics charged the leaders of Sovkino with neglecting worker and peasant audiences, and with importing ideologically harmful foreign films in order to produce profit. The charges were disingenuous: Speaker after speaker asserted that there could be no conflict between ideological considerations and desire for profit, because, they alleged, the people wanted ideologically valuable films.[6] Sovkino's leaders lamely attempted to defend themselves, but in the great political atmosphere it was already impossible to point out that the demands imposed on them were contradictory and, therefore, impossible to carry out.

The main theme of the final resolution of the conference was that Soviet directors must make films that were accessible to the millions. This phrase, in fact, became a cliché in discussions of film in the following decade. As stated, the slogan was a repudiation of artistic experimentation as practiced by the best directors. In the following years this resolution was always the starting point of attacks against the experimentally minded directors.

The feature film should become an instrument of communist education and agitation and a weapon of the Party in the education and organization of the masses around the basic tasks in the period of building socialism (industrialization, rationalization of production, collectivization of agriculture, resolution of the problems of cultural revolution, struggle against bureaucratism, enlivening the work of the soviets, strengthening the military potential of the country, problems of the international revolutionary movement in the West and in the East).

From this it seems clear that the demand for films accessible to the millions was not accompanied by a license to make films that millions would actually want to see. It would be, therefore, wrong to regard the defeat of experimentation as a victory for popular cinema. As a direct result of the cultural revolution the choice available for audiences came to be drastically limited. Comedies and romances, the most popular genres, suffered the most.[7]

Although the resolution of the conference stated that the Party could not support one artistic group against another, this was, in effect, an empty phrase. As other aspects of the discussion and final resolution show, the Party was taking an explicit position against artistic experimentation and ideological heterodoxy. By insisting that films must be immediately comprehensible to all, the politicians dealt a major blow to creative filmmakers. At the same time the pronouncements of the conference were still vague enough to leave the door open for debate. The politicians knew much better what they did not like than what they did. At least for the following two or three years, that is during the "cultural revolution," radical critics came up with some outlandish ideas about films and filmmaking, often contradicting one another. In any case, the profound changes that came about in Soviet film culture in the next few years were not the outcome of internal debate among filmmakers; these changes were imposed from the outside.[8]

From this point on changes in personnel in the film industry became increasingly widespread, culminating in the spring of 1930 with the elimination of Sovkino, and the creation of Soiuzkino, with a new leadership. Soiuzkino was to have greater authority over the studios in the national republics.[9] The change was a consequence of the Soviet belief in the advantages of centralized authority. The first head of Soiuzkino was M. I. Riutin, a fairly well-known figure of the right opposition, who would soon acquire some fame as the author of a two-hundred-page "Appeal to All Party Members" in which he expressed an anti-Stalin point of view. He was immediately arrested and in 1937 executed.[10] After Riutin's arrest, his place was taken by B. Z. Shumiatskii, who had served the Soviet state in various capacities but, prior to his appointment, knew nothing about films. When he complained about his lack of preparation and background in the industry he was to lead, he was told: "We believe you will find your way. You have revolutionary firmness and great experience in party and government work. And what concerns the specifics of the film, you will learn quickly."[11] That the government chose such a man to head Soiuzkino meant that it regarded films more than ever not as a medium of art but as a political tool. The new chief strengthened the censorship apparatus in Soviet studios.[12]

The other cinema organization that had to go through restructuring was ARK, the Association of Revolutionary Cinematography. (In 1928 ARK was renamed ARRK, Association of Revolutionary Workers of Cinematography, in order to stress the "proletarian" credentials of the organization.) ARK had been established in 1924 by young and experimental filmmakers, who believed that cinema was a new and important form of art. Most of the members of the great generation of directors, such as Kuleshov, Eisenstein, Pudovkin, Vertov, Kozintsev, and Trauberg, belonged to this organization. The members of ARK defined themselves in opposition to the pre-revolutionary directors, who had made commercially successful films. Beyond a common interest in the new and experimental, the members of ARK disagreed with one another on a variety of issues. The organization published several journals, such as *Kinozhurnal ARK, Kinofront, Proletarskoe kino,* and *Kino i kultura*. These journals, especially the last two, became a major platform for debates.

The organization became an important actor in the "cultural revolution." On the one hand, it joined the attack on the leadership of Sovkino for its "commercial deviation" and on the other, it became itself the target of increasingly bitter attack. The fate of ARK came to be intertwined with that of RAPP (Russian Association of Proletarian Writers). There was some overlap in personnel and also overlap in worldview. Both organizations advocated a profound break with prerevolutionary, "bourgeois" culture. To this extent they carried out the traditions of Proletkul't. However, it would be an error to see ARRK simply as the equivalent of RAPP in the film world. Unlike RAPP, which managed to dominate literature during the years of the "cultural revolution," ARRK did not achieve a similar status. The Party's main current slogan, that films should be accessible to the masses, could not easily be reconciled with the artistic background and principles of the leading figures of ARRK. The organization was periodically purged; it was frequently accused of supporting "formalism" and other "bourgeois" ideas.[13] But perhaps because ARRK was not important enough, when the Party repudiated "cultural revolution" and dissolved RAPP, it did not consider it necessary also to dissolve ARRK. It was simply renamed RossARK and allowed to linger for a couple of years. It was finally closed down in 1935 as a result of a second film conference.

The third major film organization was ODSK, the Society of Friends of Soviet Cinema. This society was one of the dozens of single-issue mass "voluntary" organizations that dotted the political landscape of NEP Russia. Its tasks were to bring cinema to the masses, to explain the political significance of individual pictures to audiences, and to canvass audiences and thereby act as a contact between the viewers and the film industry. Cells of ODSK in factories and schools organized discussions of films and gave an opportunity to the filmgoers to express their views. Indeed, ODSK accomplished something by collecting money for buying mobile projectors for the countryside. The most important task of the organization, however, was mobilization. The Party created an organization to mobilize the masses for the cinema, which in itself had the task of mobilizing the masses for socialist construction. The Bolsheviks instinctively understood that making people belong to organizations and perform functions, however insignificant those functions were in themselves, was an excellent agitational tool.[14]

The chief task assigned to the movie industry during the industrialization drive was mobilization of the Soviet people. Under these circumstances ODSK, together with the Komsomol and the trade unions, was instructed again and again to help bring films to the workers and peasants. The critics were never satisfied with the accomplishments. However, unlike the other two film organizations, ODSK did not have to go through a major reorganization. It was dissolved in 1934; by this time the political environment was altogether different, and the voluntary organizations did not suit the spirit of the times.

By the time the radical impulse petered out and the "cultural revolution" was over, Soviet film organizations had come under far more direct political control than Sovkino ever experienced. For its part ARRK, both maker and victim of the "cultural revolution," was for all practical purposes destroyed. The "cultural revolution" eliminated whatever autonomy film organizations had once possessed.

The critics

It may be that from the point of view of making movies the reorganizations of the industry was more important than the writings of the critics. In order to get a sense, however, of the atmosphere of the period, it is necessary to read critics. We must recall what was going on in the country at the time. Collectivization and industrialization forced millions to give up a way of life, and this social transformation was carried out with extraordinary brutality. It is not surprising, therefore, that the character of public discourse also changed even when it concerned such seemingly distant and unimportant matters as film. Saber rattling, sinister warnings, and threats became a regular feature of film criticism. When it was all over and superficially calmer days had returned, it was evident that the sabers had claimed many victims.

In November 1929, for example, *Kino i zhizn'* published an editorial that demanded increased vigilance. The editorial warned that the class enemy was carrying out a new and dangerous offensive. The sign of the offensive on the "movie front" was the appearance of petit-bourgeois, anti-Marxist, and anti-Leninist ideas, such as formalism and "mechanical materialism." The editorial ended:

We will unmask any hesitation concerning the Marxist ideological position in film arts, any kind of ideological uncertainty, any kind of compromise with deviation of whatever form.[15]

Artists had reason to worry.

The "cultural revolution" saw a riotous flourishing of ideas in film criticism. Many of these ideas were soon discarded, but others became part of the official canon of Soviet art criticism. In this feverish and murderous age, the "soldiers" of the "cultural revolution," the critics, understood that the new political order demanded a new attitude toward filmmaking. They carried out a radical attack. Their violent assault on filmmakers did great harm to the cause of Soviet cinema. The language and tone of criticism was extremely intemperate, even by Soviet standards. The critics respected neither past achievements nor international reputations. They treated Eisenstein and

Pudovkin no better, or perhaps even worse, than second-rate figures who were just making their first films.[16] No one, including the critics themselves, who often quarreled with one another, escaped criticism.

Some fundamental issues passed out of the realm of possible debate: Artistic experimentation and simple mass entertainment joined apoliticism as indefensible artistic values. Heated discussion continued on other subjects, however, such as whether the best means of agitation was the feature film, and each side, of course, claimed for itself the mantle of Marxism. Critical writing in this period generally avoided discussion of aesthetic features of filmmaking and, whatever individual critics' motivation may have been, such a perspective would inevitably have been denounced as "formalist," if not worse. Thus, critical evaluation of the past and present of Soviet cinema was couched exclusively in terms of the political usefulness of films. It was widely argued that the medium had failed in its most important task: It had not become a significant instrument of political education.

In April 1929, a minor director by the name of P. Petrov-Bytov published an article in *Zhizn' iskusstva* entitled provocatively, "We do not have a Soviet cinematography."

When people speak of Soviet cinematography, they wave a flag inscribed: *Strike, Battleship Potemkin, October, Mother, The End of St. Petersburg,* and they add the more recent *The New Babylon, Zvenigora,* and *Arsenal.* But do the 120 million workers and peasants march under this flag? I say with full confidence that they do not. And they never have. I do not deny the value of these films. Of course they are valuable. They have considerable formal values. We should learn from these films as we learn from the bourgeois classics. But it is premature to make these films into the flag of Soviet cinematography. We cannot begin Soviet cinematography with these films.[17]

Petrov-Bytov went on to argue that the films of the great directors could not serve as instruments of agitation, because the audiences were not interested in them. He recommended that the directors get to know working-class life before they made films for the workers. He also argued that directors should make films for peasants based on simple stories, told in simple language, on topics of interest to peasants, such as:

the cow that was sick with tuberculosis; the dirty, muddy cowshed that had to be remade into something clean and well lighted; the child, who is close to the heart of the peasant woman and needed a nursery; the hooligans, that can be found in the *kolkhozes . . .*

The trouble with such sensible advice was that those who attempted to follow it and tried to depict worker and peasant life more or less realistically were then abused for their efforts. They were criticized for "mechanical materialism" or "mechanical realism," a fault that was no better than "formalism." Such films also did not serve the purposes of agitators. The critics argued that leftist deviation (i.e., making avant-garde revolutionary films that audiences could not understand) had the same source as rightist deviation (i.e., pandering to the taste of the audiences) – namely, a petit-bourgeois mentality.[18]

Petrov-Bytov was harshly attacked for this article. His critics considered his views to be a revival of the ideology of the Proletkul't, inasmuch as it seemed to them that Petrov-Bytov did not want to allow nonproletarian artists to make their contributions to the development of Soviet culture. He was described on the one hand as an ultraleftist and, on the other, blamed for underestimating the intelligence of the workers by suggesting that they did not understand *Battleship Potemkin* and *Arsenal*. His ultraleftist views were considered to be just as dangerous as rightist deviation. Rightist deviation was a code name for directors who wanted to make entertaining films, that is, the kind the workers really wanted.[19]

Some critics believed that films had not become useful propaganda instruments because they did not show individual heroes who would have inspired the masses by their examples. Indeed, Eisenstein and Dovzhenko had self-consciously avoided depicting individual heroes and recognizable characters with whom the audience could identify. Instead, they worked with "types," figures that stood for a social class or an idea. Eisenstein had little use for professional actors. He remained faithful to his Proletkul't background, and continued to believe that the masses, and not individuals, made history, and that Soviet films were more "advanced" and "progressive" than "bourgeois" films precisely because they did not dwell on psychology and did not stress the role of the individual. More traditional directors who aimed at telling a story, of course, did depict individuals. But these films did not have the revolutionary drama of Eisenstein's and Dovzhenko's best work. The critics did not demand a realistic depiction of individuals. They wanted heroes. They were groping their way toward socialist realism.[20]

Some went so far as to deny the need for feature films at all. V. Sutyrin, writing in the first issue of ARRK's new journal, *Proletarskoe kino* (December, 1931), advocated that film should primarily be an agent of agitation and education. It was a harmful and dangerous idea, he maintained, that the best vehicle of agitation was an interesting and amusing film, a film with a story, that is, a feature film. Indeed, he wanted to demolish the notion that film was an art at all. He appealed to the authority of Lenin and plausibly maintained that Lenin never regarded film as one of the arts. Sutyrin argued that only 10 percent of all books published belonged to the genre of belles lettres and the proper proportion in movies should be the same. In his view the mistaken idea that the primary function of films was to entertain came from the bourgeoisie, which slyly used movies for their own ulterior purposes: carrying out propaganda and making profit. The proletarian state, however, must use the medium differently. It must establish special auditoriums in schools and factories for agitation and instruction.[21]

M. Kokorin, writing in the same issue, took a similar point of view. Like all Soviet publicists, he believed that the capitalists were exceptionally clever in their use of propaganda. A news item announcing that all American warships in the future would be equipped with movie theaters seemed to him decisive evidence of the capitalists' intention to exploit the propaganda potential of cinema. It would be folly to do less in this area than the bourgeois states, he warned.[22]

Kokorin saw the greatest danger in what he called "right-opportunist elements," who in his view, continued to smuggle in individualism and social political skepticism, and to stay away from themes of everyday life. He called their apoliticism a wrecking activity, an activity more dangerous than open hostility to the Soviet order. This was a frightening charge to make in 1931.

In the age of the "cultural revolution," two other major criticisms were leveled against the best directors. One was that they attributed too much significance to montage. The preoccupation with montage, according to the radical critics, was essentially a "formalist" position. It is, of course, true that Eisenstein, Kuleshov, and Pudovkin, among others, saw in montage the very essence of film art. An unsigned editorial in the first issue of *Proletarskoe kino,* a publication of ARRK, described as the most important task in the struggle against "bourgeois ideology" "to subject to withering criticism the theory that montage was the basis of film." The editorial singled out Eisenstein for particular criticism: "It is essential to subject to criticism the vulgar-materialist, mechanical theory of Eisenstein's montage of attractions, and his other ideas that are alien to Marxism."[23] The proposition that concern with montage was "formalism" and therefore "reactionary" became a generally accepted principle of Soviet film criticism.

The second point of the critics was connected with the attack on the primacy of montage. In their view the emphasis on montage gave the director too much control over the final product. Indeed, the kind of films that Eisenstein or Dovzhenko made could not be based on precise scripts. These directors were brilliant improvisers. Now the critics attacked the directors for not taking the scripts seriously enough. They considered it intolerable that the directors dealt with their scripts in cavalier fashion, improvising as they were going along. In the early 1930s such liberties could not be taken any longer in the Soviet Union. After all, what was the point of approving a "politically correct" script, if the director was in a position to change it?

One motivation for criticizing the importance of montage was that many important films employing this technique had been experimental and essentially plotless. As such, they did not fit with the current demand of the Party for widely accessible films, "films for millions," as the slogan went.[24]

Vertov, Eisenstein, Pudovkin, Dovzhenko, and Kuleshov

The audiences did not care about the fine points of film criticism; they were interested in movies. As a result of reorganization, constant attacks and pressure, the character of those movies gradually changed. The critics and responsible officials at the studios became ever more demanding. Directors were criticized for "flaws" that had not been noticed a year or two before.

Already in 1929, P. A. Bliakhin, an official of Sovkino, wrote of the previous movie season that 50 percent of the films made were questionable from an ideological point of view and 10 percent of the films were not allowed to be shown at all because of their ideological faults.[25] Bliakhin did not add that such unsatisfactory (from the regime's point of view) results were reached after 36 percent of the previously approved scenarios had been banned by the authorities before the films were made.[26] Ideological errors mentioned by Bliakhin include (among others) the depiction of a governor's remorse after ordering the shooting of unarmed workers (in *The White Eagle*), attributing decisive influence to individual heroism rather than to the masses in the Civil War *(Kastus Kalinovskii)*, and idealizing individual terror, "which was a Socialist Revolutionary idea" *(His Career)*. We may point out that Bliakhin was the author of the script of *The Little Red Devils,* an immensely successful film made in 1923, one, however, without a significant ideological content. Times have changed.

In spite of the relentless attacks, the work of the directors changed only gradually. After all, directors with highly developed individual styles, such as Dovzhenko and Eisenstein, could not from one day to the next abandon their way of making films and follow the recommendations of their critics. But the change did come. The experimental impulse petered out, films became less interesting, and the golden age came to an end. The Soviet regime destroyed its best artists.

Kuleshov, Eisenstein, Vertov, and Pudovkin considered themselves "revolutionaries." They rather naïvely took it for granted that their work in creating a new form of art was the equivalent in the cultural sphere to what was occurring around them in the sociopolitical sphere. They liked to think that their artistic medium was the art form of the proletariat. They considered themselves radicals in the sense of advocating a decisive break with "bourgeois" notions of art. It was one of the dreadful ironies of the cultural revolution that the more "radical" and "leftist" the artist was, the more likely he was to suffer. The versatile and nonpolitical Ia. Protazanov weathered the changes better than members of the avant-garde.

We can best appreciate the changes that occurred in Soviet film by looking at the creative biographies of the most able directors. Vertov, Eisenstein, Pudovkin, Dovzhenko, and Kuleshov had a great deal in common. They all regarded themselves as good Bolsheviks, even though they were not members of the Party. They were also, in spite of their extraordinary achieve-

ments, very young. Pudovkin, the oldest, was only 37 in 1930. Also Kuleshov and Pudovkin had some prerevolutionary experience; they all had started
their work after the Revolution, and at the end of the 1920s they were at
the height of their creative powers. There was every reason to expect that
they would contribute much more to the development of cinema as an art
form. The five men responded differently to the pressures generated by the
"cultural revolution."

Vertov's story is the most poignant. As the enfant terrible of Soviet cinema in the 1920s, it was he who insisted most strongly that film must become an instrument of class struggle, that there had to be a sharp distinction
between Soviet and "bourgeois" ways of making movies, that the task of
the filmmaker was above all to record class struggle and the creation of the
new world. In his "left" radicalism Vertov denied not only the need for
professional actors, but also rejected films that told stories. He wrote:

1. Film drama is the opium of the people.
2. Down with the immortal kings and queens of the stage! Long live the ordinary
   mortal, filmed in life at his daily tasks!
3. Down with the bourgeois fairy-tale script! Long live life as it is.
4. Film-drama and religion are deadly weapons in the hands of the capitalists. By
   showing our revolutionary way of life, we will wrest that weapon from the enemy's hands.[27]

Yet, when the prosaic NEP period was over, the new radicals had no need
for Vertov's art. In 1930 Vertov made his first sound film, *Enthusiasm* (with
the subtitle *Symphony of the Don Basin*). His avowed purpose was to show
the work of miners and metalworkers of the Donbass. He used the new
instrument of sound with great inventiveness, both synchronically and asyn-
chronically. Generally, audiences found this film, like his earlier films, boring. Although Vertov had already been heavily attacked in the 1920s, the
venom of the critics was new. He was blamed – with justice – for being
primarily interested in artistic experimentation. The film was suppressed. In
the age of "films for the millions," Vertov had no role to play.

Eisenstein was lucky in that he spent the years of bitterest attack, 1929–
32, out of the country. His absence, however, did not spare him from vili-
fication. The critics rejected all the principal elements of his aesthetics. His
enemies spread rumors that he planned to stay abroad, in order to give the
impression that he was anti-Soviet. On his return he found it impossible to
recommence his work. Shumiatskii, the director of Soiuzkino, the de facto
minister of film production, suggested that Eisenstein make a comedy, a task
for which his talents were unsuited. Between 1929 and 1938 no new Eisenstein film appeared in Soviet cinemas. However, Eisenstein, unlike other
major figures of the avant-garde, survived as an artist. When political circumstances changed before and during World War II, he once again made
superb films.[28]

Unlike Eisenstein, Vsevolod I. Pudovkin did not stop filmmaking. He made his film *A Simple Case* in 1930, but he had to recut it several times before it could be shown in 1932. As the title suggests, the film was indeed a simple story about a philandering husband and a good and forgiving wife. It condemned the husband's behavior and by no stretch of the imagination could it be considered immoral. But times were not favorable for making films on such "risqué" topics, and Pudovkin was mercilessly attacked.

His next work, the first with a sound track, is one of the most dishonest and distasteful products of the Stalin era. The film, *Deserter*, contrasts the happy and prosperous lives of the Soviet workers with that of the oppressed and starving German proletarians. Although parts of the film were shot in Germany, Pudovkin was no more able to capture the flavor of life in a capitalist country than other Soviet directors.

Hitler's coming to power forced Pudovkin to leave Germany before the film was completed. Yet in *Deserter* the Social Democrats are portrayed as the chief evil of capitalist Germany for "betraying the workers" and the Nazis do not even appear. Of course, the idea that the Social Democrats rather than the Nazis were the worst enemies of the proletariat was not Pudovkin's but came directly from the leaderships of the Comintern and the Soviet government. However, no one forced the director to make a film on this topic.

In *Deserter* the central figure is a German worker, Karl Renn, who seizes an opportunity to go to the Soviet Union while in the midst of a bitter strike. There he observes the free and prosperous lives of Soviet workers and is tempted to "desert" from his duty in class struggle and stay in socialist Russia. However, by getting to know the class-conscious Soviet people, he comes to understand his responsibility and returns to his native land to continue the struggle. One might mention that when the film was made and first shown, the Soviet Union was experiencing its worst famine in history with millions of victims.

The critics could not fault the ideological content of this film. Nevertheless, they were not altogether satisfied. They complained about Pudovkin's experimental use of sound, and about a certain abstractness in his presentation. According to their understanding, this film, too, was "formalist."[29]

Pudovkin did not direct another film for five years. The films he made at the end of his career did not even approach the artistic level of his early works.

Of the major directors it was Aleksandr P. Dovzhenko who continued longest to produce masterpieces. This is somewhat surprising considering Dovzhenko's extraordinary originality. The films that he made in the late 1920s, *Zvenigora* and *Arsenal*, are rather difficult to follow. Even more than the other great directors, Dovzhenko thought in terms of images and cared little about presenting a coherent story.[30]

The film *Earth*, first shown in 1930, was very different from *Arsenal.* Although ostensibly dealing with class warfare and collectivization in the

Ukraine, it is, in fact, a celebration of nature and the peasant way of life. This film, too, is full of extraordinary and haunting images. The reaction to the film was predictable. Although most critics recognized Dovzhenko's genius, they found the content reactionary. P. Bliakhin complained in *Izvestiia* that the film did not mobilize the masses for struggle against the *kulaks*. He raised a question as to whether the film should be allowed to be shown at all, but in the end answered affirmatively.[31] *Kino i zhizn'* sponsored a discussion of the film. The general consensus was that while Dovzhenko was a talented artist, the film was ideologically harmful and its style made it incomprehensible for worker and peasant audiences. Demian Bednyi called it a *"kulak* film" and R. A. Kedrov, the secretary of ODSK, described it as "not our film." Several participants complained that the director was interested in "biological rather than social processes." Dovzhenko was particularly condemned for "unhealthy eroticism" in showing a naked woman. (In fact, the woman tore off her dress because of her despair at the death of her lover. This was hardly an erotic situation.) This scene was later cut from the version shown in Soviet theaters.[32] Ia. Rudoi in the November issue of *Kino i zhizn'* reasoned along the following lines about the ideological content of *Earth:* The film is full of symbolism. Symbolism logically follows from mysticism, which is the ideology of the most reactionary elements of the class enemy. The film, therefore, expresses the ideology of the bourgeoisie.[33]

Dovzhenko was stunned by the hostility of his critics, especially by Bednyi's scurrilous article. In his brief autobiography he described how, in this period, he was regarded as an unreliable fellow traveler, a counterrevolutionary, and could not do his work properly, since he was not allowed to train a crew. He wanted to make a film about the Arctic explorer, Amundsen, but was not allowed. Instead, he was told, he was to show in his next work the industrialization in the Ukraine.[34]

Indeed, he started to work on *Ivan,* which was about the building of a dam. Half of his scenario was forbidden by the studio authorities. The ultimate product shows Dovzhenko's emotional state and the intervention of the censors. The film lacks the power of the director's greatest works, such as *Arsenal* and *Earth.* Nevertheless, it is a typical Dovzhenko film, with long, lyrical passages that show the beauty of nature, against which the construction project is taking place. Dovzhenko's experimental style was still in evidence, and, as critics pointed out, this film was also inaccessible to mass audiences.[35] *Ivan* was the last of Dovzhenko's films to bear the marks of his original style and his later works are much less interesting.

None of the major artists was denounced as bitterly and as consistently as Lev V. Kuleshov. In the overheated rhetoric of the day, his name came to stand for everything that the critics disliked: "formalism," "apoliticism," and a "vulgar desire to give to the audiences what the audiences wanted." The title of his film, *The Gay Canary,* became a kind of catchphrase, a shorthand for denouncing the "enemy."

Kuleshov was an obvious choice for the role of bête noire. His fascination with the work of American directors made him particularly vulnerable. His comedy, *Extraordinary Adventures of Mr. West in the Land of the Bolsheviks,* while caricaturing the style of the adventure films, also exploited the genre. He never won over the Party activists by making a revolutionary spectacle, comparable to some of the works of Eisenstein, Dovzhenko, or Pudovkin. Even in the liberal mid-1920s Kuleshov had to struggle to have his films made. Unable to get approval and therefore financing for his best film, *By the Law,* he made it as an "experiment" on a tiny budget. While it was admired by some critics, others denounced it bitterly for the ambivalence of its message.

Kuleshov was especially vulnerable to the accusation of "formalism." He was close to V. Shklovskii, a major figure among the formalists, who had written the scenario for *By the Law.* It is not altogether untrue to say that Kuleshov in developing his views on filmmaking was influenced by formalist literary critics. He presented his views in a book entitled *The Art of the Cinema (My Experience)* and had the misfortune of publishing this book in 1929, at the height of the campaign against "formalism." Kuleshov's book was a rather modest one. In it he described the techniques of moviemaking, insisting that film was an independent form of art, profoundly different from the theater. The individual frames were simply raw material for the director. How these frames were attached to one another was the art of montage, and Kuleshov insisted on its centrality in the art of filmmaking.[36] This idea, widely shared by other directors, but developed and stressed by Kuleshov, made him the primary target for attacks on "formalism."[37]

Kuleshov was passionately denounced for his next three films, *Your Acquaintance, The Gay Canary,* and *The Two Buldis.* One suspects that the object of the attack was not the films, which were rather undistinguished, but the artist himself, who came to stand for everything that the radical critics hated. Those who attacked the films most harshly at the time did not question Kuleshov's skill as an artist, but on the contrary, pointed out that these films were especially dangerous precisely because Kuleshov was a master of the art form.

Kuleshov made *Your Acquaintance* in 1927. He had been attacked for removing himself from Soviet reality, and now made a film about contemporary life. The story of the film was based on a love triangle. As in Kuleshov's best films, the individual frames were carefully composed with a stark and effective simplicity and the actress Khokhlova once again created a complex and interesting character.[38] From the point of view of the critics the attention Kuleshov paid to problems of individuals as opposed to social issues, and his unvarnished portrayal of NEP Russia, made this a harmful film.

The director was frustrated by the negative reception of his films, and decided to appease his critics by choosing the revolutionary movement as his subject. He failed completely. The stories of his next two films, *The Gay Canary* and *The Two Buldis*, indeed sound silly, though no sillier than dozens of similar films made at the time. Both of these works were really adventure stories, with improbable events, where the revolutionary movement served as a background. The artist, discouraged by his previous failures, made these films without having his heart in them.[39]

The action of *The Gay Canary* took place in a resort, occupied by the Whites. The Reds carry out underground work. In the course of the action, the film shows intrigue, romance, dance halls, and prostitutes (Figs. 22 and 23). Bliakhin, the critic, wrote with heavy irony:

See how gay and even romantic the work of the underground was! We used to think that salons, wine, prostitutes, naked legs were not necessary accessories of underground work, indeed, on the contrary. And now, in the winter of 1929 our eyes are opened by this present to the world, *The Gay Canary*.[40]

In the opinion of Bliakhin, the workers in the audience turned away in disgust from such a film. In fact, *The Gay Canary* was Kuleshov's commercially most successful film.

In *The Two Buldis* background for the "revolutionary events" was life in the circus. As in so many other Soviet films of the time, the son brings revolutionary consciousness to his father. The old clown learns about the viciousness of the counterrevolutionaries by becoming involved in his son's struggles. The denunciation of this film in the press, if possible, was even harsher. "Felix" in *Kino i zhizn'* described the film as a provocation.[41] He placed Kuleshov at the center of a rightist group that made films for the class enemies of the proletariat.

Kuleshov's next film, *The Great Consoler,* appeared in movie theaters in 1933. It quite clearly was a response to his critics. The film is loosely based on two short stories by O. Henry and an episode in the life of the American writer. Kuleshov made no attempt to convince the viewers that they were seeing America. He did not remain faithful either to the letter or to the spirit of the short stories; and the episode in the life of O. Henry did not take place as it is depicted in this film. Kuleshov clearly intended to use the stories and the biography of the writer to make the points that he wanted to make.

The story is rather complicated. Bill Porter (O. Henry) is in prison (Fig. 24). Around him he sees nothing but injustice and cruelty. He meets Jimmy Valentine, a noble prisoner, who is tricked and mistreated by the prison authorities. Unlike Valentine, Porter, the writer, is a favorite of the prison warden and receives various privileges, such as whiskey. In his writings in prison Porter describes the world not as it really is but as he imagines it. As an insert (in the form of a silent film) we see the story of Jimmy Valentine, as presented by Porter. Here Kuleshov based himself on O. Henry's story, "The Metamorphosis of Jimmy Valentine." This part of the film is presented with irony and is amusing. The safecracker, Valentine, decides to become an honest man. He finds a loving, beautiful, and rich wife and he

Figure 22.   Poster for *The Gay Canary* (1929).

uses his skill as a safecracker only to save a little child who is accidentally locked in the safe. He succeeds in escaping his past. We see the effects of prettifying reality by literature. Dulcie, a shopgirl, is a great admirer of the writer, and under his influence, she finds it impossible to accept her terrible conditions. She was about to marry a police agent, but she is revolted by him and kills him.

Kuleshov's presentation of the effects of "consoling" is rather complex. Although Dulcie's fate is tragic, she does become a better person by reading the works of Bill Porter. Valentine also appreciates the writer. He reads the story about himself with amusement. Yet, it is clear that Kuleshov's attitude to the writer is hostile. Porter is a coward and he knows it. When he complains about injustice, he is threatened with the loss of privileges. He is bought by the authorities. Nevertheless, it is Porter who has the last and decisively important lines: "I can never write what must be written. I cannot write what I know. Maybe others will come . . ."

From a purely aesthetic point of view *The Great Consoler* is not as successful as *By the Law*. The earlier film has a wonderfully simple structure and unforgettably striking images. By contrast, the different parts of the later work are not well pulled together. Too many things are going on that are connected only by Kuleshov's main theme. Also this film has some mawkishly sentimental scenes that contrast sharply with the harsh world of *By the Law*. However, when one sees the film today, one can sense the director's controlled passion and his emotional involvement in the topic, and that makes the film extraordinarily exciting.

The Great Consoler stands by itself. It was the only film made in Stalin's time in which a director expressed a strongly held and heterodox belief concerning a significant issue. Kuleshov, who had always thought of himself as a good citizen of the Soviet state but had been tirelessly and unjustly denounced as a mouthpiece of the enemy, finally made a thoroughly anti-Soviet film. Ironically, the film was so profoundly anti-Soviet that Kuleshov's critics did not even dare to admit that they understood it. It was much less harshly denounced than his earlier and innocuous films. The emperor had no clothes, but who would dare to notice it?[42]

At age thirty-four, the grand old man of Soviet cinema sang his swan song. Aside from a few insignificant efforts, Kuleshov, who lived until 1970, never made another film. His art was destroyed by the cultural revolution, but he exited with dignity.[43]

The films of the new era

It was increasingly difficult to make films in the Soviet Union. Total production declined from 148 in 1928 to only 35 in 1933. Then the number started to rise again, but never reached the production level of the previous decade.[44] Critics made it abundantly clear to the directors what they did not want. They were much more hesitant in developing a prescription for the

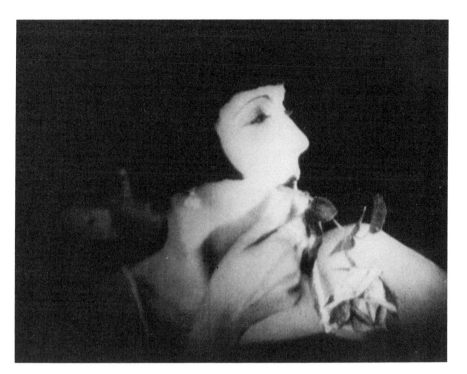

Figure 23. The heroine of *The Gay Canary* (1929).

Figure 24. The writer in prison: *The Great Consoler* (1933).

Figure 25. The popular actor Batalov in *The Road to Life* (1931).

new art. Their response to films became unpredictable. As a result, though the cultural revolution greatly reduced the varieties of styles and subject matter presented in Soviet films, no uniform style had yet emerged. As compared with what was to come, the cinema of the years of 1930–3 was still remarkably heterogeneous.

How difficult the position of the director was could be best seen by an examination of the reception of the first Soviet sound film. *The Road to Life* was made by N. Ekk in 1931. The film dealt with a contemporary topic, juvenile delinquency. It told a story simply and effectively and therefore it was very popular with the audiences. The film showed the positive effect of labor on the children. Unlike the works of Eisenstein and Dovzhenko, it contained no symbolism. The film had positive heroes with which the audiences could identify (Fig. 25). One would think that this work was bound to please the critics.

It did not. The film was greeted with a storm of abuse. The reasons for the violent attacks are hard to fathom today. A. Mikhailov wrote a particularly ugly and vituperative review in *Proletarskoe kino*.[45] He considered the film a typical melodrama and objected to an exhibition of sympathy

Figure 26. The heroine of *Alone* (1931), a female teacher, is taken to a hospital.

that cut across classes. In his view the film made the audiences sorry for the juvenile delinquents without presenting a class analysis, and without showing how the problem was connected with the capitalist system. For example, writes the critic, one of the boys, Kol'ka, almost becomes a criminal not because of any reason of class, but simply because his mother dies and his father takes to drink. Mikhailov described Ekk's worldview as subjective idealism and perceived in the work an admiration for bourgeois ideology. He considered the film especially dangerous in as much as "the alien element in it appeared in a masked form."

Other directors did not fare as badly as Ekk with the critics. Ironically, Kozintsev and Trauberg, whose *The New Babylon* (made in 1929) was the prime example of formalist cinema, now made a simple and moving film, *Alone*. The film, produced in 1931, was originally silent but sound was added later. The nonsynchronistic use of sound and the imaginative use of music gives the film a modernistic quality. *Alone* told the story of a woman teacher's struggle against *kulaks*, self-satisfied and selfish village authorities, for the common good. Although some critics, wrongly, attacked the film for lack of passion and for formalism, the bulk of critical response was favorable (Fig. 26).[46]

A film made by Ivan Pyr'ev in 1933, *The Conveyor Belt of Death,* received rather favorable reviews.[47] The film has a confused and complicated story, the consequence, perhaps, of its having been written and rewritten by several people over a period of three years. The film attempts to show the crisis of bourgeois society, to unmask "the beauties of bourgeois life," and to show the role of the Communist Parties in contemporary Western Europe. Pyr'ev's film, unlike *Deserter,* does deal explicitly with fascism. However, the location of the story is not only not specified, but deliberately obfuscated. The signs we see in this imaginary city are in German, French, and English. Pyr'ev created a synthetic West. He conveys the impression that fascism is a general problem in all capitalist societies. In this director's presentation, the working classes of the West are unbendingly loyal to the Soviet Union. In the climactic turning point of the film, the workers go on strike rather than produce weapons that could be used against the Soviet Union.

The film is an interesting example of Soviet perception of the West, a perception that has changed remarkably little over the decades. For a Soviet observer the most horrifying aspect of life in a capitalist society is lack of security, the ever-present fear of unemployment, and of the various social ills, prostitution has an unusual fascination.

A much better and more attractive film was Boris Barnet's *Borderlands,* which also appeared in 1933. This was Barnet's first sound film, and perhaps his masterpiece. In this film, more than in any other work of the period, the director creates human beings who are believable and attractive. At a time when other directors were groping their way toward socialist realism, Barnet managed to make a film that was humane and touching and had a strong antiwar, almost pacifist, message.

The story takes place during World War I, somewhere in the borderlands. The director contrasts the ordinary and even attractive life in a little town with the horrors of the battlefield. He shows how the life of an old ethnic German, who has lived in the town for a long time, is made impossible by the chauvinism of the local people. These same people also attack a poor, innocent German prisoner of war, who is saved only by a decent young woman and an old shoemaker. Although the film has a proper and predictable ending – German and Russian workers stop fighting one another and unite under the revolutionary flag – what remains with the viewer is the simple heroism and goodness of the young woman who comes to the aid of the unjustly abused.

The film was rather well received, though the critics did attack its ideological assumptions.[48] The prominent Soviet critic and film historian N. A. Lebedev, writing in 1956, complained about the film's pacifism and its abstract humanism and claimed that it did not show the influence of Bolsheviks in the factory or depict the enemy with "sharp satire, but instead with gentle irony."[49]

The most-discussed film of the period, Iutkevich and Ermler's *Counter-plan*, appeared in the theaters on the occasion of the fifteenth anniversary of the Revolution. This film, remarkably, contained within itself the main characteristics of the socialist realist style. Although it was first shown in 1932, it belongs to the next period of film history.

For the tasks of industrialization and collectivization, the Party successfully mobilized a small but important segment of the population. It took advantage of the genuine enthusiasm that existed for the great goals, especially among the young. Similarly, in the realm of the arts, including, of course the cinema, the leaders of the Party allowed and encouraged the radicals to carry out a full-scale attack on the existing semipluralist order. This was the "cultural revolution."

By the time the First Five-Year Plan was completed, the leaders decided that the chaos of mass mobilization had served its purpose and the country needed a reaffirmation of order and authority. At the same time the "cultural revolution" was also swiftly ended. Its accomplishment in cinema was purely destructive: The pluralism of the 1920s was no longer tolerated, but the form of art that would be suitable in the age of Stalin had not yet emerged.

Notes

1 The two most recent overviews of Soviet film in the 1920s are also the best: Denise Youngblood, *Soviet Cinema in the Silent Era, 1918–1935,* UMI Research Press, Ann Arbor, Mich., 1985, pp. 156–61, and Richard Taylor, *The Politics of the Soviet Cinema, 1917–1929,* Cambridge University Press, 1979, pp. 106–18.

2 S. Dymov, "Sovetizatsiia kino," *Zhizn' iskusstva,* Mar. 8, 1927, p. 9.

3 "K predstoiashchemu kino-soveshchaniiu," *Zhizn' iskusstva,* Sept. 27, 1927, p. 9.

4 The entire proceedings of the conference have been published and provide excellent material for the understanding of the mentality of those responsible for films. See B. S. Ol'khovyi (ed.), *Puti kino: Pervoe Vsesoiuznoe soveshchanie po kinematografii,* Tea-kino-pechat', Moscow, 1929. See also useful summaries of this important event in Youngblood, pp. 156–61, Taylor, pp. 106–18, and A. I. Rubailo, *Partiinoe rukovodstvo razvitiem kinoiskusstva, 1928–1937 gg.,* MGU, Moscow, 1976, pp. 29–36.

5 See the comments of Kirshon in Ol'khovyi, in *Puti kino,* pp. 76–80.

6 See, for example, Kosior's keynote address, in *Puti kino,* p. 17.

7 Richard Taylor argues a contrary position in his article, "Boris Shumyatsky and the Soviet Cinema in the 1930s: Ideology as Mass Entertainment," *Historical Journal of Film, Radio and Television* 6, no. 1: 43–60, 1986.

8 Recently Western historians have stressed that the "cultural revolution" was largely based on indigenous radicalism, and that therefore, it was not only a "revolution from above" but also a "revolution from below." See the essays in S. Fitzpatrick (ed.), *Cultural Revolution in Russia, 1928–1931,* Indiana University Press, Bloomington, 1978. The experience of the film industry does not bear out such a

generalization. Clearly, it was not workers and peasants who demanded more "revolutionary" films. Nor were the film directors themselves interested in devoting their art to serving the twists and turns of the Party line. Of course, it would be naïve to think that the Politburo decided on the course of necessary changes in the film industry and then carried out the decisions. However, events in this industry reflected the political struggle then devastating the country. Party functionaries who were anxious to do away with the political order as it had existed in the NEP period influenced the developments in the film world.

9 The change from Sovkino to Soiuzkino, strangely, was not mentioned in the press. In June 1930, Soiuzkino was described as "former" Sovkino and that was all. Youngblood, p. 190.

10 On Riutin's platform and his fate, see Robert C. Tucker, *Stalin in Power: The Revolution from Above, 1928–1941*, Norton, New York, 1990, pp. 211–12. The fact that Riutin headed Soiuzkino appears nowhere in the printed literature. My information comes from Richard Taylor who kindly shared his material with me. He learned about Riutin's role from the Soviet film scholar, Rashit Yangirov, and then found archival confirmation in the central state archives, TsGALI (f.2497 op. 1. ed. khr. 10). I am most grateful to Richard Taylor.

11 B. Bagaev, *Boris Shumiatskii*, Krasnoiarsk, 1974, p. 186.

12 I will describe the working of the censorship apparatus in detail in a later chapter.

13 See, for example "Arkovets," "ARRK nuzhno reorganizovat'," *Kino i zhizn'*, Feb. 1, 1930.

14 See on ODSK, for example, I. Naumov, "ODSK v derevne," *Kino i zhizn'*, Dec. 20, 1929, and M. Nikanorov, "Obshchestvo Druzei Sovetskogo Kino," *Kino i kultura*, Jan. 1929.

15 "Bol'she klassovoi bditel'nosti!" *Kino i zhizn'*, Nov. 30, 1929.

16 See, for example, K. Iukov, the chairman of ARRK, denouncing Eisenstein and Pudovkin. He writes: "In essence they bring in idealist, bourgeois ideas under the guise of sociology and Marxism. They all say that the essence of film is montage. But this is an anti-Marxist position." "K bor'be za proletarskoe kino," *Proletarskoe kino*, Feb. 1932, p. 26.

17 *Zhizn' iskusstva*, Apr. 21, 1929, p. 8.

18 See, for example, A. Piotrovskii, "Pravyi i levyi," *Zhizn' iskusstva*, Feb. 10, 1929. Soon Piotrovskii became the object of bitter attack and his career as a critic ended.

19 See S. Podol'skii, "Puti sovetskogo kino," *Zhizn' iskusstva*, May 19, 1929.

20 V. Nedobrovo, "Pochemu net geroia v sovetskom kino?" *Zhizn' iskusstva*, Aug. 16, 1927.

21 V. Sutyrin, "O sotsialisticheskoi rekonstruktsii kinematografii," *Proletarskoe kino*, Dec. 1931, pp. 6–16.

22 "Za kino bol'shevistskogo nastupleniia," ibid., p. 18.

23 *Proletarskoe kino*, Jan. 1932, pp. 2–3.

24 Taylor makes this point in "Boris Shumyatsky," pp. 50–4.

25 P. A. Bliakhin, "K itogam kino-sezona," *Kino i kultura*, Jan. 1929, pp. 3–24.

26 John David Rimberg, *The Motion Picture in the Soviet Union, 1918–1952: A Sociological Analysis*, Arno Press, New York, 1973, p. 72.

27 Dziga Vertov, *Kino-eye: The Writings of Dziga Vertov*, ed. Annette Michelson, University of California Press, Berkeley, 1984, p. 71.

28 There is a large literature on Eisenstein. The best works in English are Marie Seton, *Sergei M. Eisenstein*, A. A. Wyn, New York, 1952; Yon Barna, *Eisenstein*, Secker and Warburg, London, 1973; Jacques Aumont, *Montage Eisenstein*, Indiana University Press, Bloomington, 1987.

29 See the review of A. Matskin in *Izvestiia*, Sept. 21, 1933. Also, Youngblood, pp. 228–9.

30 On Dovzhenko, see Iurii Barabas, *Dovzhenko. Nekotorye voprosy estetiki i poetiki*, Khudozhestvennaia literatura, Moscow, 1968, and Vance Kepley, *In Service of the State: The Cinema of Alexander Dovzhenko*, University of Wisconsin Press, Madison, 1986.

31 *Izvestiia*, Mar. 29, 1930.

32 *Kino i zhizn'*, Apr. 24, 1930, pp. 5–9.

33 *Kino i zhizn'*, Nov. 1930, p. 7.

34 Alexander Dovzhenko, *The Poet as Filmmaker: Selected Writings*, ed. Marco Carynnyk, MIT Press, Cambridge, 1973, pp. 15–16.

35 B. Grossman-Rashchin, "Mysli ob Ivane," *Sovetskoe kino* 9: 4, 1933.

36 Kuleshov, "Art of the Cinema," in R. Levaco (ed.), *Kuleshov on Film*, University of California Press, Berkeley, 1974, p. 48.

37 See among the many denunciations K. Iukov, "K bor'be za proletarskoe kino," *Proletarskoe kino* 2: 2, 1931.

38 See a detailed description of the film in E. Gromov, *Lev Vladimirovich Kuleshov*, Moscow, Iskusstov, 1984, pp. 209–15. Gromov's study is by far the best on Kuleshov.

39 L. Kuleshov, *Gody tvorcheskikh poiskov*, Propaganda Bureau of Soviet Film Art, Moscow, 1969.

40 Bliakhin, "K itogam kino-sezona," pp. 10–11.

41 "Burzhuaznye vliiania v sovetskom kino," *Kino i zhizn'* no. 2, 1930.

42 There was a rather extensive discussion of the film in the cinema press. Critics pretended that the film was about America and criticized Kuleshov for not revealing the social background of Valentine and not dealing with the social contradictions in America. V. Rossolovskaia, "Velikii uteshitel', " *Sovetskoe kino*, Nov. 1933, p. 48. Rossolovskaia adds with perhaps unconscious irony: "There is no reason to think that the historical O. Henry was bothered by censorship at all." V. Voloshchenko writing in the next issue of the same journal says explicitly: "In front of us there is one of the films most alien to a Soviet viewer that ever appeared on the screen." He regarded the film as reactionary because, "if it is about capitalist society, then it gives a picture of hopelessness, for there is no room for protest." *Sovetskoe kino*, Dec. 1933, pp. 26–8.

43 In the course of the fearful years of the 1930s it became a common practice for artists to denounce one another in desperate attempts to save themselves. There is a blemish even on Kuleshov's record, who by and large behaved better and more courageously than others. A critic by the name of M. Shneider in 1926 wrote him a personal letter in which he praised *By the Law* and added that Kuleshov would be better appreciated in France than in the Soviet Union. Later Shneider joined Kuleshov's critics, denouncing him as a formalist and for similar offenses. At a meeting of ARRK in 1931 Kuleshov read aloud Shneider's letter, which led to the critic's

exclusion from the organization. The exclusion, however, did not end Shneider's career as a critic. See two versions of this incident. Youngblood, pp. 199–200, is not sympathetic to Kuleshov, and Gromov, pp. 251–3, takes Kuleshov's side.

44 Youngblood, p. 244.

45 *Proletarskoe kino* 5–6: 25–9, 1931. One wonders if Mikhailov's critique was influenced at all by the fact that he himself had recently been denounced as "eclectic and un-Marxist" in *Kino i zhizn'*, Apr. 11, 1930, p. 7.

46 G. Kozintsev, *Glubokii ekran*, Iskusstvo, Moscow, 1971.

47 K. Iukov, "Konveyer smerti," *Sovetskoe kino* 12: 16, 1933. Iukov correctly noted that the many themes of the film do not support one another. He also complained that the director "did not analyze the problem of overproduction in capitalist societies."

48 Bela Balash, "Novye fil'my," *Sovetskoe kino* 3–4: 19–24, 1933. "Balash," of course, is the famous Hungarian critic and theorist, Béla Balázs.

49 *Ocherki istorii sovetskogo kino, vol. 1, 1917–1934*, Iskusstvo, Moscow, 1956, p. 336.

CHAPTER 6

The industry, 1933–1941

At the end of the 1920s Soviet film enjoyed a well-deserved worldwide reputation. Within a short time, however, the fame and influence of the great Soviet directors were lost; the "golden age" was brief, and the eclipse sudden and long lasting. The coming of sound film made the famous "Russian montage" outdated and was a factor in the decline. But far more important in destroying the reputation of Soviet cinema were the political changes that took place in the 1930s.

Stalinist historians, writing before the time of *glasnost'*, have always depicted the history of the Soviet Union as an unbroken unit. In their view the principles on which Soviet society rested were enunciated by V. I. Lenin, and ever since the leaders of the Party needed merely to interpret those eternal principles. Ironically, conservative Westerners have very much agreed. They too have believed that the basic features of Soviet society were created at the time of Lenin and since then there have been only surface modifications.

In fact Soviet history has been full of shifts in policies and principles. This should not be surprising. When the Bolsheviks came to power they had only vague ideas about the society they planned to build, and they had no models to follow; their political, economic, and social system developed as a result of constant improvisation. They were among the great improvisers of the century.

Perhaps the most significant turning point in Soviet history was the ending of the NEP system. It collapsed under the weight of its own contradictions. What would take its place, however, was not at all clear even to those who actively participated in the work of its destruction. The change from the pluralism of the NEP to the orthodox Stalinism of the 1930s came about in two stages. Soviet publicists called the first period, the First Five-Year Plan, a "cultural revolution." This was a time of genuine enthusiasm, a revival of the utopian and egalitarian spirit of the revolution, but also a time of wild anarchy and of destructive attacks on institutions and human beings. By contrast what followed was a period of vast changes in the social and economic structure of the country, extraordinarily cruel repression, the establishment of a new orthodoxy, and with it the creation of a conservative social and artistic order. The transformation of Soviet culture, therefore, can be understood only in the context of the cataclysmic changes that shook the entire political and economic system. The artists were cajoled and coerced to come up with principles and methods that would be suitable in the new order. Only rarely were they passive victims; most of the time they collaborated.

Marxists have always insisted that art could not be taken out of the social context in which it was created. Indeed, the films that were made in the Stalinist 1930s reflected a murderous political system. Whenever we discuss a film of the period we must remember that it was made at a time when there was a high price to pay for political heterodoxy, when friends and relatives of the directors disappeared in the purges, when people were compelled to denounce each other, and when criticisms acquired a sinister meaning. Also, the audiences who went to see the production dramas or the often-silly comedies above all craved a relief from their terror-filled and bleak world.

The organization of the industry and the problems of production

A peculiar feature of Soviet political discourse has been a strange mixture of extravagant self-congratulation with almost equally extravagant self-criticism. On the one hand, publicists have claimed that the Revolution had already created a just and progressive society; on the other, the regime has always set itself such ambitious goals that these could not possibly have been realized. Film journals of the 1930s claimed that Soviet cinema surpassed all others in artistic quality and at the same time complained about the failures, "ideological rejects," and the inability of the industry to fulfill the plans.

The desire to achieve the impossible and the inevitable disillusionment that followed from the failures, the ever-present tension between the ideal and the recalcitrant reality, led to the characteristic Soviet mania for reorganization. Soviet leaders seemed to believe that if they reshuffled the organizations once more, the problems could be solved, the difficulties would disappear. The film industry had more than its share of reorganizations.

At the beginning of 1930 Sovkino, which had been blamed for real and imagined failures of Soviet cinema, was replaced by Soiuzkino. The basic difference between the organizational structures was that while Sovkino's authority was limited to the Russian Federal Republic, Soiuzkino oversaw the film industry for the entire Soviet Union. The new organization was headed by Boris Shumiatskii. During the next eight years he seemed enormously powerful. He suggested topics to prominent directors and participated in the discussion of individual projects. He was the ultimate censor, who could and did stop production at any stage. This extent of involvement would have been unthinkable for a Soviet bureaucrat in the previous decade.

Understandably, some directors and artists saw Shumiatskii as the personification of restrictions under which they had to labor and thus hated him. He had particularly bad relations with the greatest directors, Kuleshov and Eisenstein. Other directors, however, such as Leonid Trauberg and Iulii Raizman, regarded him as one who protected them from outside pressures and let them get on with their jobs.[1] How much power did an individual bureaucrat such as Shumiatskii really have? He represented rather than made policy. He was a small part of a large system, which he did not design and could not have changed. He finally lost his job in 1938 and was executed as a Trotskyist, Bukharinist saboteur.[2]

Shumiatskii's views, however, are important, for he represented the mentality of the ruling elite. In 1935 he published a book, *Kinematografia millionov* (Cinematography of the Millions), in which he presented his views on the art of filmmaking.[3] This book was written with the brutal directness of a simple man. He denounced the "formalists," a group that included all the great directors, with passion. As far as he was concerned there was little to choose between an Eisenstein, a Vertov, or a Kuleshov. If their theories sounded different, the source of their ideology was the same: a petit-bourgeois rebellion against the rotten bourgeois culture. In Shumiatskii's view the directors, perhaps paradoxically, represented the same despised culture against which they were rebelling. He saw, for example, in Vertov's denial of the existence of art an expression of nihilism that was a characteristic of capitalism in its dying stage. Some of these rebels, wrote Shumiatskii, ended up on the side of the Bolsheviks, others on the side of fascists; it simply depended on whether they happened to live in the Soviet Union or in Italy. The chief of the movie industry was saying – and in this he was correct – that we should not take the avant-garde artists' affirmed beliefs in Bolshevism seriously; their Bolshevism was nothing more than simple rebelliousness. Shumiatskii was unimpressed by the great works of the previous decade. *Battleship Potemkin* seemed schematic and dry to him. The insistence on depicting the masses as the moving force in history was an expression of the "petit-bourgeois notion of equality." As far as he was concerned, the great artistic leap forward took place with the coming of socialist realism.[4]

The newly created Soiuzkino under Shumiatskii's leadership assumed responsibility for all activities relevant to filmmaking. As such, its creation was a centralizing move. The studios, the factories producing materials for filmmaking, and institutes for training cadres now came under the same organization. The amount of autonomy that studios had enjoyed in the previous decade came to be greatly reduced. It was an aspect of reducing variety, imposing conformity. Such a move corresponded to the spirit of the times.

Soiuzkino under Shumiatskii introduced into filmmaking the management principles that were applied in manufacturing: a strict following of plans, industrial discipline, and financial accountability. *Sovetskoe kino,* the leading film journal, soon blamed Soiuzkino for applying industrial methods too blindly, not understanding the peculiarities of the creative process, and overcentralization – that is, the suppression of local initiative. It was particularly harmful, in the view of the writer of the editorial, for the film studios in the national republics.[5]

The next restructuring, or *perestroika,* as it was called at the time, took place in early 1933 with the establishment of the Chief Directorate of Film and Photoindustry (GUKF). The name of the organization was simplified in 1937 to GUK, Chief Directorate of the Film Industry. This organization was directly subordinated to Sovnarkom, making it, for all practical purposes, the equivalent to a commissariat. As an editorial in *Sovetskoe kino* pointed out, the significance of the move was that it showed once again that the Party attributed great significance to films as a method of propaganda. Further, by establishing republican equivalents of GUKF it drew the republican governments and Party organizations into filmmaking. The government attempted to have it both ways: On the one hand, there was now an organization that directed cinema for the entire Soviet Union; on the other, the authorities tried to escape the harmful effects of overcentralization by creating republican equivalents of GUKF.

In January 1935 the Party organized a conference of filmmakers. The contrast between this and the 1928 conference was great: In 1928 Party activists were attempting to work out principles on which Soviet film, appropriate for the age, should be based. That conference was a turning point in the history of Soviet cinema, for it signaled the beginning of the end of a great age. The second conference heralded no comparable change of direction. In 1928 primarily party functionaries gave speeches; in 1935 it was the directors themselves who were allowed to speak. They said what they were forced to say. It was a sorry spectacle: The directors, one after another, denounced what had been best in Soviet film. They exercised self-criticism, and they attacked one another. Eisenstein, who was a world renowned symbol of the great age of the past, was subjected to particularly heavy attack. He and Kuleshov stood outside of the pack; Eisenstein, because he did not renounce his past, and Kuleshov, because at one point he courageously came to the defense of Eisenstein and described the motivation of the attacks on the great director as jealousy.[6]

In January 1936 GUKF came to be subordinated to a newly created Committee for Artistic Affairs, headed by the veteran Proletkultist, V. Pletnev. Shumiatskii was named deputy chairman. It is impossible to establish whether this committee limited Shumiatskii's authority in any way. However, when in the course of 1937 GUK and later Shumiatskii in person was increasingly frequently criticized in the press, it must have been evident to contemporaries that the previously all-powerful seeming leader of Soviet cinema was in danger of being arrested. Indeed, he was arrested in January 1938. The last major reshuffle of the decade, in March 1938, created the Committee of Cinematography, under the Council of Commissars.[7] S. S. Dukel'skii was chosen to head the new organization. Compared with Dukel'skii, Shumiatskii seemed like a sophisticated gentleman and a patron of the arts. Dukel'skii came from the NKVD (People's Commissariat for Internal Affairs) and his ambition was to bring order into the film industry. He resented the independence of well-known directors and decided to strike at the root of their independence: Up to this time the directors received income at least partially in proportion to the number of tickets sold. The new boss ended this system.[8] He made entirely arbitrary decisions, at one point, for example, stopping all projects that dealt with the past in favor of presenting contemporary topics. He enjoyed summoning directors singly or as a group and lecturing them. He could not understand why the director needed more than three thousand meters of raw film for a three-thousand-meter completed film. After a year and a half on this job S. S. Dukel'skii was named minister of the Navy, and his post was given to I. Bol'shakov who managed to retain it during the war and in the difficult postwar years.[9] In 1938 the studios of the national republics were once again brought under the same organization. This committee took responsibility for all matters connected to filmmaking. These responsibilities included the administration of factories that produced raw film, the supervision of the laboratories that copied the completed work, and the organization of the distribution network and all activities that were connected with the work of bringing movies to the peasants in the countryside. Thus the film industry came to be centralized to an even greater extent than before.[10]

The Soviet film industry in the 1930s could boast considerable achievements. It was at this time that the USSR liberated itself from dependence on foreign products; domestic factories finally started to produce the raw material necessary for filmmaking. The task of building a new industry was difficult for it was necessary to start at the very beginning. In the course of the 1920s the Soviet Union imported everything: cameras, lamps, chemicals, projectors, and, most important, all of its film stock.[11] In 1931 the first Soviet factory started to produce raw film and soon after a second factory opened. At first the domestic product was very poor, but gradually the quality improved, though never equaling Western standards.[12] Without domestically produced and relatively ample film stock the work of bringing movies to the peasants, cinefication, would have been impossible. The supply of raw film enabled the USSR to produce enough copies of films for the vast country, and by 1938 there were five laboratories that were devoted exclusively to the work of duplication. In the course of the 1930s Soviet factories also started to produce 16mm film, particularly appropriate for the portable projectors used in the villages. However, the production of 16mm film was on a small scale and was soon abandoned altogether.[13] In 1934 portable sound projectors began to be produced. The output of factories making raw film was considered unsatisfactory by the authorities, and therefore they planned to increase this output five times in the following two or three years.[14] The Soviet Union also started to make its own film cameras and studio lamps. New film studios opened in Moscow, Leningrad, Kiev, and Minsk. As a result of Soviet gigantomania, the studios in Moscow and Leningrad were among the largest in the world. For Shumiatskii, these had only been the beginning. He had ambitious plans: He wanted to imitate the Americans by building a Soviet Hollywood in the Crimea. In 1935, at a time when artistic contacts between the Soviet Union and the Western world became increasingly tenuous, he traveled to America to study the American industry. Like so many other plans of the period, the projected Soviet Hollywood never materialized.

Although there were more and larger studios, these were not nearly as well equipped as studios in the West. Soviet industry could not yet produce studio lamps of great intensity. The same film stock was used for different lighting conditions. As a result, Soviet films often appeared gray and out of focus. The studios that had been built for making silent films were not properly soundproofed and therefore the quality of sound reproduction remained unsatisfactory.[15]

The viewing public

The second great Soviet achievement depended on the first: The leaders of the industry managed greatly to expand the size of the viewing public. In purely numerical terms the Soviet accomplishment was impressive. From 1928 to the last prewar year (1940), the number of movie tickets sold tripled. In 1940 there were 900 million admissions.[16] At the same time the number of cinema installations grew from 7,331 in 1928 to 29,274 in 1940. (This number included movable projectors set up in villages.) In 1928 only 2,389 were in the countryside, but in 1940 there were 17,571.[17]

In the 1930s cinema enjoyed an ever-increasing popularity all over the world. What took place in the Soviet Union was part of a worldwide trend; in this respect at least, the country was not falling behind. During this decade movie going became a significant part of the life of the average Soviet citizen. In the 1920s Soviet film journals wrote a great deal about "cinefication," and yet achievements were modest; by contrast, in the Stalinist age there was little discussion of this topic; however, this was the time that the problem was seriously tackled. Of course, the gap between cities and villages remained wide; and it could not have been otherwise. Cities continued to be better supplied, there were better and more cinemas, and there was a wider choice available for urbanites. The activists from the countryside continued to complain about the unavailability of suitable films, about the difficulties of organizing traveling exhibitions into regions without permanent projectors, indeed, without electricity.[18] However, in retrospect, it is the achievements that are striking. The primary reason for this success was collectivization: Many collective farms bought projectors from their own meager funds, and when projectors were not available, farms provided hospitality to Party organized groups traveling with movable projectors. The collective farms finally gave the Bolsheviks an organizational base in the villages that they had lacked in the previous decade.

In discussing film attendance in the Soviet Union in the 1930s, we must remember that cinema was one of the very few remaining forms of entertainment available for the Soviet people, not only in the villages but also in the cities. People, especially the young, went to the cinema not so much to see a particular film but because there was literally nothing else to do. Some of the cinemas, especially in the center of Moscow and Leningrad, had buffets and, on occasion, even small orchestras playing in the foyer. These movie houses represented an appearance of well-being and comfort that were in vivid contrast to the drab environment in which the people lived. Many people went to see the same film over and over again and therefore the number of tickets sold does not serve as conclusive proof of the popularity of a certain work.[19]

Although the number of moviegoers greatly increased in the 1930s, the choice of films available came to be very much reduced. This happened partially because now the Bolsheviks acted on their long-held conviction and stopped foreign imports. They were anxious to establish their independence in every branch of the economy, but they attributed particular significance to the film industry. They assumed that this move would provide a larger audience for domestic products, and they took it for granted that Soviet studios would be able to satisfy the need.

Soviet audiences already in the 1920s unmistakably showed that they preferred the products of Hollywood to the work of domestic filmmakers, and the importation of American films had been enormously profitable. Soviet leaders were dismayed, for they believed that even the most innocuous seeming foreign films carried hidden ideological poison. But beyond their Marxist beliefs, the Bolsheviks were influenced by that deeply held prejudice against the products of American popular culture – an attitude widely shared by the Russian intelligentsia, indeed, by educated people everywhere in the world. American films, as far as they were concerned, were vulgar. The political system, however, greatly changed from the 1920s to the age of Stalin. Whereas during the NEP period Bolsheviks were – for the sake of profit – willing to accept inevitable ideological damage, in the 1930s they drew a clear and sharp line.

In the 1930s Soviet audiences saw almost no foreign films. In the mid-1930s, for example, French Communist intellectuals decided to make a film about the horrors of Western unemployment. They gave the finished product to their Soviet comrades as a present. However, the film could not be shown in the Soviet Union, because the authorities found that the French unemployed were too well dressed and therefore the film could not serve a propaganda function.[20] The list of films allowed to be exhibited in the USSR for 1936, for example, includes only three foreign titles. It is worthwhile to quote the catalog description in its entirety:

Pet'ka, a Hungarian film, made in 1935, is about the adventures of an unemployed girl in a capitalist city. As a consequence of her personal qualities she overcomes difficulties and achieves personal happiness. In spite of prettifying the capitalist world, the film, against the wishes of its makers, shows the difficult conditions of the workers.[21]

Under the Roofs of Paris, a French film made by René Clair in 1930, which shows the lives of déclassé elements. It is the history of a street singer.

The Betrayal of Marvin Blake, an American film, made in 1932 by Warner Brothers and directed by Michael Curtiz, about the struggle of small cotton growers against the great landowners.[22]

(This last film, whose U.S. title is *Cabin in the Cotton,* was insignificant, distinguished only by the presence of Bette Davis.) And that was all.

The choice available for the audiences drastically narrowed not only because foreign films were for all practical reasons excluded from Soviet cinemas, but because domestic production started to fall at the time of the "cultural revolution" and did not recover for decades.

The film industry was caught up in the momentous changes that were taking place at the time of the First Five-Year Plan. From the point of view of the government, filmmaking was an industry like all others, and it had to work on the basis of plans. From 1934 on plans specified not only the number of films to be made and by which studios, but also thematic plans specifying topics and genres.[23] It was, therefore, all the more galling that the industry in the 1930s never came close to fulfilling the plans. Year after year brought new disappointments. The studios made no more than 20 to 30 percent of the planned films.[24] In 1935 Shumiatskii talked in an optimistic vein about the need for 300 films a year.[25] In fact, the plan for that year called for only 120, and the industry produced no more than 43. In 1936 the plan was reduced from 165 to 111, but only 46 were actually made; in 1937 GUK promised 62 films but completed only 24 feature films.[26]

Publicists, writing in film journals, constantly agonized over this question: Why did Soviet studios produce so few films? How could a single American studio produce in a year as many films as the entire enormous Soviet industry? Why was it that when more and larger studios existed in the Soviet Union, and when the country freed itself from dependence on foreign material, it still could not come close to the production figures of the 1920s? Observers pointed out that not only were Western studios far more productive, but productivity in the Soviet Union greatly declined. In the mid-1920s an average film was produced in three or four months; by contrast, in the 1930s it took fourteen months, or five times longer. In some instances it took more than two years to complete a film. The answer to the question why so few films, as will be shown in the next chapter, was to be found in the changing character of censorship.[27]

The coming of sound

The development of the technology for making films with sound tracks had profound political, technological, and artistic implications for Soviet cinema. From a purely politicoagitational point of view talkies were, of course, preferable. The agitators were interested in conveying a message, and that could be undoubtedly better and more unambiguously expressed in words. In the early 1930s there were still many illiterates in the country, and these could now be directly addressed. To be sure, the Soviet Union was a multilingual country, and therefore different versions would have to be prepared for the national republics; however, that task was relatively minor.

From an artistic point of view, matters stood differently. Many famous artists of the silent era, not only Russian, but also foreigners, such as Griffith and Chaplin, had worried that sound would destroy their medium. As far as they were concerned, the essence of film art was the substitution of movement and mimicry for sound. For many artists the new technological development meant a cheapening and coarsening of films, and a danger that cinema would be reduced to filmed theater, meaning that it would cease to be an independent form of art. The great figures of Soviet film, Kuleshov, Eisenstein, Vertov, and Pudovkin, were more self-conscious innovators than others. For them, and for other theorists of Soviet cinema, the claim of film to be an independent art form was based on montage. They believed that adding realistic sound, reproducing dialogue, would inevitably destroy montage as they knew it. This was so because the addition of dialogue was bound to slow down the tempo of cutting; it takes longer for the ear to comprehend a dialogue than for the eye to make sense of a picture.

As artists the great Russian directors had much to lose. They were obviously concerned that their highly individual styles, appropriate for the silent age, could not be easily adopted to suit the new environment. In a most immediate sense, they saw that the films that brought them world renown would lose their audience appeal, at least in the West, where the sound film quickly conquered. Eisenstein, Pudovkin, and Aleksandrov expressed their views in a brief and famous statement published in *Zhizn' iskusstva* in 1928.[28] This interesting and important statement by three major directors expressed the views of other theorists.[29] Further, film theorists believed that films with realistic dialogues would destroy the international character of cinema. They saw the success of "talkies" in the West and realized that sound was inevitably coming. They proposed to find a way out of the dilemma by nonrealistic use of sound as counterpoint. They clothed this notion in Marxist dialectic: The artistic idea would emerge from the

clash between sound and picture. Instead of dialogues, they believed monologue could accompany the films of the future. For monologue would not
destroy montage and they could not imagine film art without montage. That
is, they did not object to the use of sound as such; they objected to the
realistic dialogue of talking pictures.

Sound is a double-edged invention and its most probable application will be along
the line of least resistance, i.e. in the field of the satisfaction of simple curiosity.
  In the first place there will be commercial exploitation of the most salable goods,
i.e. of talking pictures – and those in which sound is recoded in a natural manner,
synchronizing exactly with the movement on the screen and creating a certain "illusion" of people talking, objects making a noise, etc.

A certain elitism is implied. Sound films would be successful, presumably,
because this was what people would want to see. But as many critics correctly pointed out, for some directors the protection and independence of
cinematic art was more important than serving an audience. Only a few
years before, the theoretically minded directors had defended their art by
arguing that it was something essentially different from theater because of
the possibilities offered by montage. Now they were afraid that their recently won victory would be reversed.
  The discussion concerning the introduction of sound and the kind of
sound films Soviet studios should produce became subsumed in the larger
campaign that was taking place at the time. The best directors came under
heavy and politically inspired attack for making films that were not accessible for the average Soviet viewer. The slogan "cinema for the millions,"
popularized at the conference devoted to cinema in March 1928, in effect
meant a prohibition of artistic experimentation. Eisenstein's and Pudovkin's
ideas concerning "contrapuntal" use of sound was perceived as part of the
"formalist" approach. But times were unfavorable for the innovators and
they were bound to lose. By the end of the "cultural revolution" the battle
was decided. Nikolai Lebedev, a functionary in the film industry, a theore-
tician and historian of Soviet film, would ridicule in 1933 the pronouncements of two eminent literary theorists and, indeed, formalists, Viktor
Shklovskii and Iurii Tynianov, by quoting from what they had said just a
few years earlier. Shklovskii wrote in 1927: "Talking film is as little needed
as a singing book"; and Tynianov had argued that sound and montage cannot be reconciled.[30] Lebedev described such views as reactionary. Few such
"reactionary" films were in fact made. The most famous example was Pudovkin's film, *Deserter,* which was attacked precisely for this quality. The
films that the Soviet Union would produce in the course of the 1930s were
conventional talkies, and with a few and not very successful exceptions,
contrapuntal sound was never given a chance.
  Soviet directors had an opportunity to observe the birth of sound film
from a distance, for domestic industry could follow only with some delay.

Technologically, the Soviet Union was backward. While in the West the first sound films appeared in 1926 and 1927, in the Soviet Union in the late 1920s the industry had only reached an experimental stage. At a time when the huge American industry had almost completed the transition, the Soviet Union was just producing its first sound film.

Two groups worked on the process of equipping films with sound: one in Moscow under the leadership of P. Tager and another in Leningrad under A. Shorin. The technicians faced a number of difficulties arising primarily from the poor quality of Soviet-made microphones.[31] The first Soviet sound films were made only in 1930. The Soviet filmmakers were proud of their domestically developed system of sound reproduction, and all through the 1930s the Shorin or Tager sound system was included among the credits at the beginning of the film.

It was relatively easy to produce films with sound tracks. The real difficulty was to equip the enormous country with enough sound projectors. In May 1931 there was only a single cinema in the Soviet Union capable of playing sound films. Exactly two years later out of the 32,000 projectors there were still only 300 capable of reproducing sound.[32]

Progress was exasperatingly slow. As late as January 1938 there were still more silent projectors in the country than ones equipped with sound (11,242 vs. 17,332).[33] This situation required that almost all Soviet films that were made in that year also had to come out in silent versions. Not surprisingly, sound came first to city theaters. The mobile projectors, still dominant in the countryside, were almost without exception without sound. A catalog of permitted films printed in 1943 shows 277 sound films and 175 silents.

These numbers show that while directors preferred to use the new technology, for a long time there were not enough films for the viewers. Further, the industry dealt with the emergency by producing silent versions of sound films. Such efforts meant a duplication of work and an inefficient use of scarce resources. It was clear to contemporary observers, however, that in the Soviet Union silent and sound films had to coexist for some time.[34]

Through the early 1930s Soviet filmmakers faced an impossible dilemma. If they made sound films, these could not be shown to large audiences, and therefore the directors were denounced for disregarding the interests of the "mass viewer." If they continued to make silent films, they would lose their share of the market abroad, where interest in silent films disappeared almost immediately with the appearance of sound. Also, they left themselves open to the charge that their interest in silent film was a sign of their attachment to "formalism." Most directors had a desire to participate in what was new and wanted to make sound films. Some directors were denounced as reactionary, because they did not make silent films and were therefore disregarding the mass viewer, whereas others were denounced for opposing sound. The politically correct attitude was to approve sound but for the right reasons. Nevertheless, the Soviet Union continued to produce silent films until 1936, far longer than the United States or any country in Western Europe.

Notes

1 The literature hostile to Shumiatskii is too large to enumerate. It is fair to say that writers on individual great directors, such as Eisenstein and Kuleshov, chose the head of the industry as their bête noir. Richard Taylor, "Boris Shumyatsky and the Soviet Cinema in the 1930s: Ideology as Mass Entertainment," *Historical Journal of Film, Radio and Television 6*, no. 1: 60–1, 1986. Among writers on Soviet cinema Taylor's evaluation is unique inasmuch as he takes a rather favorable attitude toward Shumiatskii.

2 Interestingly, the 640-page Soviet film encyclopedia, published in 1987, has no entry on Shumiatskii. *Kino. Entsiklopedicheskii slovar'*, Sovetskaia entsiklopediia, Moscow, 1987.

3 *Kinematografiia millionov*, Kinofotoizdat, Moscow, 1935.

4 Ibid., pp. 48–60.

5 *Sovetskoe kino 1–2; 1–5*, 1933.

6 On this conference, see E. Zil'ber and I. I. Krinkin, "Preodolenie empirizma. K itogam Vsesoiuznogo soveshchaniia tvorcheskikh rabotnikov kino," *Iskusstvo kino* 3: 7–10, 1935. See also a good summary in Youngblood, *Soviet Cinema in the Silent Era, 1917–1935*, UMI Press, Ann Arbor, Mich., 1985. pp. 230–2 and Ian Christie and Richard Taylor (ed.), *The Film Factory: Russian and Soviet Cinema Documents, 1896–1939*, Harvard University Press, Cambridge, 1988, pp. 348–58, where excerpts are reproduced. Taylor in his introductory comments to the document presents a different interpretation of the conference from what is offered here.

7 *Iskusstvo kino*, Mar. 1938, pp. 6–7.

8 Information from Mark Zak in private conversation, Dec. 1990.

9 Mikhail Romm, "Semen Semenovich Dukel'skii," *Alef*, Feb. 6, 1989, pp. 34–9. *Alef* is an Israeli journal. This article was taken from *Sovetskii ekran*. Romm died in 1971. This is an excerpt from his diaries.

10 *Ezhegodnik Sovetskoi kinematografii za 1938 god*, Goskinoizdat, Moscow, 1939, pp. 6–10.

11 "Partiia proveriaet svoi riady," *Sovetskoe kino* 10: 1, 1933.

12 A. Richard, "Kino v SSSR," *Sovetskoe kino* 7: 77, 1935. This article is a translation from a French journal, *La Cinématographie française*.

13 *Ezhegodnik za 1938 god*, p. 288.

14 I. Sidorov, "Kinopromyshlennost' v iubileinom godu," *Sovetskoe kino* 11–12, 168–9, 1934.

15 Richard, p. 78, and "Pered litsom partiinogo s''ezda," *Sovetskoe kino* 1: 3, 1934.

16 *Sovetskoe khoziaistvo*.

17 Christie and Taylor, p. 423.

18 See, for example, complaints from activists in *Kino*, May 17, 1937. An activist from Cheliabinsk wrote that the same film had to be shown over and over again to the peasants because nothing else was available. In *Kino*, Sept. 4, 1940, an activist from Stalingrad district made the same complaint.

19 Maia Turovskaia, a Soviet sociologist of cinema, made this point forcefully

in her unpublished paper presented at a conference of Soviet and American film historians in Washington, D.C., December 1990. Turovskaia concluded that since the authorities made more copies of those films that they approved of, and showed them more often and for longer periods, the best measure of genuine popularity of a certain work was how many people saw a film per copy. According to this calculation *Karo*, an Armenian film made in 1937 and hardly known by film scholars, was the most popular film of the 1930s.

20 Ervin Sinko, *Egy regeny regenye. Moszkvai naplojegyzetek, 1935–1937*, Magveto, Budapest, 1988, p. 198. The argument has been made that the importation of foreign films stopped because of the shortage of convertible currency. How important a consideration that was as compared with the demands of ideology is impossible to say. But examples, such as those given by Sinko, make one think that the primary motivation was ideological.

21 This film, starring Francisca Gaal, was phenomenally successful. People stood in line for hours to buy tickets. Sinko, a communist, was appalled. Ibid, pp. 335–6.

22 *Repertuarnyi ukazatel'*, Moscow, Kinofotoizdat, 1936.

23 *Sovetskie khudozhestvennye fil'my. Annotirovannyi katalog*, 4 vols., Iskusstvo, Moscow, 1961–8. Different contemporary sources give slightly different numbers concerning the yearly output of studios. After all, it is a matter of definition what exactly constitutes a film. However, the magnitude of the change in the number of films produced is indisputable. Information concerning genres is from "Sovetskaia kinematografiia pered litsom partiinogo s''ezda," *Sovetskoe kino* 1: 5, 1934.

24 "Kak realizuetsia plan vypuska fil'mov," *Iskusstvo kino* 11: 36–40, 1936.

25 A. Dubrovskii, "O 'predeliakh' i vozmozhnostiakh sovetskoi kinematografii," *Iskusstvo kino* 1: 23, 1938. Although Dubrovskii does not say so, what Shumiatskii had had in mind was making three hundred films yearly by 1940. Shumiatskii had assumed that Soviet Hollywood would be constructed.

26 G. Ermolaev, "Chto tormozit razvitie sovetskogo kino," *Pravda*, Jan. 9, 1938. In 1937 GUKF was renamed GUK without changing either its organization or functions.

27 I. Sidorov, "Kinopromyshlennost' v iubileinom godu," *Sovetskoe kino* 11–12: 170, 1934.

28 Aug. 5, 1928. The statement is translated in Christie and Taylor, pp. 234–5.

29 See, for example, Béla Balázs, *Theory of the Film*, D. Dobson, London, 1952. Remarkably, Balázs writing in the late 1940s still found no reason to revise his earlier negative views on the use of sound. He continued to believe that sound had destroyed silent cinema, but that the art of sound film had not yet been born (pp. 194–221).

30 N. Lebedev, "O spetsifike kino," *Sovetskoe kino* 10: 61, 1933. Lebedev was also a founder of ARK and a scenarist.

31 *Ocherki istorii sovetskogo kino*, vol. 1, pp. 262–6.

32 *Sovetskoe kino* 1–2: 4, 1933.

33 *Ezhegodnik za 1938*, p. 292.

34 V. Sutyrin, *Proletarskoe kino* 1: 8, 1931.

CHAPTER 7

Censorship, 1933–1941

In any discussion of Stalinist films the nature of censorship is inevitably a central issue. Unfortunately, the word "censorship" is something of a misnomer. One should not imagine that the problem of the Soviet artist was that he had to submit his completed work for an examination by a censor or a body of censors. The representatives of the Party, those responsible for ideological purity, were in fact cowriters and codirectors, who participated in every stage of the production of the film from the first glimmer of an idea to the last cut.

The difficulties of making films

To the question, often asked by Soviet publicists at the time, why could the industry not fulfill its plans and provide the public with enough films, there was an easy answer. It became almost impossibly difficult to make a film in the Soviet Union. None of the difficulties faced by the artists were entirely new: Glavrepetkom, the State Repertoire Committee, in February 1923 ordered the studios to submit every completed film for approval and no changes in the finished work could be made without the agreement of Glavrepetkom. Nevertheless, in the 1920s, at a time when state-owned and private companies competed, when several artistic trends could coexist, considerable creative freedom remained. The great deterioration began with the party cinema conference in March 1928. The cultural revolution in cinema meant a purge in every film organization and a merciless attack on artistic experimentation in the name of the struggle against "formalism." It was at this time that the number of Soviet films began to decline.

Although script hunger was as old as the film industry, in the 1930s the problem became more serious. This deterioration happened partially because the issue became entangled with a theoretical discussion concerning the relative importance of directors and scenarists in filmmaking. What took place could not accurately be described as a debate, for only one side could be articulated. Times favored the screenplay writers. Publicists denounced the idea as "formalist" that the film primarily belonged to the director.[1]

140

There were two main reasons why the Stalinist politicians objected to giving primary responsibility for the artistic product to the director. First of all, as socialist realist film developed, more and more precise requirements concerning an acceptable story line were set for the filmmakers, and only the scenarists could satisfy these demands. Second, by giving the director a measure of artistic freedom, there was a danger that at least some of them would experiment, would put their own individual stamp on the product, or, according to the terminology of the time, produce "formalist" cinema.

Sovetskoe kino in an editorial expressed it clearly:

We are struggling for great, full-blooded art, for an art of great social content. Is this not, above all, a struggle for scenarios? It is obvious that above all and most importantly the scenario determines that circle of ideas which will be fixed in the future film, and it is the scenario which gives the director material whose ideological quality determines the political correctness and artistic convincingness of the film.[2]

Four years later it was necessary to repeat the correct line. N. Otten wrote in *Iskusstvo kino:*

The very understanding of the role of the scenario is different in different stages of the development of cinematography. The scenario developed as a service for the director at the time of shooting, as his notation book prepared for him by his literary co-worker, his helpmate. But in the final stage of development of cinematography, the scenario is an independent, complete literary product, indicating what should be expressed on film, describing frame by frame the ideas, characters, and their development. . . . This struggle [for recognition of the importance of scenario] in spite of the abundance of fine words from all sides, is far from finished. The struggle continues above all against the survival of montage cinematography, in other words against the survival of formalism, which asserts the unconditional priority of the director against all other creators of the film, primarily against the scenarist and actor.[3]

It was intolerable for the director not to follow precisely the script that had been evaluated exhaustively. The director disregarding his scenario led to making but not exhibiting many films, and consequently to the loss of a great deal of money. No wonder the industry year after year failed to live up to the financial plan. It was necessary to cut the director down to size; the scenarist was to get equal credit, and carry equal responsibility. Soviet emphasis on the primacy of the script (i.e., the written word) over the work of the director (i.e., the image) was profoundly antithetical to the very notion of cinematic art. None of the outstanding figures of the silent era could produce first-rate work and at the same time satisfy the political demands, which called for nothing more than providing illustrations for a written text.

The bulk of films of the early 1930s was written by the directors themselves, but this arrangement was considered unsatisfactory by the authorities. They would have liked to attract well-known writers for the task. They had attempted to conclude agreements with authors concerning the delivery of screenplays, but this campaign did not bring sufficient results. Not enough material was delivered and many of the completed scenarios were not allowed to proceed to shooting. Between 1929 and 1933 Sovkino and Soiuzkino drew up 58 contracts with writers, out of which only 7 became completed films.[4] In 1933 Soiuzfil'm paid out advances for writing 129 scripts. Of these only 13 were accepted for production.[5] Nevertheless, as time went on it became increasingly rare for the director to write his own script. Indeed, GUKF considered passing a regulation that would have forbidden directors to write their own material. This did not happen, for there were so few scripts that the industry could not afford to impose on itself further restrictions.[6]

The task of the scenarist was not an easy one. The number of steps between developing an idea and seeing the finished product was considerable. The writer first submitted a synopsis to the scenario department of the studio. These departments, set up in December 1929, included representatives from the district Party committee and the Komsomol. (By regulation Party and Komsomol representatives were to make up at least a third of the committee.) In addition there were people from ODSK (Society of the Friends of Soviet Cinema), ARRK (Association of Revolutionary Workers in Cinematography), as long as these organizations existed, and from the Party, trade-union, and Komsomol organizations of the studios. Only after the writer's idea was approved would he proceed with the work. The finished script was then examined by another set of censors, called editors and consultants.

In the course of the 1930s the extent of control and intervention became more and more extraordinary. Beginning in April 1933, the scenario had to be discussed by the studio's party organization before it was to go into production. Finally GUKF had to approve each and every project. After March 1938 the scenario department of the Cinema Committee approved every submitted project. After this approval the director could not change a single word in the screenplay without explicit permission.

Even so, on each occasion changes or additions would most likely be demanded, and the writer had no control whatever over the final product. In some instances, such as in the case of *The Conveyor Belt of Death* of Ivan Pyr'ev, which was also known as *Tovar ploshchadei*, the film was remade fourteen times.[7] When one contemplates the control mechanisms that existed, it is not surprising that authors tended to shy away and that there was an inordinate amount of time lost between the conception of the film and its appearance in the cinemas of the country.

As the script problem remained unresolved, instead of simplifying the process, the authorities set up more and more supervisory organizations. In 1937 the authorities created special commissions from the representatives of the Party and of social organizations. These commissions were placed within the scenario departments and had the task of passing on submitted film projects. Sometimes workers were invited to participate in the discussions. The Komsomol demanded the evaluation and discussion of all scripts dealing with problems of youth. The Ukrainian GUK formalized the process in 1937 by ordering that all film projects be examined by representatives of the "voluntary" organizations (Komsomol, trade unions, etc.). In addition from 1934 onward almost every issue of Sovetskoe kino included scenarios, published in order to encourage public discussions.[8] It is extraordinary and yet revealing that even after all these discussions, censorship, evaluations, additions, and deletions, a large number of completed films in the 1930s remained unreleased and were considered "ideological rejects" (ideologicheskii brak). How many films remained unreleased is unclear for they were not included in the Catalog of Soviet Films, but one may reasonably estimate that about a third of the completed films were never exhibited. We know, for example, that in 1935 and 1936 alone thirty-seven films were declared to be "ideological rejects." These films cost the state 15 million rubles.[9]

A consequence of the large number of control and censorship bodies was that policy became altogether unpredictable. We can perhaps best appreciate the difficulties of filmmaking in the Soviet Union by following the tribulations of one writer. In 1935 Ervin Sinko, a Hungarian Communist, moved from Paris to Moscow in the hope that he could get his novel published and his screenplays realized in the Fatherland of Communism. Soon after his arrival he indeed signed a contract with Mezhrabpom concerning the delivery of a scenario about class struggle in contemporary France. Although the head of the scenario department, a certain Feldman, found the work satisfactory, nevertheless the author was told that at the moment the country needed comedies. Therefore they signed another contract concerning another script that was to deal with the life of French artists. This was to be a rather apolitical work, called Advertisement, making fun of the power of Western media to make and break reputations. By the time this work was delivered, Feldman had lost his job. Sinko now dealt with a Comrade Gold, who liked the screenplay, but told Sinko that circumstances had changed and therefore it would be necessary to include references to unemployed miners in France. Because Sinko found it impossible to include references to unemployed miners in work dealing with Paris intellectuals, the project was canceled. Sinko then tried his luck with Mosfil'm. He signed a contract with E. K. Sokolovskaia, the deputy director. He was to write a script about the plight of a Rumanian unemployed pregnant woman who managed to find her way to the Soviet Union. By the time he delivered the work, Sokolovskaia had been arrested. As a result, nothing came of this project either.[10]

Because there was a high price to pay for the "lack of vigilance," everyone erred on the side of prudence. In 1936 Béla Balázs, another Hungarian, made a film, Karl Brunner, which dealt with the tragedy of a German boy who is left alone after his parents were arrested by the Nazis as Communists. The film had to be taken off the screens. Someone maintained that it was based on the true story of the son of Ruth Fischer, a Trotskyist. Balázs argued in vain that he did not even know that Fischer had a son.[11]

The politicians set up extraordinarily complex control mechanisms because they were absolutely certain that cinema possessed great power. Under these circumstances it was not enough to prohibit some topics and styles. Intervention became prescriptive as well as proscriptive. Problems in filmmaking were treated as issues of greatest significance, and many of the top leaders, including the highest one of them all, were not too busy to devote their attention to films. For example Jay Leyda, who was in the Soviet Union in the 1930s and acquainted with many of the prominent directors, tells us in his book that Sergei Kirov, the head of the Leningrad Party organization, concerned himself personally with the making of *Counterplan* from the inception of the project, and gave "advice."[12] We learn from Shumiatskii that in this same film the idea for the famous episode in which the party secretary drinks vodka with the old worker came from the leadership of Soiuzkino.[13]

Film distribution was controlled just as strictly as filmmaking. GUKF every year published a book that included lists of all the films and newsreels that were allowed to be shown and those forbidden. The second list was usually considerably longer than the first. The list of forbidden films for 1936 contained most of the successful films of the silent era, including all the films of Kuleshov and several of the works of Dovzhenko, Protazanov, Kozintsev, and Trauberg. Among the forbidden films were *Aelita, The White Eagle, The Gay Canary, The Girl with the Hatbox, The House in the Snowdrift, Evdokia Rozhnovskaia, His Call, The Cross and the Mauser, The Death Ray, The Bear's Wedding, Father Sergius, By the Law, Polikushka, Happiness, Third Meshchanskaia Street (Bed and Sofa), Turksib, The Devil's Wheel,* and *The Miracle Maker.*[14]

The authorities tightly controlled not only films but also projectors. All of them had to be registered with *soiuzkinoprokat.* This registration was a complex process. A recognized body, such as a trade union, a Komsomol cell, or collective farm, assumed formal responsibility for the work. They had to certify that they had technical personnel available and therefore the projector would be cared for and that the projector would be used according to the cinefication plans. The Soviet government obviously spared no effort to prevent the showing of works that it considered ideologically dubious.[15]

The supreme censor

Although Stalin was very much interested in movies, he had not the slightest understanding of this medium of art. He did not comprehend the visual aspect of filmmaking and considered the word to be primarily important. In his view the director was merely a technician who carried out the instructions of the scenarist. Directors benefited from Stalin's misunderstanding:

With few exceptions, they survived. By contrast, scriptwriters and officials of the industry lived in a dangerous world and dozens of them became victims of the terror.[16]

Stalin lavished an extraordinary amount of attention on the cinema. From the mid-1930s to the end of his days, he was the chief censor. He personally saw and approved every single film exhibited in the Soviet Union. Just like his German colleague, Goebbels, he micromanaged the film industry: He suggested changes, altered titles, reviewed scripts, and recommended topics. His extraordinary preoccupation with cinema is shown by the fact that when the editors of the fourteenth volume of his collected works, so far unpublished, gathered material for the year 1940, they found that in that year there were only three pieces of writings that survive and all these concern his opinions about film scenarios.[17]

Stalin alone could afford to be liberal. Perhaps the most morally reprehensible Soviet film of the 1930s was Ivan A. Pyr'ev's *Party Card*. The film, completed in 1936, was about the need for vigilance. The enemy, the son of a *kulak*, hides his real essence and feelings, pretending to be an honest Soviet citizen. He steals the Party card of his wife, which is then used for a nefarious purpose. The film was made at a time of the national campaign for exchanging Party cards and thereby purging undesirable elements. Among the goals of the film was to contribute to the cult of the Party card, the losing of which was considered to be a major infraction of Party discipline. Many Party members carried their cards in a little canvas bag on a chain on their necks.[18] The enemy is unmasked at the end by his wife (Fig. 27). The leadership of Mosfil'm for some reason found this film "unsuccessful, false and distorting Soviet reality." Stalin had a different opinion. He changed the title of the film from the proposed *Anka* to *Party Card* and approved its distribution. Pyr'ev's next film, *The Rich Bride*, had exactly the same fate (Fig. 28). Shumiatskii without comment shelved it, and the director once again successfully appealed to a higher authority. The appearance of the film in the movie houses coincided with Shumiatskii's arrest.[19] Leyda informs us that Stalin himself intervened in order to allow Eisenstein, after the debacle of *Bezhin Meadow*, to make *Aleksandr Nevskii*.[20]

Another illustration of Stalin's personal involvement in filmmaking comes from Dovzhenko. Having been severely criticized for his previous work in *Earth* and *Ivan*, he decided to turn to Stalin himself. As Dovzhenko tells the story, Stalin, Voroshilov, Molotov, and Kirov received him twenty-two hours after he posted a letter addressed to the general secretary. He read to this distinguished company the entire script of *Aerograd* (Fig. 29). Stalin made suggestions and criticisms. On another occasion Stalin suggested to him that he make a film about the Ukrainian civil war leader, Shchors. Then Stalin summoned him. Dovzhenko continues:

I want to write in greater detail about my second visit to Comrade Stalin. I want my comrades in art to be happy and proud and our enemies to have cause for reflection. Comrade Stalin summoned me to see him. It was at the height of work on *Aerograd*

Figure 27.   Anka, the heroine of *Party Card* (1936), unmasks the enemy, her own husband.

when I was literally disappearing under the weight of the many newspaper articles about the making of *Shchors* that Joseph Vissarionovich suggested to me. There was apparently a meeting going on in Comrade Stalin's office and I entered the room during the break when he was not in the room. A couple of minutes later Comrade Stalin came in and asked first of all whether I already knew everybody. It was only when I answered in the affirmative that he began to ask very detailed questions about work on *Aerograd*, about my creative state of mind, and about whether the Air Force was giving me enough help to film aircraft. In a word, I felt that whatever help I needed to complete the film was guaranteed. But surely he has not summoned me just for that, I thought. "Now I will tell you why I summoned you," Comrade Stalin said, "Giving you some advice. I was merely thinking of what you might do in the Ukraine. But neither my words, nor newspaper articles put you under any obligation. You are a free man. If you want to make *Shchors*, do so – but, if you have other plans, do something else. Don't be embarrassed. I summoned you so you should know this."[21]

Needless to say, Dovzhenko carried out Stalin's suggestion without any hesitation.[22]

In the case of politically sensitive films such as Ermler's *The Great Citizen*, which dealt with the purge trials, Stalin's revision of the script was so

Figure 28.   Happy peasants celebrate in front of Stalin's picture in *The Rich Bride* (1937).

Figure 29.   "Friends" in *Aerograd* (1935).

extensive that we might consider him a coauthor. A letter that he wrote to Shumiatskii concerning this film in 1937 survives. Once again, it is necessary to quote directly in order to convey the extent and nature of Stalin's interventions.[23]

I read Comrade Ermler's script. I agree that it is undoubtedly politically literate. Also, it also undoubtedly has literary virtues. However, there are some errors.

1. The representatives of the "opposition" appear as older both physically and also in the sense of Party service than the representatives of the Central Committee. This is not typical and did not correspond to reality. Reality gives us the opposite picture.
2. The picture of Zheliabov must be removed: There is no analogy between the terrorists, pygmies from the camps of Zinovevists and Trotskyists, and the revolutionary, Zheliabov.
3. The reference to Stalin must be excluded. Instead of Stalin the Central Committee of the Party must be mentioned.
4. Shakhov's murder should not be the center and highest point of the scenario: This or that terrorist act pales in comparison with those being uncovered by the trial of Piatakov and Radek.

The letter continues in making instructions how the inner Party struggle must be presented.

Stalin's preoccupation with films was extraordinary. As he withdrew from the real world, in the sense of seeing actual factories, collective farms, villages, and even streets of Moscow, more and more his view of the world was determined by what he saw on the screen. Socialist realist art aimed to do away with the distinction between "is" and "ought." Through the medium of the film "reality" became what it was meant to be according to Bolshevik, Stalinist ideology. Of course, the Soviet people could not easily be taken in. After all, they experienced the dreadful conditions of the 1930s on their own skin, they knew how a collective farm in fact looked, and they knew what life was in a collective apartment. But Stalin, ironically, allowed himself to be deceived by the lies of his own Party activists, lies that he himself had generated.

Cinema came to be an essential feature of the Stalinist phenomenon, through its ability to create an alternate "reality." Nowhere else up to this time, not even in Nazi Germany, did cinema play a comparable role.[24]

Three films

Most of the rejected films simply disappeared and therefore we cannot form an opinion of them. A few films, however, although they never appeared in the cinemas, received wide and negative publicity. From examining the contemporary discussion of these films, much can be learned about the mentality of the censors to indicate exactly what disturbed them. These discussions make us appreciate the very narrow limits within which Soviet artists had to work. Let us examine three examples. The first of these, *Bezhin Meadow*, was made by the great Eisenstein; the second, *Father and Son*, by a less well-known director, Margarita A. Barskaia; and the third was Stol'per's film, *The Law of Life*, based on a script by A. Avdeenko.

Eisenstein's previous film had been *The Old and the New*, made in 1929. Then he went abroad and returned in 1932. For three years he was unable to begin work on a new film. In 1935 he accepted a commission from the Komsomol to make a film on the theme of the Pioneers' contribution to collectivization. The scenario was written by A. Rzheshevskii, a man with great experience in cinema. The title, *Bezhin Meadow*, came from a famous story by Turgenev, a story that was a part of *A Sportsman's Notebook*. Turgenev's story, dealing with peasant boys in the 1850s and of a death foretold, had so little to do with the scenario that one remains puzzled why Eisenstein chose this title. The film, in fact, was inspired by Pavlik Morozov, a Soviet hero, whose life and death was known by everyone. At the time of collectivization, Pavlik's relatives had murdered him because the boy had denounced his father as a *kulak*.[25] Rzheshevskii changed the story rather substantially: In his version it was the father who killed his own son. Nevertheless, the basic juxtaposition between duty to communism and duty to family remained.

Pavlik was a symbol for an era: The young "hero" placed his duty to society higher than his obligation to his family; in an age of denunciation, he was the ultimate denouncer. In making a film about him Eisenstein decided to add another brick to the edifice of Stalinism. He did everything within his power to produce a film that would serve the propaganda interests of the regime as he understood them. The scenario shows not even the slightest or hidden criticism of Soviet reality, for Eisenstein, like other Soviet directors, was content to do what was expected of him. Given the times, it was unthinkable to reject a demand for a change, for an addition or deletion from his work. Still, among all the famous directors Eisenstein best preserved his personal and artistic integrity. It is, therefore, doubly ironic that he was most severely denounced for a film whose ideological message was morally the most repugnant of all the work that the director had ever attempted. The Soviet authorities prevented us from seeing the work of a great artist using his enormous talent for an abominable cause.

Eisenstein, the artist, still survived. In this respect he was different from other filmmakers. It may be that he had greater self-confidence as a result of his worldwide reputation, or that he simply did not understand the unstated demands of socialist realism. He threw himself into making his first sound film with customary enthusiasm and thoroughness. Yet, he produced a film that was completely unacceptable. First of all, he put his individual stamp on it; the film was to be unmistakably his. Unconsciously, he resisted the homogenizing attempts of socialist realism. He regarded Rzheshevskii's scenario, which he liked very much, as only a starting point. In spite of all the denunciation of the "emotional scenario" (i.e., the director using the scenario as merely a source of inspiration, a starting point), he handled

Rzheshevskii's work precisely in that spirit. He liked the scenario because it was simple and therefore he could expand it. But he was not alone in his admiration for the scenario. In *Iskusstvo kino* E. Zil'ber, one of the major critics of the day, also praised Rzheshevskii's work.[26] Zil'ber particularly liked the fact that the major confrontation occurred not between father and son, but between the representatives of two worlds. That is, Rzheshevskii depicted types rather than individuals. Ironically, Eisenstein was attacked in the following year for precisely this characteristic of the film.

It was difficult to make this film and it took a very long time. The director went to extraordinary trouble to find the right people to play the roles. He chose Pavlik (Stepok, in the film) after having interviewed two thousand children. He chose the other actors as types. He carefully choreographed each of their moves. He experimented with both realistic and nonrealistic use of sound. Consciously or unconsciously, he dealt with his own individual preoccupations (such as the father–son relationship).[27] At the same time, and perhaps paradoxically, the film was more realistic than any Soviet film made in the 1930s. Unlike all other Soviet films of the period, it dealt with a genuine issue and it showed a real conflict.

Shumiatskii, without the permission or even knowledge of the director, showed an unfinished version of the film to leaders of the film industry and later to members of the Politburo.[28] Eisenstein was attacked for making a drama about the struggle between new and old, and the price that had to be paid for historical advances, rather than about a concrete situation. He was criticized for depicting collectivization as a destructive process. In particular the critics objected to scenes that portrayed an attack on a church. Eisenstein obviously captured a little of the anarchy, and the dreaded spontaneity of the period. More than a year after he started to work on the film, in August 1936, Eisenstein had to revise the scenario substantially. Ironically, his helpmate in the revision was the great Soviet writer, I. Babel, soon also to become a purge victim.

Then in March 1937, GUK ordered him to stop work on the film before its completion. Because of Eisenstein's worldwide reputation, it was Shumiatskii himself who wrote an article in *Pravda*. In it he attacked the director and explained why the shooting had to be stopped, in spite of the millions of rubles already spent.[29] Shumiatskii's article was followed by a predictable deluge of denunciations of Eisenstein, for being "abstract," for being a formalist, for cutting himself off from the people. He was criticized for not showing the leading role of the Party, and for depicting collectivization as an elemental process. In a particularly distasteful article, Veisfel'd maintained that Eisenstein's theory of filmmaking was profoundly hostile to socialism. He wrote that "in the film there is no passionate hatred for the class enemy and there is no genuine love for those who build *kolkhozes*."[30]

N. Otten attacked Eisenstein's attitude to the scenario, attributing the failure of *Bezhin Meadow* to the so-called emotional scenario, which allowed the director to regard the scenario merely as a starting point. In his view montage implied "formalism," the supremacy of the director in the creative work as against the work of the scenarist and actor. The director labored under the illusion that working with "emotional scenario" freed him from control of the leadership of the studio. Otten drew the lesson that in the future only fully developed scenarios should be allowed to be staged.[31]

Bezhin Meadow, never publicly shown and seen only by a handful of people, became one of the most discussed films of the decade. In the age of show trials, film organizations and studios in Moscow, Leningrad, and Kiev each held meetings for the purpose of discussing the "lessons" of the film. In Moscow the meeting lasted three days, March 19–21, 1937.[32] Shumiatskii himself opened the attack by blaming the director, the film studio in which it was made, and GUK itself. Although the director was responsible for the political errors, the studio and the higher bodies were guilty of "rotten liberalism," allowing Eisenstein to proceed without knowing exactly what he was up to. GUK had asked for a copy of the completed portions of the film but had not insisted on its delivery when it was not forthcoming. The head of Mosfil'm, V. Ia. Babitskii, accepted responsibility and blamed himself for not exercising daily control and therefore not stopping the project earlier. Within a short time Babitskii was arrested.[33] Zel'dovich of GUK expressed concern that a man of Eisenstein's political unreliability was allowed to work with students at the Film Institute.

Perhaps more interesting than the predictable statements of officials were the opinions expressed by Eisenstein's peers. In their speeches we find a wide spectrum from courage and decency to swinishness. An ex-student of Eisenstein, Pavlenko, whose name deserves to be remembered for his courage, defended his master at a meeting in the Kiev studio.[34] Eisenstein's former colleague, Aleksandrov, stayed away, earning himself a denunciation in *Kino* for "raising himself above the community." Others managed to speak in such a way as to avoid attacking the man whom they respected. Barnet spoke without saying anything. Roshal stressed that whatever the circumstances, artists had to trust the leaders. Shub spoke ambiguously, suggesting that Eisenstein's absence from the country during the period of the First Five-Year Plan rendered him unable to draw the correct political lessons. Dovzhenko, the archformalist reformed, saw the source of formalism in Eisenstein's lack of knowledge of the countryside. Eisenstein was an "urbanist," he said – probably an allusion to Jewishness. Pyr'ev was as harsh, as might be expected from the director of the loathsome *Party Card*. He blamed Eisenstein for not wanting to be a "Soviet person" but wishing to be somewhere else. In his evaluation the formalist Eisenstein had steadily declined after making *Battleship Potemkin*.[35]

The most bitter attack came from a third-rate director, Iu. Mar'ian. To appreciate the flavor and absurdity of Stalinist discourse it is best to quote his statement verbatim. First he blamed the director for looking down on others, for taking no pleasure in the achievements of others, and for being a loner. Then he went on:

Formalism, formalism and once again formalism. This is a terrible disease with you. Formalism condemns you to loneliness; it is a world view of pessimists, who are in conflict with our era. I should say that I hate formalism with all my being, hate its elements in works of art, even when they are done by such masters as you. I became your opponent when I saw *October*. I saw the Revolution through your eyes. I did not see *Bezhin Meadow*, only excerpts concerning the fire, but that was enough. How could you make a fire the central episode in a *kolkhoz* building? I do not understand what the artist wanted to say by that. We feel that we cannot express in our films even a part of the great thoughts which we want to express. How do you dare to give a part of your film to show a fire? This is the best testimony of your poverty. You said that the fire represented the struggle of the *kolkhoz* peasants against anarchy. But don't fascists and capitalists also fight fires? There was no socialist element in it.[36]

Eisenstein's response was extraordinary. One can sense between the lines that if he had ever sympathized with the Soviet regime, that sympathy had disappeared. He must have had loathing and hatred for the Stalinist system. First he expressed the inevitable contrition and asked his comrades' help in overcoming his errors. He asked permission to work in the theater, where mistakes could be more easily corrected. Then he went on to make an ambiguous self-criticism, which can also be read as a frontal attack on Stalinist art. He accused himself of believing

that talent and glory gave me the right to have an original vision of the October Revolution. In *The Old and the New* I once again attempted to give my own special, as if it were independent, views of the world, instead of carefully studying the statements of the Party and expressing them. I thought I had the right, but it turned out I did not.[37]

Discussions continued for months. VGIK (All-Union State Institute of Cinematography) had special meetings scheduled on April 25 and on May 13. The same themes were repeated again and again and some of the same people gave their denunciations several times. Mar'ian, for example, spoke again on April 25. During the May meeting Kuleshov also could not avoid making a speech. However, every criticism he made of his colleague, he added that he himself, Kuleshov, was just as guilty. He began:

Comrades, I must speak of the errors of Sergei Mikhailovich in a special way because my own artistic work went on the same incorrect path as the work of Sergei Mikhailovich. I have made special errors, but my artistic work is so full of errors that I cannot speak of the errors of others without remembering my own.[38]

He went on saying that the source of their (Kuleshov's and Eisenstein's) errors was that they had been too preoccupied with the artistic aspects of filmmaking and of not knowing Soviet reality. By saying that Eisenstein did not know Soviet reality, Kuleshov must have meant that his fellow director believed that he could still make a work of art with his own, individual stamp on it.

Eisenstein weathered this storm and soon – but only after Shumiatskii's arrest – started to work on his next project, *Aleksandr Nevskii*. However, the director of another much criticized film of the same season was not so fortunate.

Margarita Barskaia was, of course, a much less significant figure in the film world, having made only one previous film, *Torn Boots* (1933). This film, which took place in Germany and showed how terrible life was there, was meant for children. *Torn Boots* received very favorable notices when it appeared, and it is still regarded as one of the best films for children made in the period.[39] In 1937 she finished her second and last film, *Father and Son*. It is about the director of a major factory, who, because of his work, is unable to pay enough attention to the education of his thirteen-year-old son, Boris. He recognizes his mistake at an open Party meeting and exercises self-criticism. However, it is too late. Boris has already become a poor student and gotten into bad company. Returning home the father finds that his son has run away and joined a group of bandits. The bandits attempt to steal the property of a new school that is being built. At this point Boris's conscience awakens and he foils the attempt. The police arrest the bandits, and the film ends happily with the reconciliation of father and son. Each recognizes the mistakes he made.

This film was considered unsuitable for public exhibition. The reviewer in *Iskusstvo kino* entitled his article, "Slander against Soviet reality."[40] It was slanderous in view of the reviewer to show that Soviet children were not happy; that a good Bolshevik, a decorated hero, would not take care of his son; that Party work took up so much time that parents could not take care of their children; that Boris's schoolmates were interested only in a class trip, rather than saving Boris; that the children played in the streets, as if there were no better places to play in Moscow. Zamkovoi in particular criticized the director for not showing the construction of a new Moscow. He also detected social pessimism: Boris rarely smiled. Zamkovoi described the film as harmful and anti-Soviet. He asked rhetorically, How could the making of such a film be allowed? and held the leadership of the studio responsible. The film was withdrawn.

Kino attacked Soiuzdetfil'm, the studio where Barskaia's film was made, several times. It described the film as "fascist."[41] When the writer added that in January Shumiatskii had described the film as "not bad," the attentive reader might have concluded that the chief of the film industry was in serious trouble.

But Barskaia was arrested even before Shumiatskii and died in a camp the following year. Why she suffered a fate much worse than others is impossible to establish. Soviet terror was haphazard. (Aside from Barskaia, there was only one other director who became a victim of the purge: Aleksandr S. Kurbas, the director of such films as *The Swedish Match* and *Vendetta;* Kurbas had already been arrested in 1934.)[42]

The third film, *The Law of Life,* did appear in the cinemas in August 1940, but after a ten-day run it received a devastating review in *Pravda,* and next day the film was withdrawn.[43] The film depicted a Komsomol leader in a negative light: He lived a dissolute life, abused his power, and was hypocritical. At the end of the film, naturally, he was unmasked and removed.

The aftermath was extraordinary. On September 9 in the Kremlin, a special meeting was called in which, aside from Stalin and Zhdanov, the best-known writers, such as Fadeev, Pogodin, and Kataev, participated. The meeting, which lasted for five hours, was organized as a military tribunal. Stalin gave the main speech. Interestingly, he had not a word to say about the director, Stol'per, but devoted his entire criticism at the scenarist, Avdeenko. The terrified writer was accused not merely of misrepresenting Soviet reality, but of not loving the positive heroes, who unmask the villain at the end. He was accused of secretly preferring the villain whom he had made into a more interesting character than the positive figures.[44]

The history of these three films suggests that at the height of Stalinism it was impossible in the Soviet Union to make a film that even touched upon reality. The significant fact was not that artists could not criticize the regime or that they were required to make their films in a pro-Soviet spirit. Such matters were taken for granted. The primary requirement was to depict an altogether fictitious world that was in no way connected to Soviet life.

Notes

1 A. Dubrovskii, *Iskusstvo kino* 1: 23, 1938.

2 *Sovetskoe kino* 5–6: 1, 1933.

3 "Snova ob 'emotsional'nom stsenarii,'" *Iskusstvo kino* 5: 30, 1937.

4 B. Shumiatskii, "Tvorcheskie voprosy templana," *Sovetskoe kino* 12: 3, 1933.

5 "Partiia proveriaet svoi riady," *Sovetskoe kino* 10: 3, 1933.

6 K. Iukov, "Doklad o soveshchanii kinodramaturgov," *Sovetskoe kino* 8–9: 10, 1934.

7 "Partiia proveriaet svoi riady," *Sovetskoe kino* 10: 3, 1933.

8 A. I. Rubailo, *Partiinoe rukovodstvo razvitiem kinoiskusstva, 1928–1937 gg.,* MGU, Moscow, 1976, pp. 130–7. Information concerning censorship organizations comes from this book.

9 Ermolaev in *Pravda,* Jan. 9, 1938.

10 Sinko's story has a grimly amusing conclusion. As a naïve outsider, he did not understand what was going on around him. He sued Mosfil'm for violation of contract. He called I. Babel as his witness. Babel, who was his friend, nevertheless denied everything, and Sinko lost the case. Ervin Sinko, *Egy Regeny Regenye. Moszkvai Naplojegyzetek, 1935–1937,* Magveto, Budapest, 1985, pp. 306, 333, 361, 449, 523.

11 Sinko, p. 523. On Balázs, also see Joseph Zsuffa, *Béla Balázs: The Man and the Artist*, University of California Press, Berkeley, 1987.

12 Sinko, p. 290.

13 B. Shumiatskii, *Kinematografiia millionov*, Kinofotoizdat, Moscow, 1935, p. 124.

14 *Repertuarnyi ukazatel'*, Kinofotoizdat, Moscow, 1936. It should be remembered that the country lacked projectors capable of showing sound films and therefore there was a shortage of silent films at the time.

15 *Ezhegodnik*, 1938, pp. 299–300.

16 A few examples of victims must suffice. They included Boris Babitskii, director of Mezhrabpom and then Mosfil'm; Margarita Barskaia, actress, scenarist and director; Evgreniia Gorkusha-Shirshova, actress; Aleksandr Kurbas, actor and director; Vladimir Nil'sen, scenarist; Adrian Piotrovskii, critic and scenarist; Elena Sokolovskaia, director of Mosfil'm; and Shumiatskii. See *Sovetskii ekran* 1: 23, 1989.

17 A. Latyshev, "Stalin i kino," in *Surovaia drama naroda*, ed. Iu. P. Senokosov, Politizdat, Moscow, 1989, pp. 494–5.

18 On the cult of the membership card, see, for example, Zoltan Vas, "A kelet-Europai barati kapcsolatok," *Latohatar*, Budapest, June 1989, p. 64.

19 I. A. Pyr'ev, *Izbrannye proizvedenia*, Iskusstvo, Moscow, 1978, 1: 74–84.

20 Jay Leyda, *Kino: A History of the Russian and Soviet film*, Collier Books, New York, 1960, p. 348.

21 The story first appeared in *Izvestiia*. It was reprinted in *Iskusstvo kino* 10: 15–16, 1937. The article is translated in Ian Christie and Richard Taylor, *The Film Factory: Russian and Soviet Cinema Documents, 1896–1939*, Harvard University Press, Cambridge, 1988, pp. 383–5.

22 On Dovzhenko, see Vance Kepley, *In the Service of the State: The Cinema of A. Dovzhenko*, University of Wisconsin Press, Madison, 1986.

23 Ibid., p. 494. Zheliabov was a nineteenth-century revolutionary. Shakhov was the name of the figure based on Kirov.

24 The comparison of Nazi and Soviet film propaganda is a large and controversial topic that I will discuss in Chapter 9.

25 On Pavlik Morozov, see Iu. I Druzhnikov, *Vosnesenie Pavlika Morozova*, Overseas Publications, London, 1988.

26 E. Zil'ber, "K probleme siuzheta," *Iskusstvo kino* 3: 15, 1936.

27 For the story of making *Bezhin Meadow*, see Leyda, pp. 327–34. Leyda worked on the project as one of Eisenstein's assistants. Yon Barna, *Eisenstein*, Secker and Warburg, London, 1973, p. 241. Barna analyzes Eisenstein's relationship with his father in connection with *Ivan the Terrible*. *Bezhin Meadow* purposely or accidentally was destroyed during World War II. Naum Kleiman, the curator of the Eisenstein museum, and S. Iutkevich in 1967 succeeded in restoring something from individual frames. That brief film is full of beautifully photographed still pictures, and as a whole it is striking in its originality.

28 E. Levin, ". . . na sud obshchestvennosti . . . ," *Iskusstvo kino* 8: 76–7, 1988.

29 "O fil'me 'Bezhin lug,' " *Pravda*, Mar. 19, 1937, p. 3.

30 I. Veisfel'd, "Teoriia i praktika S. M. Eizenshteina," *Iskusstvo kino* 5: 25–8, 1937.

31 N. Otten, "Snova ob 'emotsional'nom stsenarii,' " *Iskusstvo kino* 5: 30–5, 1937.

32 *Kino* published two major articles summarizing some of the speeches and giving others verbatim. Mar. 24, 1937, pp. 1–2, and Apr. 11, 1937, p. 1.

33 A. Latyshev, "Khotelos' by vsekh poimenno nazvat'," *Sovetskii ekran* 1: 23, 1989.

34 *Kino*, Apr. 11, 1937, p. 1.

35 N. M. Lary, *Dostoevsky and Soviet Film: Visions of Demonic Realism*, Cornell University Press, Ithaca, 1986. Lary, in his chapter on Pyr'ev (pp. 111–29), gives a psychological interpretation of Pyr'ev's hatred of Eisenstein.

36 *Kino*, March 24, 1937, p. 2.

37 "Uroki bezhina luga," *Kino*, Mar. 24, 1937, pp. 1–2, and Apr. 11, 1937, p. 1.

38 *Iskusstvo kino* 8: 86–8, 1988. Kuleshov and Eisenstein had made an agreement with one another that when one of them was attacked the other would participate in it. After this meeting Kuleshov brought a box of chocolate to Eisenstein, who loved sweets. This story was told to me by Viacheslav Ivanov, who had heard it from Kuleshov's wife, Khokhlova. Interview with Ivanov on May 14, 1990.

39 *Istoriia sovetskogo kino, vol. 2, 1931–1941*, Iskusstvo, Moscow, 1973, p. 65.

40 L. Zamkovoi, "Kleveta na sovetskuiu deistvitel' nost'," *Iskusstvo kino* 7: 30–1, 1937.

41 *Kino*, May 17 and June 22, 1937.

42 The information on Barskaia's and Kurbas's fate comes from *Sovetskii ekran* 1: 23, 1989.

43 *Pravda*, Aug. 16, 1940. *Pravda* wrote:

> It is all the stranger that some papers considered the film *The Law of Life* an "event" in Soviet cinematography. For example, *Kino* uncovered in the film "sincerity," "temperament," "genuine truthfulness," "profound knowledge of the material." Would it be that the editorial board of *Kino* (and the Committee for Cinematography, which is responsible for the paper) thoughtfully and in good conscience relates to the films that are distributed! They would not have allowed the distribution of such a badly thought out and harmful film, which distorts our reality and slanders the Soviet student youth.

The newspaper, *Kino*, which reprinted the *Pravda* review in its entirety, exercised self-criticism for a previous favorable notice. *Kino*, Aug. 23, 1940.

44 The description of the meeting comes from an interview conducted with Avdeenko by Anatolii Latyshev in 1988. In his article Latyshev reproduces the entire speech by Stalin. Latyshev, "Stalin i kino," pp. 500–6.

CHAPTER 8

Socialist realism, 1933–1941

The doctrine

The doctrine of socialist realism was first defined – and imposed on all artists – at the 1934 First All-Union Congress of Soviet writers.[1] The congress included in its statutes this classic definition:

Socialist realism is the basic method of Soviet literature and literary criticism. It demands of the artist the truthful, historically concrete representation of reality in its revolutionary development. Moreover, the truthfulness and historical concreteness of the artistic representation of reality must be linked with the task of ideological transformation and education of workers in the spirit of socialism.[2]

This definition was replete with Stalinist double-talk about "truthfulness," "historical concreteness" and so on, but artists of the time understood perfectly well what was called for by the "representation of reality in its revolutionary development." The artist was to see the germs of a communist future in the present. This requirement was based on the remarkable and incorrect assumption that Marxism was a tool that enabled a Communist not only to interpret the past and present, but also to predict the future. It was impossible to reconcile the teleological requirement with realistic presentation. The world could either be depicted as it was or as it should be according to theory, but the two are obviously not the same. Furthermore, socialist realist art was to be didactic; pure entertainment was not enough; the consumer of art was to be educated.

Socialist realism, as defined by the 1934 congress, seemed to be a very simple concept. Yet it is striking that many intelligent commentators have found it necessary to struggle with a definition, and they by no means agreed with one another. Mikhail Sholokhov, a foremost practitioner of the genre, after complaining that he was not at all good in "scientific formulations," came up with this definition: "Socialist realism is the art of the truth of life, comprehended and interpreted by the artist from the point of view of devotion to Leninist party principles."[3] A. Tertz in a witty and penetrating essay maintains that the best way to understand the socialist realist art is to

157

compare it with eighteenth-century panegyric literature. For Tertz socialist realism is a variety of romanticism.[4] Vera Dunham sees the essence of Stalinist fiction in the triumph of middle-class values – that is, vulgarity; for her the texture matters more than the structure.[5]

A most helpful approach to the question is offered by Katerina Clark in her book, *The Soviet Novel.*[6] Clark suggests that since the socialist realist novels are formulaic, the best way to appreciate these works is to present the master plot on which the novels were based. Those novels that follow the master plot are socialist realist, and those that do not are not, regardless of the intentions of the author. As she points out, a socialist realist novel is always a *Bildungsroman,* that is, it is about the acquisition of consciousness. In the process of fulfilling a task, the hero, under the tutelage of a seasoned Party worker, acquires an increased understanding of himself, the world around him, the tasks of building communism, class struggle, and the need for vigilance. Indeed, the same masterplot can be found in films also. Clark argues that socialist realist art is best compared not with the classics of literature, but with cheap novels and Hollywood films. Low and middle brow tend to be formulaic not only in the Soviet Union, but everywhere.

Socialist realist films included three stock figures with depressing regularity: the Party leader, the simple person, and the enemy. The Party leader was almost always male, ascetic, dressed in a semimilitary style, unencumbered by a family or love affairs. The simple person could be male or female and was allowed to have interest in the opposite sex. Sexual relations were always chaste, the viewer could never see more than a kiss, and these relations often needed to be straightened out by the Party leader. The enemy, whose function was to wreck and destroy what the Communists were building was always a male. On occasion, but rarely, he attempted to win over the simple person to his side by lying and subterfuge, but mostly he limited his activities to blowing up things.

The official definition of socialist realism was couched in positive prescriptions, but an appreciation of what was implicitly excluded by these prescriptions yields a clearer perspective on the novels and films of the time. Because art was primarily an educational device, it had to have the ability to reach the broadest masses. The Stalinists wanted to convey the message that there was only one way to look at the world, their way, and that every deviation from their point of view was necessarily hostile. Given this position it is not surprising that irony and ambiguity were always perceived by the Stalinists as subversive. Experimentation with forms that would impede immediate comprehension, even by the half-educated, were also placed beyond bounds. The limitations imposed on the artists, of course, made it less likely, but did not altogether exclude the possibility that artistically worthwhile works would be produced.

In spite of the large body of scholarly literature on the subject and the availability of socialist realist works – some of which are amusing and not at all bad – it is still very difficult for a Westerner to envisage what it was to live in the world of socialist realist culture. Socialist realist art did not exist and could not have existed in a vacuum; however much it may have drawn on native, Russian, traditions, it came into being because politicians needed it. Without appreciating this political context, it is impossible to understand an individual work. In the Stalinist world political authorities intervened at every step of the creative process. The cost of failure was potentially high. Genuine socialist realism presupposes concentration camps in the not very distant background. Under the circumstances no honest contemplation of the human predicament was possible; no genuine issues that society faced could be examined.

Stalinist art was counterfeit; its great power resided in its ability to exchange an artificial world surreptitiously for the real one. The victims of this sleight of hand were shown an entirely imaginary and yet seemingly realistic and self-consistent universe again and again. The make-believe universe was full of references to itself. For example, there was a series of films about a mythical revolutionary figure, named Maxim. He was more real to audiences than a historical character. At the time of World War II it was Maxim who turned to the Soviet people, encouraging them to fight.[7] But because the cinema world was utterly unlike the one the viewers experienced every day, they might have started to wonder about their own sanity.

For socialist realist art to carry out its assigned social function, it had to enjoy complete monopoly. Socialist realism cannot coexist with other literary trends; the phenomenon must completely dominate the artistic world. This domination is the source of its power: The consumer of art must get the impression that there is no other way to look at the world than the one that is presented to him. As long as the reader or the viewer has a choice he does not yet live in the world of socialist realist culture. The Stalinist 1930s was the age of socialist realism, not because a new doctrine was suddenly discovered; the crucial variable was the willingness of the political system to suppress every portrayal of the world that did not conform to the current doctrinal "reality." Classics of socialist realism, novels such as Furmanov's *Chapaev* and Gorky's *Mother* and Iutkevich and Ermler's film *Counterplan*, appeared years before the concept of socialist realism was defined. One might plausibly argue that these precursors became truly socialist realist only in the mid-1930s. Soviet cultural life was unique; it could be compared with nothing that had ever existed before.

A thematic survey

Before analyzing some typical socialist realist films let us first survey the topics that were most frequently chosen by directors.

In the 1920s Soviet researchers were the first to attempt audience surveys. They used a variety of imaginative methods in order to find out how audiences responded to films. Such work was not done and could not have been done in the Stalinist 1930s. Beyond anecdotal evidence we know very little about which films were popular and why. Only through a laborious method of studying newspaper advertisements can we establish how long a film was playing in the major cities, but we know very little about the rest of the country.

We have, however, a reliable source concerning the films that were publicly shown – *Sovetskie khudozhestvennye fil'my. Annotirovannyi katalog.*[8] This extremely useful work allows us to account for every film exhibited. Some caveats, however, must be introduced. The catalog impartially includes twenty-minute shorts and major productions. It enumerates films that were made in obscure studios in Ashkhabad or Tashkent and presumably had limited distribution, and films from Mosfil'm and Lenfil'm, which were seen all around the country. Giving equal weight to each product would be somewhat misleading in trying to establish what the average viewer actually saw.

In the eight years from 1933 to 1940 inclusive, 308 Soviet films were distributed. This number does not include cartoons but does include shorts, films made for children, filmed concerts and operas, and movies withdrawn for political reasons from distribution immediately after their premiere.

As in the previous decades film versions of nineteenth-century classics remained popular. Twenty such films were made in these eight years. Scenarists made use of Chekhov, Gogol, and Pushkin most frequently, but Dostoevsky, Lermontov, and Ostrovskii were also not neglected.[9] Among foreigners it was only Balzac and Hugo who had this honor. The stress on contemporary relevance sometimes distorted the original beyond recognition. A. Ivanovskii, for example, placed the action of Pushkin's tale *Dubrovskii* at the time of the Civil War.[10]

The Soviet Union produced fifty-four films for children in this period, more than one-sixth of all films distributed. In some instances it is difficult to draw a distinction between films for adults and for children. For example, M. Donskoi's trilogy (*The Childhood of Maksim Gorkii, My Apprenticeship,* and *My Universities*) – based on Gorky's autobiography and certainly among the best films of the decade – was made by Soiuzdetfil'm (Union Children Film), a studio devoted to juvenile films.[11] Some of these fifty-four films were shorts. Others dramatized fairy tales and classics, such as the works of Mark Twain, Jules Verne, and Samuil Marshak. The bulk of the films, however, comprised dramas aimed at the education of children in the proper communist spirit.[12]

All Soviet films made in the 1930s were didactic and, naturally, it was considered especially important to educate the young. The same ideological concerns prominent in films for adult audiences permeate the films for children. The young viewers saw children in the West suffering from poverty and oppression, while happy life in the Soviet Union was depicted with

fairy-tale realism. In order to hold a child's attention, however, a film director must tell an absorbing story. Iu. Menzhinskaia, writing in *Proletarskoe
kino* in 1931, complained that the favorite film character of Soviet children
was Zorro, and that the children preferred American films because they
were more exciting.[13] Although foreign competition in the 1930s disappeared, the adventure story remained the dominant vehicle for these tendentious children's films. When the action was placed in the past it usually
involved children who helped revolutionaries, whereas present-day stories
showed children catching spies and saboteurs. Films for the young – even
more than those which were made for adult audiences – stressed the importance of the collective. Film after film showed that the erring child was saved
by the collective, and that no matter how bright and brave a child was, he
could not set himself against his comrades.

We may divide feature films into three categories: (1) historical spectacles, (2) revolutionary stories, and (3) contemporary dramas. The first of
these was the smallest group. The most prominent of these were V. Petrov's
Peter the First, Eisenstein's *Aleksandr Nevskii*, Pudovkin's *Minin and Pozharskii* and *Suvorov*, P. Petrov-Bytov's *Pugachev*, and Preobrazhenskaia's
Stepan Razin. The didactic purpose of the films was explicit: They were to
educate Soviet audiences in the spirit of the new nationalism of the 1930s.
From these films audiences learned that the Russians had always been handsome, heroic, and truthful whereas their enemies were always cowardly,
cruel, ugly, and stupid. If Russians have resisted foreign invaders heroically
in the past, the present generation could do no less. Far from being avoided,
anachronism became a didactic tool. Both Pugachev and Stenka Razin, peasant
rebels of the seventeenth and eighteenth centuries, analyze class relations in
Marxist terms and before their executions foresee another, victorious revolution.

The stories of sixty-one films were placed at the time of the Revolution
and Civil War. These included such well-known films as *Chapaev*, *We Are
from Kronstadt*, *The Deputy from the Baltic* (Fig. 30), and the Maxim trilogy: *The Youth of Maxim*, *The Return of Maxim*, and *The Vyborg Side*
(Fig. 31). Most of these films simply used the background of the Civil War
to tell an adventure story. Every national republic that had a film studio
made at least one (but usually more than one) film on the establishment of
Soviet power. The Armenians, for example, made three films on Communists fighting the Dashnaks, and Central Asian studios depicted the struggle
against the Bashmachi.

From our point of view, however, the most interesting films depicted the
contemporary world. In this period twelve films were made that could be
called construction dramas. Among these the best known were *Counterplan*, *The Miners*, and *Komsomolsk*. These films always focused on heavy
industry: The workers, who seemingly never grew tired in spite of their
heroic accomplishments, built power stations, bridges, and railroads, mined

Figure 30.   The great actor N. Cherkasov as Polezhaev in *The Deputy from the Baltic* (1936).

coal, and so on. The material conditions of workers in these films – for example in Komsomolsk – were depicted as rather dismal. We are to understand that the young enthusiasts were interested in spiritual rather than in material rewards.[14]

Twelve is a surprisingly small number when one considers the significance of economic propaganda and Stakhanovism on the Soviet agenda. One would have expected that filmmakers would have used their talents to advance "socialist construction" by showing the excitement of struggling for the fulfillment of the plan. One suspects that directors found it difficult to make interesting films on the topic and therefore tended to avoid them. It may be, although we cannot know for certain, that audience preferences also mattered. The workers did not want to see themselves in their hours of relaxation. They were much more drawn to exotic locales. They wanted heroes larger than life, and contrary to ideology, these did not fit well into a factory environment. Two of the most successful films of this category were *The Courageous Seven,* which was made by Gerasimov in 1936, and Raizman's *Flyers,* made in 1935. In Gerasimov's film young Soviet heroes

Figure 31.   Stalin portrayed in *The Vyborg Side* (1938).

struggle against the hardships imposed by nature; Raizman's film attempted
to capture the excitement of flying and at the same time show the importance of discipline. These films were among the best in the decade and can
be watched today with enjoyment; because of their subject matter neither
of these conformed neatly to the socialist realist formula. *Flyers* depicts with
surprising delicacy a love affair.

   The collective farm was only slightly more popular than the factory. Seventeen films dealt with the problems of building collective farms or living in
them. Whereas the bulk of construction dramas dealt with the problems of
overcoming saboteurs, *kolkhoz* films were more likely to be musical comedies. Soviet audiences who learned about the life of the peasants entirely
from movies must have imagined that life in the countryside was a round of
dancing and singing.

   Pilots, explorers, and geologists were the most popular choices for representing the new Soviet hero. Five films dealt with explorers and geologists
while fifteen films had pilots as their heroes or dealt one way or another
with the love of flying. The theme of flying became ever more popular in the

course of the decade. Eight of the fifteen films were made between 1938 and 1940.

A few films were devoted to some social issue of the day. One of them, a rather attractive and humane film, *The Last Camp,* dealt with the problem of settling gypsies in a collective farm (Fig. 32). The "ordinary" gypsies overcome resistance from their own leaders and some prejudice on the part of the Russians and assimilate into happy *kolkhoz* life. Another film, *Searchers for Happiness,* is about Jews who settle in Birobidzhan. Those who are content to work in the *kolkhoz* find their place easily, but the man who searches for gold is disappointed and attempts an illegal border crossing, falling into the hands of the NKVD. Remarkably, in 1936 E. Cherviakov made *Prisoners* on the basis of N. Pogodin's scenario set in a concentration camp. Prisoners are building the White Sea Canal. The film depicts ordinary criminals with more sympathy than the members of the imprisoned intelligentsia. Honest labor and the wise and tactful behavior of the Chekists, however, reform the common criminals and the saboteur engineers.

Possessed by the magnitude of the creative undertaking and by the interesting work are also the ex-saboteur engineers, Sadovskii and Botkin. People who seemed to have been lost for socialist society are born anew as a result of creative work. And at the lock of the new canal appears the first ship. Among the passengers are the outstanding workers of the construction – Botkin, Sadovskii, Kostia, Sonia, and many others. In front of them there is a broad road to a new and constructive life.[15]

By far the most frequent theme in films dealing with contemporary life was the struggle against saboteurs. This is hardly surprising. It was an age of denunciations, phony trials, and the "uncovering" of unbelievable plots. Although it is likely that sabotage did not exist at all in the 1930s, in the world of Stalinist discourse the unmasking of the hidden enemy was a dominant theme. Film directors lent their talents to the creation of an atmosphere of hysteria and paranoia. Their scenarios closely resembled the tales of the most vicious storyteller of them all, A. Vyshinskii, the infamous prosecutor at the purge trials. In the films, as in the confessions at the trials, the "enemy" carried out the most dastardly acts out of unreasoned hatred for decent socialist society.

In the seven years 1933–9 Soviet directors made eighty-five films that dealt with contemporary life. (This number does not include some films for children and about military adventures or about the exploits of border guards.) In thirty-three of these films the socialist hero had to overcome difficulties, such as bureaucracy, arrogance, stupidity, or natural obstacles such as storms or cold. But in more than half of the films, fifty-two, the hero unmasked hidden enemies who had committed criminal acts. The hero could never be too vigilant: In Dovzhenko's *Aerograd* the enemy turned out be his best friend, in Eisenstein's unfinished *Bezhin Meadow* it was the protagonist's father, and in Pyr'ev's *Party Card,* it was the heroine's husband.

Figure 32.   Gypsies and Russians in *The Last Camp* (1935).

By 1940, however, we witness a curious phenomenon: The internal enemy suddenly and completely disappears. Of the thirty films dealing with
contemporary topics made in 1940, not a single one focused on traitors.
The enemy, to be sure, remained, but now the wicked people were agents
smuggled over the border. The country was preparing to face a foreign foe.
Instead of encouraging the Soviet people to ferret out nonexistent internal
saboteurs, the films now preached how Russian and Georgian, Armenian
and Azerbaidzhani, must work together for the common good.

Perhaps not surprisingly, the opinion makers were obsessed with the danger posed by the foreign foe. In the 1930s more films were made about
border guards than about workers. Twenty-one films dealt with catching
foreign agents. Most of these agents were Japanese and were caught by
border guards. Eleven other films tell more or less the same story: The enemy, most often German, but sometimes Polish, attacks without a declara-
tion of war. The Soviet people respond quickly and decisively. The war is
taken to enemy territory where it is rapidly and victoriously concluded. In
retrospect, one gets the impression that Soviet publicists were whistling in
the dark.

Soviet films depicted the outside world as undifferentiated and threatening, but also uniformly miserable. The outside world as it appeared on the

screen was unrecognizable. In this world people were starving to death; brutal police were suppressing a mighty Communist movement; and the foreign workers' ultimate concern was the security of the Soviet Union. Again and again they would rather strike and starve than allow an attack on the fatherland of all workers. Given these premises, it is not surprising that a recurring motive was foreigners, whether of Russian extraction or not, coming to the USSR and finding there a happy and worthwhile life. On the basis of these works one might conclude that a basic problem of the USSR was how to keep out all the foreigners who wanted to come and live there.

The action of twenty films took place entirely or partially outside of the borders of the USSR. The foreign locales clearly reflected the twists and turns of Soviet foreign policy. Before 1935 an unnamed Western country was usually portrayed; this was a synthetic place, having signs in English, French, and German. Sometimes, however, Germany or the United States was specified. Films set in Germany in the early 1930s, such as Pudovkin's *Deserter* (made in 1933), not only did not comment on the Nazi danger but portrayed the Socialists as the main enemies of the working class. In 1935 Soviet foreign policy shifted. The Comintern called for a popular front of all progressive forces against Nazism. Soviet studios made six anti-Nazi films between the Congress of the Comintern in 1935 and the signing of the Nazi–Soviet pact in 1939. Of these the best and most prominent were *Professor Mamlok* and *The Oppenheim Family*.[16] In 1940 audiences could see several new films showing the joy of Ukrainians and Belorussians being liberated from Polish oppression.

Counterplan

In the heterogeneous culture of the 1920s it was impossible to find a "typical" film; the films differed from one another in subject matter and approach. All of the great directors developed their own highly individual styles. The struggle against formalism during the "cultural revolution" and the imposition of the doctrine of socialist realism, however, produced conformity among the artists. To be sure, there were exceptions. Eisenstein was permitted to finish only one film in the course of the decade, *Aleksandr Nevskii*. Although this is perhaps his least impressive work, it is nevertheless obvious that no one else could have made it. He was irrepressible. The movies of Barnet also had a special quality, a lyricism and humanity that made them specially appealing. In spite of these few exceptions, the films of the 1930s were made according to the requirements of discernible rules and therefore they shared a great deal with one another. They easily fit into a few categories. We can best understand the character of Stalinist cinema by examining in detail a few works. We shall look at *Counterplan* as the example of a production drama, *Chapaev* as a representative of the historical–revolutionary genre, and *Shining Path* as a typical Stalinist comedy.

The choice of any three films out of several hundred is bound to be subjective, and therefore in need of justification. *Counterplan* was a very important film in the history of Soviet cinema, one that was widely discussed at the time. The leaders of the film industry considered this film as a pattern to be followed, and therefore its release can be regarded as the beginning of an era. It is generally agreed that *Chapaev* was the most successful socialist realist film ever made, both in terms of audience appeal, and in artistic quality. *Shining Path* is perhaps less well known than the other two films, but it well illustrates the qualities of socialist realist comedy. This film represented the end of the era, the last of a string of successful comedies made by G. Aleksandrov (*Happy Fellows, Circus, Volga-Volga*).

Ermler and Iutkevich were instructed to make a film on industrialization in January 1932, but they were given neither a script nor precise instructions. Ermler wrote later: "I had no feelings for the themes. The idea of *Counterplan* did not excite me very much, but I understand [*sic*] that it was what we needed." Although, *Counterplan* (*Vstrechnyi*) is one of the milestones of Soviet cinema, it remains almost entirely unknown in the West and is distinguished neither by artistic quality nor aesthetic innovation. When the film was completed in October, it was heavily criticized by the collective at Sovkino and had to be hurriedly recut.[17] Even contemporary critics agreed that it contained nothing new artistically.[18] The film was to be completed for the fifteenth anniversary of the Revolution. It was important, however, because it offered a model and set the tone for many future films. Significantly, *Counterplan* was made two years before the official doctrine of socialist realism was articulated. But that should not be surprising. Socialist realism did not come down from on high as a fully developed theory imposed on entirely unwilling artists. The doctrine grew out of a mixture of influences: Russian literary tradition, Marxist–Leninist ideology, and the political atmosphere prevailing in the country.

The period of the "cultural revolution" was a time of searching. It was like the process of natural selection: Mutation threw up many new varieties, such as, for example, Dovzhenko's *Earth* and *Ivan*, Pudovkin's *A Simple Case* and *Deserter*, and Kuleshov's adventure films *The Two Buldis* and *The Gay Canary*. The artists were trying to find a model, a style of filmmaking suitable for the new era. The trial-and-error process was cruel, inasmuch as those who failed to please the artistic and political authorities were denounced and had reason to fear for their future. *Counterplan* was the successful mutant: It contained all the necessary elements.

Like all socialist films, it had a veneer of realism. No strange juxtapositions or cuttings disturb a plausible urban locale. We see familiar landmarks of Leningrad, a factory interior, and apartments, which are, to be sure, nicer than most people in the audience had ever seen, but believeable nonetheless. Yet the world that is depicted here is completely imagined: People in the film do not behave as human beings have ever behaved. Instead they represent types and talk and act as they should according to Stalinist myths.

The action of *Counterplan* takes place in a factory. The choice of locale was slightly unusual: None of the major films of the previous decade had dealt with the problems of production in a contemporary factory. However, during the period of industrialization it was inevitable that production dramas would play a role in the film world, albeit not as large as one might have expected. The obvious purpose of these works was to mobilize the people to work with greater enthusiasm for the grand task of industrialization. Indeed, Aleksandr Macheret's *Jobs and Men,* another production drama, appeared in the movie theaters almost at the same time as *Counterplan.* (*Jobs and Men* was first shown in October 1932, and *Counterplan* had its premiere on November 7.)

Unfortunately the English title *Counterplan* gives no hint of the meaning of the Russian *Vstrechnyi*, a well-known term in the ideological jargon of the period of the First Five-Year Plan. The workers of a factory expressed their enthusiasm for industrialization by presenting their own "vstrechnyi" plan to the authorities, a "counterplan" by definition more ambitious than the original. The action of the film revolves around the difficulties of fulfilling this counterplan, the completion of an electricity-generating turbine ahead of schedule. The film has a *Perils of Pauline* quality: When one difficulty is successfully surmounted another appears. Will our heroes, in spite of all, succeed in carrying out the ambitious "counterplan"?

A socialist realist film is always about the acquisition of consciousness. In the film not only are the difficulties overcome, but in the process some of the heroes acquire a superior understanding of the world. This higher degree of consciousness never arrives by itself, simply as learning from experience. There is always an instructor, representing the Party. In *Counterplan* there are two processes of education going on at the same time.

One story line concerns an old skilled worker, Babchenko. He is a respected and devoted worker, but he represents the old world: He drinks and, instead of measuring the finished product, he simply estimates (Fig. 33). He is entrusted with making a crucial part of the turbine, but the part is spoiled because Babchenko makes a mistake. In the course of the film he learns to give up his daily vodka, acquires respect for the Party leadership, and learns to work properly according to modern methods. At the end of the film he is ready to join the Party (Fig. 34).

The other student is Pasha, the head of a section in the factory, a young cadre and a good friend of the Party Secretary. He is a devoted Party member and there is nothing more important in his life than carrying out his responsibilities. Yet he is not on the same level of consciousness as the Party secretary, Vasia. Vasia intuits that a saboteur is at work. He knows how to

Figure 33.   Babchenko, the naïve hero in *Counterplan* (1932).

talk to the workers and motivate the downcast Babchenko. Above all, unlike Pasha, he would never admit defeat. He articulates the message of the
day: "Numbers! If numbers are against the fulfillment of the plan then they
are hostile numbers! And the people who bring them forward they are not
our people, but they are enemies. . . . How is it that you did not know
numbers can also be Party numbers?" Under Vasia's tutelage, Pasha becomes a better communist.

   During the "cultural revolution" directors were attacked for dehuman-
izing history by presenting the masses as heroes and not providing Soviet
audiences with worthwhile models to follow. Critics correctly maintained
that heroless movies were boring for mass audiences. Socialist realist films
always provided an individual hero. In *Counterplan* this essential role is
played by Vasia, the progenitor of dozens of others. His job, secretary of
the factory party organization, was the appropriate job for a positive hero.
He is an attractive man; in his military uniform he looks a bit like the young
Stalin. (There were no physically unattractive, positive heroes in Soviet films.)
He has a nice sense of humor, and he loves to sing and play the guitar.

   Soviet directors had to struggle with the difficult problem: how to make the positive hero believable? Ermler and Iutkevich attempted to humanize the Party secretary by adding a love story. Vasia is secretly in love with his friend's wife, Katia. Katia and Pasha quarrel and Vasia hopes that Katia now will reciprocate his feelings. In a lyrical and rather attractive interlude the two young people walk the streets of Leningrad at the time of white nights. We see construction everywhere in the beautiful city. Like Dovzhenko in *Ivan*, the directors attempted to aestheticize building sites. Vasia's love story, however, is bound to be a sad one. Katia tells him that she really loves Pasha and is planning to return to him. Vasia, of course, does not reveal his feelings; he suffers silently. It was this episode that was most heavily attacked by the critics, who considered the love story false and not connected to the rest of the film.[19]

If it was difficult to make the positive hero lifelike, it was entirely impossible to create a believable negative character. The problem was that the party line, to say nothing of Soviet power, could not possibly be opposed on morally acceptable grounds. A negative hero in a socialist realist film, therefore, is always an Iago-like character, who wants to do evil for the sake of evil. But Shakespeare's Iago has grandeur; he is intelligent, perceptive, and a skillful manipulator of his antagonists. In his desire to harm Othello, he is a figure of superhuman proportions. A Soviet director, however, could not give to his negative character majesty and courage, thereby making him a worthy opponent.

Counterplan has a typical negative hero. He is a member of the old intelligentsia, the engineer Aleksei Skvortsov. In explaining his wicked motives to his mother, all he can say is: "They are eliminating us as a class. If there will be no electricity, there will be no communists!" He is a relatively unimportant figure and appears only for a few minutes on the screen. He does not even carry out active sabotage. He simply knows that the drawings are incorrect and he fails to correct them. He is a small, cringing figure, dominated by his mother, who calls him Aleshenka. In the 1920s Ermler, the only Party member among the major directors, had made several appealing films about the plight of the old intelligentsia. But in this film, made at the time of specialist baiting and phony trials, he lent his talent and reputation to the unattractive task of justifying the murderous policy of the regime.

The dramaturgical weakness of *Counterplan* is that the adversaries are unevenly matched. There is little tension, for it is easy to defeat an enemy such as Skvortsov. In this respect also the film is typical of Soviet cinematography of the 1930s. Few movies had fully developed negative characters and in many they were completely absent. For reasons of dramaturgy it was easier to combat nature than a human enemy and therefore a large number of films dealt with the heroic deeds of Soviet people against natural obstacles. By contrast, films with negative heroes, such as Ermler's *Great Citizen* and especially Pyr'ev's *Party Card,* are the most repellent and morally

Figure 34.   Babchenko the communist: *Counterplan* (1932).

reprehensible products of the decade because they explicitly and consciously justified mass murder.

Counterplan is a schematic work. It is meant to illustrate, among other things, the policy of the Party toward the intelligentsia. As well as Skvortsov, we meet an "honest" old engineer, Lazarev, who is dismayed that he cannot be a good Party member because of his social background, and a worker, Chutochkin, who is training to be an engineer. He is a representative of the future, proletarian intelligentsia. At the end of the film the "good" engineer promises Chutochkin to instruct him.

Unlike the great films of the silent era, or even such works of the 1930s as *Chapaev* or *The Road to Life, Counterplan* did not age well. Seeing the film almost sixty years after it was made, one is struck not only by the newborn clichés but also by the patronizing attitude in socialist realist films that was particularly apparent in this one. The film depicts its characters as infantile. They are all like children in their one-dimensionality: They have no doubts; they have no internal lives; they speak in slogans. With the exception of the saboteur, they are all absorbed in the problems of fulfilling the plan. When Pasha and Katia get a fine new apartment, they cannot enjoy it: They are too upset by events in the factory. The infantilization is most disturbing in the depiction of Babchenko. He is utterly childlike: He receives a kitten as a present, he cries when his work is not going well, and he is transparently manipulated by the Party secretary.

It is easy to see, however, why *Counterplan* was such an important film in its time. It dealt with a contemporary topic from a "correct" point of view, and at the same time it could attract an audience. It was not as wildly successful as some earlier films, such as *The Bear's Wedding* or Ilinskii's comedies, but it filled movie houses. Without a trace of "formalism," which might have alienated mass audiences, it had a bit of humor and likable characters. Dmitri Shostakovich's music made a considerable contribution. It was the first film music to become widely known and very popular. Indeed, some of the songs outlived the film. The authorities were encouraged: It was possible to make a politically correct film that people would actually want to see.

Chapaev

A socialist realist film dealing with contemporary problems, such as *Counterplan*, depicted the world as it should be according to Stalinist understanding of Marxism–Leninism; a film dealing with a historical topic portrayed the world as it ought to have been. Because the regime derived its legitimacy from the Revolution and the Civil War that followed it, a "proper" depiction of those events was just as important, if not more so, than the correct handling of contemporary issues. On November 7, 1934, on the seventeenth anniversary of the Revolution and exactly two years after the premiere of *Counterplan*, Grigorii and Sergei Vasiliev's *Chapaev* appeared in the cinemas. This film was the prototypical depiction of the Bolshevik victory in the Civil War.

Chapaev was the most popular socialist realist film ever made in the Soviet Union. In five years over fifty million tickets were sold.[20] Even those who were not favorably disposed toward the regime enjoyed it. When emigrés from the Soviet Union were interviewed by American sociologists after World War II, the ex-Soviet citizens recalled this film more often than any other and reported favorable responses.[21] Foreign critics, such as Harry T. Smith of the *New York Times,* praised it as "the best Soviet sound film."[22] Shumiatskii, the boss of Soviet filmmaking, went so far as to call it the best film in the history of Soviet cinema, "the very apex of Soviet film art."[23] The film has aged well and has continued to entertain audiences decades after it was made. For example Boris Vasil'ev, writing in 1982 in *Ekran,* repeated Shumiatskii's evaluation and also called it the best Soviet film ever made.[24]

Why the film was popular with audiences does not require an elaborate explanation. People enjoyed it because it was an exciting action film, competently made, and easy to understand. It was also humorous and touching. It had well-drawn characters with whom the audience could identify. Its success shows that, though it was difficult, it was not altogether impossible to construct a popular film according to even the strictest interpretation of the canons of socialist realism.

The central character of the film was, of course, based on the historical figure V. I. Chapaev, who commanded a rifle division against various anti-Bolshevik armies on the eastern front in the Civil War. The historical Chapaev was a man of peasant background, who had served as a noncommissioned officer in World War I and joined the Bolshevik Party in September 1917. In 1918 he spent a few months studying in the Academy of the General Staff. Although he was an able leader and a man of undoubted courage, it is unlikely that his name would be widely remembered had he not had as his political commissar D. A. Furmanov. Chapaev became a national hero because Furmanov published a successful book about him in 1923.

The book was extremely important, not because of its literary qualities, but because its content anticipated what would become one of the central myths of the Revolution. Lenin's chief contribution to Marxist theory and, more important, to revolutionary practice was the notion that only conscious revolutionaries (i.e., Bolsheviks) could bring class consciousness first to the workers and then to the entire people. In the Leninist view a successful revolution, therefore, was impossible without the guiding role of the Bolsheviks. It was this accomplishment of the Party that justified its continued "leading role," and thus justified the entire existing political system. Perhaps the most important political task assigned to Soviet artists was showing that the Party had in fact been the indispensable guiding force.[25]

Furmanov, as if by accident, devoted his work to this essential theme. As commissar, he represented the Party in Chapaev's unit, and as such acted as a political instructor to the commander. By writing about his relationship with Chapaev, and perhaps unconsciously exaggerating his own significance, he gave a picture of the role of the Communist Party that was considered to be politically correct. Interestingly, he was not certain whether he was publishing memoirs, a novel, or party literature. For example, while he gave Chapaev and Frunze their real names, he called himself in his book Klychkov, indicating that he did not aim at a simple recollection of facts. It soon transpired, however, that historical accuracy did not much matter. What was far more important was a depiction of Bolshevik understanding of higher historical truth. Furmanov turned Chapaev into the prototypical hero: an uneducated peasant who was courageous, who instinctively understood that the Bolsheviks were correct, and yet would have been condemned to defeat without the guidance of the Party's representative, the commissar.

Furmanov also shows another crucial element of the Bolshevik image of their revolution: the "worker–peasant alliance," or, more accurately, the

Figure 35.   Chapaev the fighter: *Chapaev* (1934).

tutelage of the peasants by the workers. According to the author, Chapaev's army was formed when he incorporated into his peasant partisan band a unit of class-conscious workers from Ivanovo-Voznesensk. Up to that point he had commanded only an unreliable band of peasant partisans.

Furmanov's story had almost everything necessary for a socialist realist film. Nevertheless the writers of the scenario, working on the script for two full years, introduced changes to emphasize these features further. The commander–commissar relationship is at the very heart of the story. While the novelist was content simply to assert that Klychkov instructed Chapaev, the scenarists provided many details in showing the peasant hero's education. The film shows how the commissar (here called not Klychkov but Furmanov) turned the commander into a conscious fighter for communism (Fig. 35). When the two men first meet, Chapaev is less than delighted to have someone looking over his shoulder. But because the commissar time and again shows his usefulness, Chapaev is dismayed when, toward the end of the film, Furmanov is sent elsewhere by the higher authorities. Furmanov is constantly instructing, stressing the importance of discipline and the impor-

Figure 36.   Chapaev explains strategy: *Chapaev* (1934).

tance of the Party. He even pays attention to the proper attire of the commander.

Ironically, the scenarists made Furmanov into more of a hero, more into
a larger-than-life character than the writer made himself out to be. For example, in the original story Furmanov stresses that the commissar at first
had little understanding of military matters and was rather frightened in
battles. This aspect of the commissar's character is missing from the film.
As a result, in the film Furmanov is a much more one-dimensional and less
interesting figure than in the original story. He operates in the background
most of the time and is a somewhat shadowy figure. He is a typical Soviet
positive hero with all its dullness and improbability.

Chapaev, by contrast, has weaknesses and faults, but these actually make
him into a more interesting and attractive character. His faults are a necessary part of the overall design. He needs his faults in order to be able to
"grow." He is shown as a man of little learning. He does not know that
Bolsheviks and Communists are the same people and has no knowledge of
the differences between the Second and Third Internationals. He is somewhat vain and is quick tempered, but he has the right instincts, a nice sense
of humor, and a dashing style (Fig. 36). He can also see into the future. As

a socialist realist hero, in the present he can see the germs of the future. To Petia, his orderly, and to Petia's sweetheart, Anna, Chapaev explains that after the victory an eternal happy life will follow.

Anna and Petia's love story is another change from the novel to the film. The relationship of Anna, a worker, and Petia, a peasant lad, further emphasizes the importance of the theme that all working people are on the same side in the great battle. For dramatic purposes the film version needed a picture of the enemy. Furmanov, on the basis of his own experiences, of course, could not have depicted White officers. Colonel Borozdin, the White officer in the film, is perhaps the most successfully drawn negative character in socialist realist cinema. To be sure, he is multidimensional only in comparison to other negative figures. The most positive thing about him is that he is "cultured" for we see him playing Beethoven's "Moonlight" sonata.[26] Maybe we can also consider it a positive feature that Borozdin can recognize Lenin's genius. He quotes the Bolshevik leader on the significance of the rear in war. But of course Lenin's stature was so great that even his most determined enemies could not fail to recognize it. Otherwise the colonel is an enemy of the people and a cruel man who has the brother of his faithful orderly flogged to death. As a result of this episode, the hitherto loyal orderly, Potapov, learns the class essence of the struggle and defects to the Reds.

There is a significant contrast between the enemies in *Counterplan* and in *Chapaev*. Although Borozdin is no more attractive than Skvortsov, nevertheless, he is not a cringing figure but possesses considerable strength and authority. His strength makes him to be a more dangerous enemy and, incidentally, makes the film more interesting. It was acceptable for a Soviet director to depict an aristocrat at the time of the Civil War as a convinced opponent of the socialist Revolution; but a filmmaker simply could not envisage that degree of wickedness that was necessary to stand against socialist construction and the Stalinist state.

At the end of the film Chapaev dies a heroic death. He is wounded, but continues to fight until another bullet strikes him. A socialist realist film, however, is by definition optimistic. It ends in a major key. Chapaev's death is avenged by the victory of the Red forces. The hero might die, but the cause is invincible.

Shining Path

It might appear paradoxical that, during a time of mass murder, deportations and starvations, comedy flourished. But on reflection it is understandable that people during hard times wanted escape from their troubles and misery. It would be a mistake to think that directors no longer cared about popularity. People wanted to see comedies and the directors were happy to oblige, all the more so because they were encouraged by politicians who

Figure 37.   Animals at the banquet: *Happy Fellows* (1934).

maintained that such films were most appropriate for the glorious present. Films were to demonstrate Stalin's famous saying: "Life has become gayer, comrades!" The authorities wanted comedies.

In the same decade audiences in the United States, which had suffered the effects of a dreadful economic depression, also flocked to the cinemas to see comedies and musicals. Americans and Russians alike craved laughter and entertainment. Although the Soviet people could see almost no foreign works, the directors were well acquainted with the films of Western directors. (They saw Western films in special exhibitions in their studios.) Soviet directors were greatly influenced by American films, in particular, by musical comedies. Given the existing political system, naturally, biting social satires and parodies could not be made. Under the circumstances all or almost all Soviet comedies belonged to the category of musicals.

By far the most successful Soviet director at the box office and maker of musicals was G. V. Aleksandrov. His films, *Happy Fellows* (Fig. 37), *Circus, Volga-Volga,* and *Shining Path* entertained millions of Soviet citizens. People in the cities and in the villages became familiar with the songs of Isaac

Dunaevskii that were composed for these comedies. Aleksandrov's principal actress and wife, Liubov' Orlova, was the darling of Soviet audiences and the favorite of I. V. Stalin. It was said that the dictator in particular loved *Volga-Volga* (Fig. 38).

The original title of *Shining Path* had been *Cinderella*. It had received wide prerelease publicity under that title: Even *Cinderella* matchboxes and perfumes were made to coincide with the release of a much-awaited new Aleksandrov musical comedy. Soviet filmmakers were influenced by Hollywood not only in making musicals but also in marketing the finished product. But intervention came from the highest level. Stalin did not like it as much as *Volga-Volga*, but nonetheless liked it very much. The title, however, would not do; something more contemporary, something broader was needed. Incredibly, he took the trouble to draw up a list of twelve titles and it was from this list that Aleksandrov chose *Shining Path*.[27]

The principles of socialist realism applied not only to contemporary dramas and revolutionary–historical spectacles, but also to comedies. The defining characteristics of socialist realism, that is, the overcoming of difficulties and the acquisition of socialist consciousness under the guidance of the Party, can be found in the works of Aleksandrov just as well as in the film dramas of the period. In these comedies the negative hero, who is, of course, always defeated, represents the "survival of the past." In *Volga-Volga,* for example, the negative hero is called Byralov, "man of the past."

Shining Path, first shown in October 1940, not only has the characteristics of a socialist realist film but is an unconscious parody. The fairy-tale aspect of socialist realism, elsewhere implicit, here becomes explicit: A fairy godmother appears, and cars can fly. Bringing the supernatural into a socialist realist film created an uneasy coexistence. In spite of the flying car, Aleksandrov and Orlova went to great length to reproduce the actual motions of a textile worker.[28]

In this film the socialist realist hero typically grows through overcoming difficulties under the tutelage of the wise Party representative. Tania, an illiterate peasant girl working in a private hotel, becomes a national hero. Her mentor, the Party secretary, is the fairy godmother from Cinderella.

Interestingly, in Soviet films the heroine – but not necessarily the hero – is always provided with an ultimately happy love story. Still an uneducated servant girl, Tania is attracted to the dashing, young engineer, Lebedev, who is new in town (Fig. 39). Lebedev recognizes her qualities and treats her well. But the gap between them in education and political consciousness is too great for a happy relationship. He becomes one of her instructors on the "shining path" to the beautiful future. He resists the allures of the equivalents of the ugly sisters from the original Cinderella, and at the end of the film, the two young lovers, now suitable for one another, walk hand in hand. The love story, however, is so elliptically presented that it is not at all

Figure 38.   Poster for *Volga-Volga* (1938).

clear what the relationship of these two people has been while the years went by. A love story is rarely, if ever, at the center of a socialist realist film.

The modern equivalent of the prince's palace is the textile factory, where Tania is taken by the fairy godmother/Party secretary. Tania in her dream sees a vision of the palace/factory, which looks remarkably like MGU (Moscow State University), to be constructed only ten years later. The concept of beauty that was to produce that finest example of Stalinist architecture was already present in this film by Aleksandrov.

Even at the outset, this socialist realist Cinderella is no mere kitchen maid. She is an uneducated genius, who constantly thinks up clever labor-saving devices. When her mistress's jealousy costs her her job at the hotel, Tania is hired as a cleaning woman in a factory. She studies in order to better herself and soon becomes a worker. Native talent, to be developed under Party guidance, is always a characteristic of the naïve socialist realist hero. Tania has limitless ambition to contribute to socialist construction. Not satisfied to handle eight machines at once, she wants to work on sixteen. In these scenes the film verges on being a parody of the Stakhanovite movement, the main mobilization device of the regime for higher productivity. We are now in 1935, and the hidebound director of the factory resists Tania's bold attempts to rationalize and produce more and more. The difficulty is overcome by supernatural intervention. Tania had turned with her problems to the chairman of the Council of People's Commissars, V. M. Molotov. Now, when she is about to be judged by the conservative leadership in the factory, she is saved by a telegram from Molotov himself. Needless to say all obstacles immediately disappear and Tania is celebrated as a hero.

Tania's attitude to work is that of a proper Soviet person. Her interest in her work is all-consuming. When her colleagues are happily celebrating New Year's Eve, she sits by herself crying because she has had trouble handling her machine. As her achievements become more and more fantastic, and at one point she is working on 240 machines, she learns that someone in the country bettered her record. For a moment she is dismayed, and she weeps. But then, of course, she understands the true nature of socialist competition, takes pleasure in the achievement of her competitor, and promises to work even harder.

Shining Path, as all of Aleksandrov's comedies, was aimed at uneducated audiences, and the humor is rarely above slapstick. In *Happy Fellows*, for example, the most memorable moment is a scene in which a pig gets on a banquet table and makes a big mess. In *Shining Path* vulgarity is most painful at the end of the film. It concludes with an approximately ten-minute-long coda, only loosely related to the rest of the work. Aleksandrov abandons the jocular tone. Tania is now a national hero, she has become an engineer, received the order of Lenin in the Kremlin, and is walking in the grounds of the VDNKh (Exhibition of the Achievements of the National Economy) (Fig. 40). This was a permanent exhibition that, in 1940 when

Figure 39. Liubov' Orlova as the naïve heroine Tania in *Shining Path* (1940).

Figure 40. Tania the Communist: *Shining Path* (1940).

the film was made, was still limited to agriculture. By including the textile industry here, Aleksandrov shows himself a good socialist realist artist, able to see the future in the present, depicting VDNKh as it would become in the following decade. Tania's companion in happiness is Lebedev, who has become the director of the factory. VDNKh with its gaudy buildings and statues is presented as the vision of the beautiful socialist future. As these Soviet heroes show their handsome profiles to the audience, an invisible female chorus gives voice to the message: "We were born in order to make the fairy tale reality."[29]

Soviet cinema in an age of terror

Recent scholarly literature has tended to underemphasize the gap between the Stalinist Soviet Union and the rest of the world. Western revisionist historians since the late 1970s have depicted the Soviet Union in the 1930s as if it was just like any other state, with interest groups struggling against one another and a population not very much affected by the terror.[30] At the same time, film scholars looking for parallels and similarities, and starting out with the assumption that cinema has never been free anywhere, have placed Stalinist films comfortably within the history of world cinema.

There can be no question that Hollywood, for example, in the 1930s had some similarities with the situation that prevailed in the Soviet Union. In the United States as in the Soviet Union, owners of studios were people who had little knowledge of the art of cinema, and yet did not hesitate to interfere in every aspect of the creative process. The directors everywhere resented this interference. In Hollywood, again, as in the Soviet Union, directors were expected to follow the script slavishly. American managers, like Shumiatskii, attempted to introduce industrial discipline in the creative process. No doubt, one could continue to list similarities.

How much significance we attribute to the similarities as against the differences is, to a considerable extent, a subjective judgment. In the view of this author, similarities were only superficial, for the peoples of the Soviet Union lived in an altogether different world, and Soviet cinema well reflected the peculiarities of that world. American artists who displeased studio owners had to fear for their jobs; Soviet artists feared for their lives, and this fear manifested itself in their work. The many studios of Hollywood competed with one another, and since the ignorant owners wanted to make money, they insisted on making films that would appeal to audiences. In this sense the owners represented the simple viewer. By contrast, Shumiatskii, the boss of the Soviet film industry, represented the interests of a criminal state.

The Soviet system, as it developed in the 1930s, destroyed millions of its own citizens and contrary to the views of some Western historians, the terror affected all layers of society. Cinema both reflected the terror and also contributed to an atmosphere of hysteria. One needs no particularly sophisticated methods of analysis to recognize that Soviet films made in the 1930s conveyed the message that the enemy was everywhere: The parents, children, friends, and lovers of the naïve heroes turned out to be traitors. The enemy could appear in the guise of a good worker and even show false enthusiasm for the building of socialism. No one could be trusted. Films, of course, did not exist in a vacuum: Soviet reality confirmed their vicious message.

Notes

1 *Soviet Writers' Congress, 1934. The Debate of Socialist Realism and Modernism,* Lawrence and Wishart, London, 1977.

2 Abram Tertz, *On Socialist Realism,* Pantheon, New York, 1960, p. 24.

3 C. Vaughan James, *Soviet Socialist Realism: Origin and Theory,* St. Martin's Press, New York, 1973, p. 121.

4 Tertz.

5 Vera Dunham, *In Stalin's Time: Middle-Class Values in Soviet Fiction.* Cambridge University Press, 1976.

6 Katerina Clark, *The Soviet Novel,* University of Chicago Press, Chicago, 1981.

7 The Maxim trilogy was directed by G. Kozintsev and L. Trauberg. Maxim reappeared in *Fighting Film Albums* in 1941.

8 Published in four volumes by Iskusstvo, Moscow, 1961–8 (hereafter cited as *S.kh.f.*).

9 On Dostoevsky in Soviet films, see N. Lary, *Dostoevsky and Soviet Film: Vision of Demonic Realism,* Cornell University Press, Ithaca, 1986.

10 *Istoriia Sovetskogo kino,* Iskusstvo, Moscow, 1973, 2: 262.

11 In 1936 one of the oldest and best studios in the land, Mezhrabpomfil'm, which had been established in 1924 and made some of the best films of the golden age, was renamed Soiuzdetfil'm, and started to produce movies almost exclusively for children. Soviet publicists proudly and correctly point out that the Soviet Union was the first country in the world to have a major studio entirely devoted to making films for children. Aside from this studio, others also continued to make movies for young audiences. *Kino, Eritsiklopededicskii slovar',* Sovetskaia Entsiklopediia, Moscow, 1982, p. 476.

12 One of these films, *The Siberians,* was directed by the great Lev Kuleshov. It was an embarrassment. It told the story of two boys who search for and think they find the pipe that I. V. Stalin used in his Siberian exile. Although it turns out that the boys bring the wrong pipe, The Great Friend of All Children nevertheless invites them for a visit. N. Zorkaia, *Portrety,* Iskusstvo, Moscow, 1966, p. 51.

13 *Proletarskoe kino* 2–3: 64–67, 1931.

14 As an amusing sidelight, we might mention that, of course, the films depicting

the contemporary world were full of pictures of Stalin. In the Soviet Union, films of the 1930s continued to be shown, at least on television, until very recently. These films, however, have been "reconstructed" in the 1960s. The reconstruction meant, among other things, the removal of pictures of Stalin, which have been substituted with pictures of Lenin. However, Soviet technology was still very poor to carry out this deceit successfully. The picture of Lenin, where Stalin used to be, always flickers. It creates the strange impression that the founder of the state is still alive and looking down on what is going on around him.

15 *S.kh.f.* 2: 92.

16 Richard Taylor and K. R. M. Short, "Soviet Cinema and the International Menace, 1928–1939," *Historical Journal of Film, Radio and Television* 2: 131–56, 1986.

17 Denise Youngblood, "Cinema as Social Criticism: The Early Films of Fridrich Ermler," in Anna Lawton (ed.), *Red Screen: Image Making and Social Impact,* Harper Collins, New York, 1991.

18 The film was widely reviewed at the time. See, for example, L. Ginzburg, "Fil'm o liudiakh, stroiashchikh sotsialism," *Pravda,* Nov. 27, 1932, p. 4, and Bella Balash (Béla Balázs), "Novye fil'my. Novye zhizneoshchushchenie," *Sovetskoe kino* 3–4: 19–24, 1933.

19 See, for example, V. Pudovkin, "Sovietskaia kinematografiia i zadachi RossARRK," *Sovetskoe kino* 7: 4, 1933, and R. Messer, *Geroi sovetskoi kinematografi,* Isskustvo, Moscow, 1938, p. 21.

20 John David Rimberg, *The Motion Picture in the Soviet Union, 1918–1952: A Sociological Analysis,* Arno Press, New York, 1973, p. 202.

21 Ibid., p. 150.

22 *New York Times,* Jan. 15, 1935, p. 22.

23 B. Shumiatskii, *Kinematografiia millionov,* Kinofotoizdat, Moscow, 1935, p. 148.

24 "Vpered, k 'Chapaevu'!" *Ekran, Sbornik,* Iskusstvo, Moscow, 1982, p. 22.

25 Clark, pp. 84–9. Clark's interpretation of Furmanov's work is similar to the one developed here. See also Stephen Crofts, "Ideology and Form: Soviet Socialist Realism and Chapaev," *Essays in Poetics* 2, no. 1: 43–59, 1977, and Marc Ferro, "The Fiction Film and Historical Analysis," in Paul Smith (ed.), *The Historian and Film,* Cambridge University Press, 1976. Ferror presents an interesting analysis of how the audiences understood the film in 1934 in light of recent history. Among contemporary essays the best are by N. Otten, "Dramaturgiia fil'ma. Tri varianta tsenariia 'Chapaev,' " in *Sovetskoe kino* 7: 58–66, 1935, and D. Velikorodnyi, " 'Chapaev' podarok 15-letnego iubiliara," *Sovetskoe kino* 11–12: 110–14, 1934.

26 As Ferro points out, the choice of the "Moonlight" sonata is a wink at the audience. Most people knew that this was Lenin's favorite music, and that the Bolshevik leader said that it was intolerable to listen to beautiful music when great cruelties were committed. While the colonel was playing, the brother of his orderly was being flogged to death. Ferro, p. 89.

27 G. V. Aleksandrov, *Epokha i kino,* Izdatel'stvo politicheskoi literatury, Moscow, 1983, p. 257.

28 Ibid., p. 258.
29 Ibid., p. 255.
30 See the works of J. Arch Getty, Lynne Viola, Roberta Manning, Robert Thurston, and Gabor Rittersporn.

CHAPTER 9

Films of World War II

The comparative context

All belligerent countries during World War II used the instrument of the cinema as a means of indoctrination. Films depicted the heroism of soldiers and civilians, attempted to increase vigilance by presenting insidious foreign spies, and deepened the hatred against the enemy by showing his atrocities. Inevitably, Soviet works of the period shared a great deal with propaganda efforts made in other countries. Yet, when one attempts to put Soviet films in the context of propaganda films made elsewhere, one is struck by the contrasts more than by the similarities.

Soviet film was unique because only the Communists succeeded in completely mobilizing their industry. Judged on the basis of their movies, Russians and Americans seemed to have been engaged in different wars. For the American people, protected by two oceans and a fabulous industrial might, the war never grew into a life-and-death struggle. Washington was content to use its limited powers to influence the products of Hollywood. Its intervention was largely limited to withholding in a few instances export licenses. Studios made propaganda films – some of them vicious in their anti-Japanese racism – because audiences were willing to pay to see them.

American directors made as many war movies as the market demanded. The huge United States industry between 1942 and 1944 produced 1,313 feature films and of these only 374 dealt with at least some aspect of the war.[1] The great majority of films the Americans saw in those years could have been made just about any time. Patriotic as the Americans may have been, the topic of the war did not dominate the national imagination. A favorite American hero, Humphrey Bogart's Rick of *Casablanca*, showed his commitment to his country's cause and his essential decency, so to speak, in spite of himself. He would have been ashamed to speak of patriotism. In a Soviet picture such a character could not have appeared: For the Russians no amount of talk of the love of motherland was too much.

The Germans, unlike the Americans, did fight a total war, and their government, unlike the one in Washington, did have the means to ensure that

186

the studios produced exactly what it wanted. Joseph Goebbels, the minister of propaganda, was a theorist of the modern means of indoctrination and had a fascination with movies. He took such an interest in casting and in other details that he could be considered as the producer of some films. He was, of course, well aware of the political potential of cinema and, indeed, under his leadership the Nazis produced some of the most repulsive and scurrilous films ever made. No film could surpass *The Eternal Jew* in vicious hate mongering.[2] The Germans made several movies with the intention of teaching their people to think of Slavs as inferior; historical pictures that instilled pride in German history; and others that taught hatred of the British by depicting them as hypocritical, unscrupulous, and cowardly. Nazi documentaries showed the "marvelous" achievements of German arms and attempted to strengthen in their audiences a pride in their "race" and a love of war.[3]

Yet, the German film industry in its lack of complete mobilization was closer to the American than to the Soviet. The great majority of movies that the Germans saw had nothing to do with propaganda. In 1945, at the time of the Allied occupation of Germany, the victors considered it necessary to ban only 208 Nazi films out of a total production of 1,363.[4] The great bulk of the films that were shown comprised historical romances, melodramas, and musicals, that is, escapist entertainment. The audiences were enticed by a promise of amusement, but once they were in the theaters they were exposed to newsreels that sometimes lasted thirty to forty minutes. From the Nazi point of view such an arrangement was satisfactory. They assumed that larger doses of propaganda would turn people away. How apolitical most German films were can be seen from the fact that the Soviet Union, which had captured them at the end of the war – and therefore did not have to pay for them – did not hesitate to distribute them widely for Soviet audiences.[5]

If at the end of the war some committee had attempted to screen apolitical, nonideological Soviet films out of the seventy or eighty feature films that had been made in the Soviet Union, it would have passed only a handful: perhaps some films made for children, some film versions of concerts, and perhaps two or three others that had been based on nineteenth-century classics. All other films were more or less explicitly propaganda. How are we to explain the contrast between the wartime cinema of the two totalitarian countries?

First of all, Nazi rule was much younger. The Nazis nationalized the film industry only shortly before the outbreak of the war, and the "untrained" audiences would have rebelled at a heavy dose of obvious propaganda. They had to be humored. Directors and actors had a degree of freedom that would have been unthinkable in Stalin's Russia. They could bargain with Goebbels. They could emigrate or threaten to emigrate and, of course, many of them did just that. They could refuse roles and on occasion had to be cajoled to accept others. More importantly, the Nazi regime did not have the same degree of control over its artists because it did not desire such controls. Nazi ideology was not comparable to the Soviet version of Marxism; it was only a hodgepodge of half-baked thoughts that did not and could not claim relevance to all aspects of human existence. Goebbels was satisfied with prophylactic censorship and with the transmission of a few themes, because he did not have a coherent worldview to transmit.[6]

The Stalinist regime managed to mobilize the entire society and economy for the purposes of the war. The film industry was a small but not insignificant part of this total mobilization. To evaluate wartime Soviet cinema in purely aesthetic terms would therefore miss the point. The politicians, and presumably the filmmakers themselves, wanted to have pictures (documentaries and feature films alike) to raise the morale of the Soviet people. In our evaluation of wartime Soviet film the central question must be how well the filmmakers carried out their essential task.

Documentaries

In every country the purest form of war propaganda was the newsreels.[7] The peculiarity of the Soviet case was that the Soviets did not draw a sharp line between feature films and documentaries. On the one hand, documentaries at times included staged scenes; on the other, directors made feature films about real persons. The spirit and even the text of these two types of films were often very similar.

It is instructive to compare the attitude of the imperial government in World War I with that of the Soviet in World War II. During the first war only five cameramen operated in the front lines;[8] in the course of the second war thousands of cameramen shot approximately three and a half million meters of film. The Soviet government, by not stinting on resources, produced a remarkable chronicle of the monumental war effort.[9]

By World War II, the Soviet film industry possessed an impressive tradition of making documentaries and had artists of considerable experience. Perhaps this long tradition explains the speed with which the documentary makers could turn to their new tasks. The first wartime newsreel appeared in the movie theaters only three days after the outbreak of the war, on June 25, 1941. From that time on, a new edition came out every three days.[10]

When in the fall of 1941 film studios were evacuated from the capital, the documentary makers remained in Moscow. It was here that the raw film was cut, edited, and provided with accompanying material, such as maps and texts explaining the military action and exhorting the people. It is easy to imagine that the filmmakers had to perform their tasks under very difficult circumstances. Because Moscow was threatened by the enemy during the first autumn and winter of the war, it was difficult to obtain even the most elementary technical necessities for filmmaking. In evaluating the quality of the first newsreels, we must remember the circumstances in which they were made.

The first works were the least successful. It took some time for the cameramen to learn to work under the new circumstances. During the first months documentary makers rarely photographed actual military action, but were content to film second- and third-echelon troops. They filmed maneuvers and presented their versions as if they were actual battles. Contemporary audiences as a rule saw through the pretense.[11] In order to improve the work of filmmakers, the Red Army set up special film groups at the headquarters of army units. These groups were headed by the most prominent documentary makers. These leaders had the authority to send out cameramen to segments of the front they considered the most important. This organizational arrangement lasted through the end of the war.[12]

The main problem, however, was neither inexperience nor organizational flaws. The problem was that reality was hardly suitable to show. Very little happened during the first four or five months of the war that could be honestly told in such a way as to increase the self-confidence of the people and convince them that the war would ultimately be won. When the Soviet people most needed encouragement, documentaries – which, after all, were to a large extent dependent on reality – could least provide it.

The most memorable of the early newsreels dealt not with battles, but with the home front. A newsreel made in July 1941, for example, showed the intent and serious faces of the listeners to Stalin's famous first wartime speech. Looking at the faces of those men and women today, we get a vivid sense of the mood of that dark and anxious period.[13]

Already during the first autumn of the war, directors made full-length documentaries out of newsreel material. The first of these, *Our Moscow*, was made by M. Ia. Slutskii, who with R. L. Karmen (Fig. 41) became the most prolific and famous documentary maker of the war. Slutskii's film, for which he received a Stalin prize, dealt with the capital's preparation for the siege. Needless to say, the film did not show the panic that seized at least a part of the inhabitants. Instead, it depicted the air defense batteries and the soldiers who manned them, and citizens who heroically endured hardships, carried out their tasks, and, at times of air raids, took refuge in subway stations.[14]

The next documentary, *The Defeat of German Armies outside Moscow*, made by L. V. Varlamov and I. P. Kopalin, became perhaps the most effective Soviet documentary of the war. Clearly, the effect was achieved on the basis of the inherent material, rather than by the extraordinary artistry of the filmmakers. Soviet people (and also antifascists everywhere) were desperately eager to see pictures of the first great strategic defeat of the Nazis. The film attracted huge audiences, and the people stood in line to see it. Watching the film reinforced the electrifying effect of the news. The movie did not present the actual strategic picture of the battle, and it contained not a single map.[15] However, the audiences did not come to receive instructions in military affairs; they wanted to see defeated, bedraggled, humiliated German soldiers. The most effective scenes, therefore, were the ones showing German prisoners of war being led through Moscow, and pictures of destroyed German tanks and other war material strewn around the snowy fields.[16]

Aside from domestic propaganda, Soviet documentaries – and especially the one depicting the victory of the Red army at Moscow, shown in Britain and in the United States under the title *Moscow Strikes Back* – had international success. They won public support for the Soviet ally and made large-scale aid more popular. In 1942 *Moscow Strikes Back* received the award from the New York film critics for best "war-fact" film.[17]

Following the success of early documentaries, filmmakers made dozens of full-length films. The defense of Stalingrad, the siege of Leningrad, the battle for Sevastopol, the battle for Orel, and later the liberation of Eastern European countries all became subjects for full-length films. A particularly successful film was *A Day of the War* made by Slutskii, which depicted one day, June 13, 1942, in the life of the Soviet Union. The film was based on the pattern of an earlier picture of Slutskii, completed not long before the outbreak of the war: *A Day of the New World*. On the latter occasion Slutskii edited the work of about 160 cameramen filming in different parts of the country. The film showed life on the front, but also workers in their effort to support the soldiers by providing them with weapons.[18]

One documentary, first shown in the fall of 1943, deserves special attention. This was *Battle for our Soviet Ukraine* by Dovzhenko. Because it was made by one of the greatest Soviet directors, not surprisingly this was aesthetically the most satisfying film. Particularly memorable was the lovingly photographed landscape of Dovzhenko's native Ukraine. The picture, as many other documentaries, started out by showing the peacetime life of the country and then it turned to the depiction of the course of the war. Dovzhenko was the first among Soviet directors to use captured German newsreels for his work. For example, he intercut the faces of smiling Germans and suffering Ukrainians.[19] Dovzhenko's text in its laconic style very much reminds the viewer of the intertitles of his famous silent films.[20]

Dovzhenko was, of course, an artist of great originality. Other documentaries rarely bore the stamp of their creators. To what extent, therefore, can one talk about a particular Soviet style of documentary making? The Nazis, as well as the Soviets, understood the significance of documentaries, and accumulated a great wealth of material. We can take it for granted that the courage of the cameramen on two sides of the battle line was about equal. In any case, such matters cannot be measured. Further, because of the nature of the subject matter documentaries made anywhere had a great deal in common. They all showed rolling tanks, batteries firing followed by explosions (usually not caused by the batteries just seen), soldiers marching,

Figure 41.   Roman Karmen, the most prominent Russian documentary filmmaker in World War II, in 1944.

and so on. Without accompanying texts we can rarely make sense of what we are seeing. All newsreel makers "cheated," staging events for the camera. For example, the famous scene in which two groups of White-clad Soviet soldiers meet, after having completed the encirclement of General Paulus's 6th Army at Stalingrad, was in fact filmed several days after the event. Even from internal evidence it is often clear that newsreels depicting the firing of a gun followed by an explosion could not possibly have photographed that particular explosion. In this sense Soviet documentaries were neither less nor more honest than others made elsewhere.

It is in the accompanying text that we see best the peculiar Soviet style.

American breeziness and flippancy or British understatements would have been completely out of place in a Soviet product. The voice of the Soviet commentator was always solemn and often bombastic – as if a human observer were not commenting on pictures, but history itself was speaking. Perhaps needless to add, each and every newsreel contained references to the genius of Stalin's leadership.

Soviet documentaries also differed from others made elsewhere in their willingness to show suffering and devastation. This was particularly true during the later period of the war, when filmmakers no longer had to fear that painting too dark a picture might undermine faith in the ultimate victory. The Germans, who also suffered greatly in the war, preferred to skip over such matters and instead presented victorious armies marching forward. The difference between the Russian and German attitude to the depiction of suffering was caused primarily by the fact that the Germans started the war. Depicting war as misery could not possibly have served their propaganda goals. On the other hand, a graphic portrayal of suffering deepened the Russian's hatred of the enemy. By showing pain and suffering, Russian newsreels still have an air of reality today that is lacking in Nazi products.

Mobilizing the film industry

The quick advance of the enemy during the summer and fall of 1941 created extraordinary difficulties for Soviet cinema. One major studio, the one in Kiev, was lost within the first few weeks of the war, and by September it became impossible to continue to make feature films either in Moscow or in Leningrad. As the other major industries were moved east, so were the studios. The Central Asian cities of Tashkent, Ashkhabad, Stalinabad, and especially Alma-Ata, which became the headquarters of Mosfil'm and Lenfil'm, became filmmaking centers, and the studios in the Caucasus, Tbilisi, Baku, and Erevan acquired new importance.

In evaluating the quality of wartime films we must remember the circumstances in which they were made. Although Soviet movies had never been able to match the technical quality of Western ones, the war brought lowered standards even further. In the new studios there was not enough space (at times filming had to take place in courtyards, corridors, and even stairs and landings), the laboratories lacked necessary equipment, and even the supply of electricity was unreliable. The directors worked under great pressure to use only the minimum amount of raw film, spend as little money as possible on props, and produce a final product in no more than six months.[21] Then there was the difficult practical problem of how in torrid Central Asia to depict the ice and snow of Russia and the Ukraine, where the battles were fought. One must admire Mark Donskoi's still that made the viewer feel the harsh winter of the Ukraine in *The Rainbow*, which was actually shot in

Alma-Ata. Similarly, it is remarkable to realize that the battle of Borodino for the film *Kutuzov* was also filmed in the same Central Asian studio. Working in the Caucasus and in Central Asia, directors were physically removed from the intellectual centers of the country; prominent writers and directors, discussing the problems of the industry, saw in this separation one of the sources of weakness of the wartime scenarios.[22]

Soviet technology may have been backward and the film industry unprepared for the extraordinary demands placed on it by the demands of war. However, ideologically the Soviet Union was better prepared than any other belligerent in mobilizing filmmaking for the purposes of winning the war. In such matters a nondemocratic country possesses considerable advantages.

First of all, the well-functioning propaganda machine could easily and at a moment's notice change the message. During the first half of 1941 studios turned out anti-British and anti-Polish movies. For example, a film appeared in the theaters in April that depicted the White general, Iudenich, as a tool of the British *(The Defeat of Iudenich)*. *The Girl from the Other Side,* which came out at the same time, portrayed an Iranian girl who helped the Soviet authorities to unmask a British agent.[23] Needless to say, such films disappeared from the movie houses on June 22. Eisenstein, by contrast, could derive at least a little satisfaction that his passionately anti-German diatribe, *Aleksandr Nevskii,* which had been banned for the duration of the Soviet–Nazi alliance, would be soon shown again.[24]

Second, and more important, the Soviet leaders had an exceptionally clear understanding of the importance of the film as a propaganda device, and therefore they never stinted, even at the worst moment, on spending scarce resources. Even at the darkest period of the war, filmmaking never stopped and only barely slowed down.

Of course, it was not enough to make movies; they had to be distributed and shown. The intention of the government was to enable every village soviet to show at least two movies a month. In order to bring about this result, in 1944 alone the plans called for producing three thousand movable projectors and for training forty-five hundred mechanics to operate the machines. The government did not spare resources for rebuilding bombed theaters.[25]

Perhaps the most impressive achievement of Soviet filmmakers was the speed with which they turned to their new task. Already a few days after the outbreak of the war the first anti-Nazi works were already in production. The first collection of shorts appeared in movie houses on August 2 and was followed by two other collections in August. These were called *Boevye kinosborniki* (Fighting Film Collections). Each *kinosbornik* consisted of several shorts, as few as two or as many as six, and they were not individually titled, but numbered. Numbers 1–5 made up a series entitled, *Victory Will Be Ours,* a line from Molotov's first wartime speech. Seven collections were made in 1941 and five more in 1942. At that time they were discontinued; the film industry by then could make full-length feature films, and therefore there was no more need for them. Although film novellas continued to be made, no more collections were put together. These collections were shown not only in the theaters of the land but also to soldiers at the front. By all available evidence the soldiers enjoyed them.

The *kinosborniki* were obviously the revival of the *agitki*, the short agitational films used by the Bolsheviks in the Civil War. At that time the shortage of raw material and the lack of technical equipment forced the directors to make shots that were used primarily to spread the Bolshevik message among the peasants. These films appealed to an uneducated audience and proved useful in spite of their extraordinary simplicity of message and unabashed didacticism. Now that the Bolsheviks once again felt threatened, they turned to the use of a propaganda instrument that had shown its worth in the past.

The content, style, and quality of the shorts that made up the *kinosborniki* greatly varied. They included humorous sketches, Allied documentaries about subjects such as the British Navy or the air war over London, and simple dramas. The first collection was tied together by the imaginary figure of Maxim, the hero of a famous film trilogy of the 1930s, who introduced the shorts.[26] The collection included a short written by Leonid Leonov, *Three in a Shell Hole*. A wounded Soviet soldier, a wounded German, and a Soviet nurse find themselves after a battle in the same shell hole. The nurse, a Soviet humanist, provides help to both of the wounded soldiers. The vicious German nevertheless is about to kill her, when the alert Soviet soldier prevents him by a well-aimed and well-timed bullet. The second collection included a short, called *The Meeting*. This movie depicts the cruelties of the Germans in occupied territories, in this instance, in Poland. The Germans execute a group of people in 1939 because one peasant saved a bottle of milk for a sick child rather than handing it over to the occupiers. One of the peasants manages to escape into the Soviet Union, and two years later meets the same cruel German officer, but this time with a weapon in his hand as a Soviet soldier. He takes revenge for all the victims, Poles, White Russians, and Russians.[27] By common consent the best of these short dramas was *Feast in Zhirmunka* in No. 6. This sketch was also based on Leonov's scenario, and it was directed by Pudovkin. Praskovia, a Soviet *kolkhoz* woman, invites the occupying Germans to a meal in her house and poisons the food. In front of her guests she eats the poisoned food in order to allay their suspicions and encourage them to eat. When the partisans arrive they find everyone dead.[28]

Perhaps more effective than the dramas were the humorous shorts. The second collection, for example, included a vignette entitled *Incident at the Telegraph Office*, made by Arnshtam and Kozintsev. The entire film consists of one scene in which we see Napoleon at the telegraph office sending Hitler this message: "I have attempted it. I do not recommend it."[29] The third collection included a short about Antosha Rybkin, a cook in the army, who aspires to be a hero. Soon the fighting gives him an opportunity to use his quick wit to fight the Nazis with weapons. The figure of Rybkin became so popular among the viewers that director K. Iudin in 1942 made a full-length picture about him, the first comedy of the war (*Antosha Rybkin*).[30] Iutkevich made a short about the new adventures of Schweik for the seventh collection (*Schweik in the Concentration Camp*), turning the famous character of Czech writer Jaroslav Hasek into an active fighter against fascism.[31] Schweik also became the hero of a full-length comedy, *New Adventures of Schweik*, in 1943.

In a discussion of wartime Soviet film, the Fighting Film Collection deserves special attention because this was a uniquely Soviet genre. In no other country would it have been possible to give the audiences such obvious propaganda. Americans, British, and even Germans would have found such products counterproductive. Soviet directors, on the other hand, had no need to disguise what they were doing. They could do this because their audiences had been prepared by decades of experience; the agitation and propaganda machinery had already been in existence. No one could question that the transmission of an ideology and the justification of the policies of the government were not merely legitimate, but even desirable enterprises. Furthermore, as before, during the war Soviet theaters presented little alternative to the viewers. Very few foreign films were shown even at a time when the alliance with Britain and the United States was the warmest.

War films

From the spring of 1942 the film industry settled down to wartime conditions and began to produce full-length movies. These works obviously varied in style and quality but shared enough in basic conceptions and point of view to allow generalizations about them. Between 1942 and 1945 the studios made seventy films. (This number does not include a few that were made especially for children, photographed versions of concerts, and science films.) Of these, forty-nine took place in the present and, with a single exception (a collective farm musical described in the annotated catalog as "vaudeville"), could be described as war films. The twenty-one "historical" pictures made up a varied category, which included versions of nineteenth-century classics, spectaculars based on the history and folklore of national minorities. One of these, however, amusingly enough, was an operetta, *Silva* (original title *Gypsy Princess*) based on the Kalman libretto.[32]

Although Soviet policymakers quickly hit upon the main propaganda themes, which then remained constant, in some peripheral matter the tone of films did change as the Red Army succeeded in turning the tide. The Soviet people acquired an unfortunate knowledge of the particular branch of evil that the Nazis represented, and, reflecting this knowledge, the films became somewhat less schematic and the Germans in them slightly more recognizable.

The theme of vigilance, which was pronounced in the early period, receded in importance. Of course, all belligerent nations were preoccupied with spies; nevertheless, in the Soviet case this preoccupation had a particular flavor, no doubt as a consequence of the recent memory of the great terror. In the early films everyone, including children and old women, unmasked spies. A particularly amusing example of this genre was *In the Sentry Box*, a short that appeared on the screens in November 1941. The film is interesting inasmuch as it is an unconscious caricature. Red Army soldiers uncover a German spy who speaks flawless Russian and is dressed in Soviet uniform. He gives himself away by not recognizing a baby picture of Stalin on the wall.[33] The movie is based on a perfectly realistic premise: No one who lived in the Soviet Union in the 1930s could possibly fail such a test. It is the subtext, however, that is important: Stalin protects his people even in the form of a picture, even as an icon. Most likely Soviet directors lost interest in making movies about spies as a result of an unconscious recognition that modern wars were won and lost not as a consequence of subversion but as a result of national mobilization.

The experience of the individual soldier in the front has been a central theme of an extraordinary number of Soviet works ever since the war. Neither audiences nor directors ever seem to tire of the topic. Interestingly, however, unlike the directors of the other belligerent countries, Soviet filmmakers made relatively few movies about actual military exploits at the time, and the approximately half dozen films that did appear came out during the last year of the war. One can only speculate about the reasons. Perhaps the struggle was too serious an affair for the Soviet people to be depicted as a series of adventures. Or maybe the directors considered the stability of the home front a greater concern than the behavior of soldiers under fire.

The most influential of the war films was made by the Vasil'ev "brothers" on the basis of the Korneichuk play, *The Front*. The picture (and the play), in a didactic fashion, juxtaposed an older and younger generation of Soviet commanders and predictably took the side of the younger, unconventional, and daring ones.[34] Other war movies, such as *Two Warriors, Days and Nights, Malakhov Kurgan, Moscow Sky,* and *Ivan Nikulin – Russian Sailor,* were all undistinguished, ineffective, and attacked even at the time for failing to show the face of the battle and the scale of the struggle.[35]

A much better subject than battles was partisan warfare. Indeed, films about partisans turned out to be the most effective and also artistically the most satisfying ones. The three most memorable films dealing with this topic share so much with one another that they form a trilogy. The first of these, *She Defends the Motherland,* was made by Fridrich Ermler and appeared in movie houses in May 1943. As so many other movies, it starts out by depicting the happy life of the Soviet people before the Nazi invasion. By recalling the wonderful past, it sends the message that the people have much to fight for. Today these scenes appear rather ludicrous. Praskovia, a simple *kolkhoz* woman, is enjoying her life with her husband and son so much that she seems unable to suppress her giggles. On the first day of the war the invaders kill her husband and soon after a German tank brutally squashes her son. Praskovia is transformed by the experience and escapes into the forest where she becomes a partisan leader. She is accepted as leader presumably because her desire for vengeance is the greatest and her hatred of the occupiers is the fiercest. Not only does she succeed, rather improbably, in finding the murderous tankist, but with her friends she manages to get him out of his tank and then kills him the same way her son was killed (Fig. 42). She returns to the village because she hears the rumor that Moscow has fallen to the enemy and she wants to shore up the courage of the villagers by telling them the truth. The Nazis capture her and are about to execute her when her fellow partisans appear and liberate her and the village.

She Defends the Motherland is an artistically primitive film that has the simplest political message: the necessity of vengeance. Ermler gave few individual characteristics to his heroine. The picture obviously gave a vicarious satisfaction to the Russians, who had suffered so much. It could not appeal to foreign audiences. When it was shown in the United States with the title, *No Greater Love*, it was judged by critics as crude and stagy.[36]

A much more complex and successful work was Mark Donskoi's *The Rainbow*, released in January 1944. It is about a woman partisan, Olena, who returns to her village to give birth. When captured, she is subjected to the most dreadful torture but does not betray her comrades. The film has many characters who, unlike those in *She Defends the Motherland*, are endowed with individual traits; as a result, the viewer can identify with them. *The Rainbow* has a powerful effect even on today's audiences largely because of its unusually graphic and detailed depiction of Nazi barbarities. For example, the Germans murder a young boy who tries to smuggle food to a prisoner (Fig. 43), and they kill a newborn babe. Olena's torture is shown in naturalistic detail. A subsidiary theme is the punishment of collaborators. The director depicts the wife of a Red Army officer who cohabits with a German with even greater loathing than he has for the Nazis themselves. When she is killed by her husband, who returns with the partisans, the audience readily accepts her death as just punishment. Similarly, the village elder who serves the Germans is punished by death.[37]

Zoia, directed by L. Arnshtam, appeared on the screens only in September 1944. Its scenario was based on the martyr death of the eighteen-year-old partisan, Zoia Kosmodem'ianskaia. She, like Olena in *The Rainbow*, endures tortures and prefers death to betraying her comrades.[38]

The most obvious feature that the three films have in common is that the

Figure 42.   Praskovia confronts the German tank with a pistol: *She Defends the Motherland* (1943).

directors chose women as their protagonists. By showing the courage and suffering of women, these works aroused hatred for the cruel enemy and at the same time taught that men could do no less than these women. The basic message here, as in so many other wartime products, is the necessity for vengeance. Two of these films depict graphically Germans killing children. No crime could be greater than that in the eyes of the Russians.

The three protagonists are positive heroes. They are presented as human beings without flaws, indeed without individual traits. They stand for an idealized image of Soviet womanhood and for patriotism. Artistically this is a source of weakness, for the viewer cannot recognize them as real human beings. By far the best of the three films is *The Rainbow*, which presents secondary characters who are better drawn and more believable than the central figure. *She Defends the Motherland* and *The Rainbow* implicitly (and *Zoia* explicitly) raise the question what makes a hero. We see Zoia as a schoolgirl admiring the historical figure of Ivan Susanin, who had saved the tsar. When tortured, Zoia says: "All through our lives we have thought about what is happiness? Now I know. Happiness is to be a fearless fighter for our country, for our fatherland, for Stalin."[39]

The films show an interesting evolution. At the end of *She Defends the*

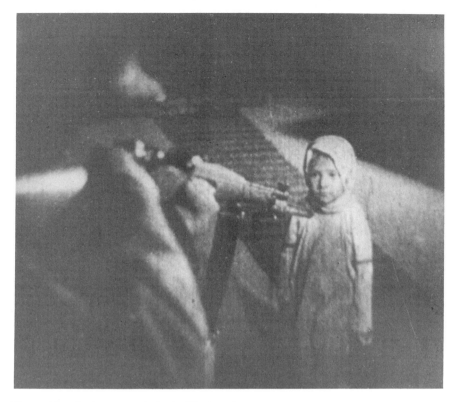

Figure 43.   An innocent victim in *The Rainbow* (1943).

Motherland, the partisans liberate the village and save the heroine from execution. In *The Rainbow* the heroine is killed, but her death is avenged when the partisans liberate her village. *Zoia*, by contrast, concludes with our witnessing a martyr death. The explanation for the differences is simple. In 1942, when the scenario of *She Defends the Motherland* was written, Soviet audiences would have found it too disheartening to watch an execution; but by the summer of 1944 the people were confident of the ultimate victory and did not need the false consolation of a phony rescue.

Movies about partisans were effective at least partially because they showed most clearly the brutality and inhumanity of the Nazi occupiers. The depiction of Nazi behavior made a great impression on contemporary audiences, because the description was fundamentally truthful: The Nazis were beastly and Soviet citizens knew it. These films conveyed the essential propaganda point: The Germans had to be resisted because they left no alternative. Because German occupation was extraordinarily brutal, resistance to it was indeed heroic – the more vicious the enemy, the more attractive the hero.

Although directors truthfully depicted Nazi atrocities, they were not successful in making the character of individual Germans believable. Especially in the early films, the Nazis were not only bestially brutal, which of course, they were, but also silly and cowardly. In the short sketch *Elixir of Courage* (1941), the Germans dare to go into the attack only under the influence of alcohol.[40] In another, *Spiders* (1942), doctors murder their own severely wounded soldiers in a German hospital.[41]

Soviet opinion makers made the conscious decision not to allow the depiction of decent Germans. In 1942 Pudovkin directed the film *Murderers Are on Their Way*, based on stories by Brecht, which attempted to show German victims of Hitler's regime and fear among ordinary citizens.[42] The film was not allowed to be distributed. In Soviet films there was to be only one type of German, hateful. A characteristic example of this approach was Romm's *Girl No. 217* (1944), which was about the life of a Soviet slave laborer with a German family. All Germans according to this film are cruel, stupid, money grubbing, and degenerate.[43]

The movies even projected the wickedness of the Germans into the past. A particularly unattractive example of this tactic was *The Golden Road* (1945), which depicted Volga Germans in 1918 as smugglers of Russian gold.[44] This work implicitly justified the mass deportations of ethnic Germans.

Films that celebrated the achievements of the home front were, of course, without German villains. Most of them also had female heroines, and aimed to show that those who labor courageously and unstintingly at home also make a contribution to victory. Gerasimov's film, *The Great Land,* first shown in August 1944, dealt with the evolution of Anna, who after her husband's departure to the front becomes an excellent worker in an evacuated factory.[45] By contrast, *Actress* is a rather silly comedy and full of improbable coincidences. It raises the rather banal question whether art is possible at the time of war. The answer is, of course, that it is not only possible but necessary.[46] None of the movies dealing with the rear presented a realistic picture. Kozintsev and Trauberg's film *Simple People,* which also dealt with evacuation, attempted to describe the confusion that prevailed at the time. The authorities found this bit of realism too much and the movie could not be publicly exhibited until 1956.[47]

Nationalism and history

The Soviet Union was a multinational empire, and this fact presented dangers and difficulties to the propagandists. The Nazis indeed attempted to take advantage of the existing national hostilities and jealousies. Especially during the second half of the war they encouraged the aspirations of the minorities against the Russians. It was the task of the Soviet opinion makers, therefore, to parry the danger. A part of this effort was the studios turning out products about the "friendship of peoples." This meant that the audiences would see, let us say, a Georgian and a Russian soldier going on a dangerous mission and the success of the mission would depend on their cooperation. At the end, either the Russian would save the Georgian, or vice versa. (Because the United States also lacked ethnic homogeneity, this particular simple idea could also be found in contemporary American films.)

The Soviet people were to fight the brutal foe in the name of patriotism. But what did Soviet patriotism mean? It meant a combination of old-fashioned pride in the nation's past and a thin veneer of Stalinism. The Soviet authorities made a conscious decision not to stress the communist nature of their regime, to deemphasize the idea of proletarian internationalism, and to counteract the notion that Moscow was the headquarters of an international revolutionary movement. Consequently only very rarely do we see communist functionaries playing a major role in organizing the home front or the guerrilla movement. (*The Secretary of the District Committee*, a film made by Ivan Pyr'ev in 1942, is unusual inasmuch as in it the leading role is played by a communist.) Those who go to their deaths fighting the enemy have the name of Stalin and motherland on their lips, not that of the Communist Party. It was, therefore, grossly unfair that after the end of the war the directors were taken to task by the politicians for having failed to show the leading role of the Party.

Harnessing the imperial Russian past for Soviet purposes was a straightforward matter. No director could overdo the depiction of past Russian glories. The succession of historical films that aimed to show past greatness in order to inspire current audiences began before the war. Eisenstein's *Aleksandr Nevskii* and Pudovkin's *Suvorov* belong to this category. During the war V. Petrov, who had made *Peter the First* (1937–9), made the film *Kutuzov* in 1944, and Eisenstein made his great film *Ivan the Terrible*. In the course of the late 1930s Stalin increasingly saw himself as a modern Ivan the Terrible. He was fascinated by the positive portrayal of the tsar by the ex-monarchist historian, R. Wipper, and the idea that Eisenstein should make a film about the sixteenth-century ruler came from Stalin himself.[48] Six months before the German attack, in January 1941, Eisenstein received his instructions from A. Zhdanov.

An expression of Russian patriotism was a reemergence of pan-Slavism. The Slav peoples of Eastern Europe were once again regarded by the propagandists as "little brothers." They, and not the proletarians of Germany and Italy, were to be allies of the Russian people in the struggle against Teutonic expansionism. This process also began before the war, but it was accelerated at the outbreak of the hostilities. Never before had Soviet filmmakers paid so much attention to Czechs, Yugoslavs, and Poles as in these years. The underground struggle of the Slav peoples against the Nazis became the topic of several films. A second-rate film about the Czech underground operating a radio station announced clearly the theme of Soviet propaganda: "The hour has come when the entire Slav people should unite for the quickest and final defeat of German fascism."[49]

The Poles, as always, posed a special problem for the pan-Slavs, for the

Poles did not like the role of "younger brother." They also claimed territories that the Soviet Union was determined to retain. In the films of the 1930s they were usually depicted in a hostile fashion. *Bogdan Khmel'nitskii*, made in 1941, was bitterly anti-Polish, and Eisenstein's portrayal of the Polish court in *Ivan the Terrible* was obviously hostile. Before the outbreak of the war, Romm made *The Dream*, which showed the miserable life of the people of the western Ukraine under Polish rule and how their dream was realized when in 1939 they could become "free citizens in a free country" – that is, when their land was annexed by the Soviet Union as a consequence of the Molotov–Ribbentrop pact.[50] Once the war started, it was inappropriate to exhibit this movie. Its premiere was postpoined until September 1943. That it was shown at that time clearly indicated that Stalin had decided that those territories would be retained at the end of the war whatever the cost.

Soviet cinema taught the audience that Russian arms in the past had always been victorious. It was more difficult to deal with the pasts of the minority peoples. Soviet studios produced during the war one major epic for each nationality: *Bogdan Khmel'nitskii* for the Ukrainians, *Georgii Saakadze* for the Georgians, *David Bek* for the Armenians, and *Arshin-Mal-Alan* for the Azerbaidzhanis. The directors, however, had to be careful to choose a hero who had shown his mettle by fighting an enemy other than the Russians. Preferably, "the friendship of people" was to be projected into the past, through films that showed, for example, that the safety and happiness of the Armenians had always depended on their alliance with the Russians.

Minority nationalism was a ticklish issue. Soviet authorities encouraged a legitimate pride in one's past, but too large a dose of such pride could be dangerous, for it encouraged demands for independence or at least autonomy, and threatened to undermine the willingness to accept the leading role of Russians. The Ukrainians, to whom the Germans appealed in particular, presented a special problem. Dovzhenko, the "film poet" of his native land, wrote a scenario that Stalin personally decided to ban because of its nationalism; during the war, the great director was restricted to making documentaries.[51]

It is striking that almost every one of the historical movies bore the title of an individual hero. Each of them aimed to show how an extraordinary person through his heroism and wisdom changed history. A characteristic example is Petrov's film *Kutuzov*. The old general was victorious not because he allowed his army to lead him, as in Tolstoy's *War and Peace*, but because he was a brilliant strategist. Gone were the days when Soviet directors celebrated the historical role of the masses. In the age of Stalin it seemed appropriate to focus on the importance of leadership and thereby support authority. Cinema reflected reality: In the Stalinist Soviet Union it was the decisions of the all-wise leader that mattered.

Today these historical films are almost unwatchable. Their exaggerated nationalism, their bombast, their unbelievable heroes, and their false pathos make the experience of watching them unpleasant. They distort history; the directors had no interest in recreating the past for its own sake. It is true that the overwhelming majority of historical films made anywhere and at any time aims to use the past in order to deal with present problems. It would be foolish to expect Soviet cinema of the war period to present us with a dispassionate depiction of some long-past event or some long-forgotten historical figure. Nevertheless it is extraordinary how brazenly the directors distorted past events, distant or recent, in order to make their points.

An entire series of films, for example, dealt with the German occupations of the Ukraine in 1918 (*Kotovskii, How the Steel Was Tempered, The Defense of Tsaritsyn,* and *Aleksandr Parkhomenko*). In these movies the directors wanted to show that the Germans had always been vicious, that the Red Army had always managed to defeat them, and that Stalin had always provided wise leadership. In order to make these points the directors faced some ticklish problems: for, in fact, the Red Army had never engaged the Germans, except for some minor skirmishes, let alone defeated them. Reality, however, did not deter the filmmakers. L. Lukov in *Aleksandr Parkhomenko* (1942) and the Vasil'ev "brothers" in *The Defense of Tsaritsyn* (1942) depicts battles that never occurred, could not have occurred, and, if they had, would have resulted in resounding defeats for the Reds.[52]

Donskoi brought to the screen the best-known Soviet novel, Nikolai Ostrovskii's *How the Steel was Tempered*. In that novel Pavel Korchagin's adventures in the German-occupied Ukraine take up only a few pages. The film version, by contrast, concentrated entirely on this period. The scenarist, in order to fill the gap, had to rearrange some incidents and make up others. In the process Korchagin is turned into a nationalist freedom fighter. Almost everyone in the audience knew that the director, to put it mildly, had not been faithful to the original, and yet none of the critics was disturbed enough as to mention it in a review.[53]

Putting it in the context of the other movies made at the time, it is extraordinary that Eisenstein was still able to produce a masterpiece. *Ivan the Terrible* (Part I, 1944; Part II, 1946), which shares a great deal with other movies in the genre, nevertheless is one of the great movies of all time. Eisenstein, too, aimed to show the victory of Russian arms and the importance of the heroic leader, and he too did not hesitate to make contemporary references. When, for example, the tsar speaks of the importance of the English alliance, the director clearly winks at his audience. However, unlike other products at the time, this one is fiercely individualistic; no one but Eisenstein could have designed the highly original composition of individual scenes. Unlike any other director of a Soviet historical film, Eisenstein created a complex and interesting character.

We started our survey of Soviet wartime cinema by pointing out that it was necessary to place it in an international context. It is just as important to look at these works within the history of Soviet film. When we attempt to do this, it is obvious that these years formed a distinct period. Naturally, not everything changed at the outbreak of the war: The celebration of patriotism, which had begun in the 1930s, accelerated at the time of the war and reached ludicrous proportions during the last years of Stalin, and the depiction of the "positive hero" of socialist realist aesthetics was a constant in the art of the Stalinist period.

The irony of the history of Soviet cinema is that during the war directors made propaganda films, which by definition distorted reality – they depicted the enemy as uniformly vicious and stupid and the Soviet people as clever and heroic – and yet these films were more realistic than anything that the studios had produced either immediately before 1941 or immediately after 1945. In the Stalinist years artists did not dare to touch upon any genuine issue facing society. Directors either turned to the past for subject matter, or depicted a never-never land of smiling and singing collective farmworkers who cheerfully competed against one another in fulfilling the plan. In this context the war, in spite of the dreadful destruction and suffering it caused, was a liberating experience. Films once again expressed genuine feeling and real pathos: The hatred for the enemy, the call for sacrifice and heroism, and the sorrow for the abused Soviet people were real and heartfelt. The directors believed in what they were saying. The period of the war was a small oasis of freedom in the film history of the Stalinist years.

Notes

1 Dorothy B. Jones, "The Hollywood War Films, 1942–1944," *Hollywood Quarterly* 1: 2, 1945–6.

2 For an analysis of this film, see Richard Taylor, *Film Propaganda: Soviet Russia and Nazi Germany*, Cambridge University Press, 1979, pp. 190–206.

3 The best analysis of Nazi documentaries is still Sigfried Kracauer's *From Caligari to Hitler: A Psychological Study of the German Cinema, 1933–1945*, Princeton University Press, Princeton, 1947, pp. 275–331.

4 David S. Hull, *Film in the Third Reich: A Study of the German Cinema, 1933–1945*, University of California Press, Berkeley, 1969, p. 8.

5 To be sure, Soviet distributors were particularly anxious to show films in which Nazi and Soviet propaganda interests coincided, such as those that attacked British colonial policies. However, these films were in a minority. Also, when necessary, Soviet censors did not hesitate to "edit" Nazi films or provide them with oral commentaries.

6 Richard Taylor in his comparative analysis of Soviet and Nazi propaganda films expressed a different point of view.

7 This book is a study of the Soviet feature film. At the time of World War II, however, the significance of the documentaries was so great that it seemed necessary to devote a few pages to this topic.

8 See Chapter 1.

9 V. Zhdan (ed.), *Kratkaia istoriia sovetskogo kino*, Moscow, 1969, p. 305.

10 R. Katsman, "Frontovaia kinokhronika," *Novyi mir* 7: 109, 1942.

11 *New York Times*, June 6, 1942. The *Times* reviewed a documentary collection called *Red Tanks*.

12 S. V. Drobashenko, "Dokumental'naia kinematografia," *Ocherki istorii Sovetskogo kino, 1935–1945*, vol. 2, Iskusstvo, Moscow, 1959, p. 562.

13 These and other Soviet documentaries are available at the Axelbank collection of the Archives of the Hoover Institution at Stanford University.

14 R. Katsman, "Frontovaia," p. 109.

15 Drobashenko, pp. 570–1.

16 R. Katsman, "Perventsy kinopublitsistiki," *Literatura i iskusstvo*, Apr. 15. 1942, p. 3.

17 *New York Times*, Aug. 17, 1942. According to *Istoriia sovetskogo kino, 1917–1967*, 4 vols., Iskusstvo, Moscow, 1969–78, 3: 21, and also *Kino. Entsiklopedicheskii slovar'*, Moscow, 1987, pp. 66, this film was chosen by the "American Academy of Film" as best film of 1942. This is, however, a misunderstanding. See also, "Fil'm 'Razgrom nemetskikh voisk pod Moskvoi' v SShA," *Literatura i iskusstvo*, Dec. 12, 1942, p. 2.

18 Drobashenko, p. 576.

19 *Literatura i iskusstvo*, Oct 23, 1943, p. 2.

20 R. Sobolev, *Aleksandr Dovzhenko*, Iskusstvo, Moscow, 1980, pp. 214–22.

21 See the letter of M. Il'in from Alma-Ata in *Literatura i iskusstvo*, Nov. 14, 1942, p. 4.

22 *Literatura i iskusstvo*, July 24, 1943, p. 1.

23 *Sovetskie khudozhestvennye fil'my. Annotirovannyi katalog*, vol. 2, Iskusstvo, Moscow, 1961, p. 265 (hereafter referred to as *S.kh.f.*).

24 Jay Leyda, *Kino. A History of the Russian and Soviet Film*, Collier Books, New York, 1960, pp. 365–6.

25 *Literatura i iskusstvo*, Feb. 12, 1944, p. 4.

26 *Pravda*, Aug. 6, 1941, p. 4.

27 *Pravda*, Aug. 11, 1941, p. 5.

28 *S.kh.f.*, p. 259, and A. Karaganov, *Vsevolod Pudovkin*, Moscow, Iskusstvo, 1983, pp. 208–9.

29 *S.kh.f.*, p. 256.

30 *Literatura i iskusstvo*, Feb. 6, 1943, p. 3.

31 *Pravda*, Dec. 10, 1941, p. 3.

32 I based my calculations on *S.kh.f.*, pp. 252–361.

33 *S.kh.f.*, p. 262.

34 *S.kh.f.*, p. 324.

35 See for example the review of *Malakhov Kurgan* in *Pravda*, Dec. 10, 1944. The review, rather amusingly, objected to sailors using vulgar language.

36 *Literatura i iskusstvo*, May 22, 1943, p. 2. *New York Times*, Feb. 5, 1944.

37 *Literatura i iskusstvo*, Jan. 29, 1944, p. 3.

38 *Literatura i iskusstvo*, Sept. 23, 1944, p. 2.

39 *Pravda*, Sept. 22, 1944.

40 *S.kh.f.*, p. 260.

41 *S.kh.f.*, p. 294.

42 Karaganov, pp. 209–10.

43 *S.kh.f.*, p. 341.

44 *S.kh.f.*, p. 352.
45 *S.kh.f.*, p. 325.
46 *S.kh.f.*, p. 331.
47 S. S. Ginzburg, "Khudozhestvennye fil'my o bor'be sovetskogo naroda protiv fashistskikh zakhvatchikov," in *Ocherki*, pp. 662–3.
48 On Stalin's relationship to Ivan the Terrible, see Robert C. Tucker, *Stalin in Power: The Revolution from Above, 1928–1941*, Norton, New York, 1990, pp. 277–78.
49 The title of the film was *Elusive Ian*. See *S.kh.f.*, p. 305 and *Ogonek* 27: 14, 1943.
50 *S.kh.f.*, pp. 271–2.
51 *Alexander Dovzhenko: The Poet as Filmmaker: Selected Writings*, ed. Marco Carynnyk, Cambridge, Mass., 1973, pp. 30–1.
52 *Pravda*, Mar. 28, 1942, p. 3 and *Pravda*, July 22, 1942, p. 4.
53 *Literatura i iskusstvo*, Sept. 26, 1942, p. 2.

PART III

The death of Soviet film

CHAPTER 10

Film hunger, 1945–1953

Stalin's last years were the gloomiest in Soviet history. Although the number of victims and the percentage of the population incarcerated most likely had not increased since the 1930s and the Soviet people were spared the gruesome and frightening spectacles of the great trials, new and unattractive themes appeared in public discourse. The lunatic excesses of a Stalinist version of patriotism turned into chauvinism, xenophobia, and anti-Semitism, and the show of adulation of Stalin reached pagan proportions.

The chief source of gloom was unrealized hopes. People believed that after so much suffering they would have a better and freer life. During the war the policymakers for tactical reasons underemphasized the communist nature of the regime. The Soviet people, who had shown their fundamental loyalty to the system, now hoped that they would be rewarded by being allowed to live in a less-repressive order. Stalin and his fellow leaders, however, had different views; they saw dangers rather than opportunities. Indeed, the country emerged from the war devastated and the losses in terms of death and destruction were extraordinary. The Stalinists believed that in order to ensure the security of the regime, the social discipline that had been loosened during the war now had to be tightened. The importance of communist ideology had to be reasserted.

Soviet soldiers and millions of other citizens acquired firsthand information concerning the impressive material civilization of the West. They could not but see that the standard of living of Westerners had been much higher than their own. Such contacts were bound to be subversive because they undermined the claims of the Party about the Soviet Union being the most advanced and progressive society on earth. Propaganda dealt with this problem by an increasingly shrill assertion of Soviet superiority. At a time when the West appeared overwhelmingly rich, successful, and powerful, propagandists in an ever-more brazen and ridiculous fashion claimed Russian superiority not only for the "wonderful" present but also projected it into the past.

Even more depressing than the new themes of propaganda and the violent denunciation of all kinds of enemies was the further narrowing of the public sphere. The regime placed more and more topics beyond legitimate discourse. The newspapers and periodicals discussed fewer and fewer meaningful issues: A handful of themes came to be repeated endlessly. Looking at the press of the day, such as *Pravda* and *Kul'tura i zhizn'* (Culture and Life), the organ of the *agitprop* section of the Central Committee, one cannot form a picture of the life of the people. The gap between public discussions and reality further widened.

Cultural life, including filmmaking, reflected this political order. The artistic and intellectual worlds lost their last vestiges of autonomy; intellectual and artistic disputes were decided by politicians. Entire branches of science were destroyed by outsiders. No medium of art escaped the attention of the Party ideologists.

Once again, cinema suffered the heaviest blows. In these years filmmaking as an art form died. In the late 1930s, a period of great repression, some enjoyable films were still produced. By contrast, the postwar years were entirely sterile. Postwar history provides us with a case study of the role and function of cinema in conditions of extreme repression.

The period of few films

According to the Catalog of Soviet Feature Films, the studios of the country in 1945 produced 18 films; in 1946, 22; in 1947, 22; in 1948, 16; in 1949, 17; in 1950, 12; in 1951, 9; in 1952, 23; and in 1953, 44. Even these numbers do not show the magnitude of the change. The catalog includes works that could not fairly be described as films. Especially after 1951 a large percentage of films were only photographed versions of theatrical performances. A camera was set in front of the stage and simply recorded what was taking place in front of it. Two such "films" were made in 1951, 14 in 1952, and 17 in 1953. These films were made in order to bring theater to the provinces, and perhaps also for the benefit of Stalin, who according to some authors loved the theater, but because of his dread of appearing in public did not attend performances.[1] The catalog also includes short films made for children and experimental stereoscopic films. Furthermore, many of the films made in this period, and therefore included in the production figures, did not reach the cinemas until years after Stalin's death. Among these were *The Star, The Fires of Baku,* the second part of *Ivan the Terrible, A Great Life,* and *Simple People.* In the early 1950s the enormous Soviet film industry with its many studios gave the audiences no more than four or five feature films a year. Major studios stood idle and such giants as Mosfil'm completed but one or two films. *Kul'tura i zhizn'* complained that in 1947 Soiuzdetfil'm, the studios in Tbilisi, Baku, Alma-Ata, Tashkent, Askhabad, Sverdlovsk, and Riga produced not a single film. Mosfil'm produced one – *Spring* – but that was in fact made in Prague.[2] Compare this output with the yearly 400–500 films produced in Hollywood or the 200–300 films made in India or Japan.[3]

Why did Soviet production decline so precipitously? Clearly, the diminished production could not be entirely the result of the extensive damage caused by the war. After all, at a time when the country was engaged in a life-and-death struggle and the work had to be carried out under far less favorable circumstances, more films were produced. Furthermore, as the economy recovered – and it did recover remarkably rapidly – the number of films not only did not increase, but decreased.

Pointing to the quick recovery is not to deny that the industry continued to face serious technical problems. The studios in Kiev, Odessa, and Yalta had been destroyed and had to be rebuilt. A raw-film factory in the little town of Shostka (between Kiev and Kursk) was also destroyed.[4] The removal to Central Asia of the major studios from Moscow and Leningrad and then their return was also a difficult task, no doubt causing damage to equipment. The Soviet studios from the time of their establishment had always been technologically backward compared to their Western counterparts and the war damage, at least temporarily, further widened the gap.

The conquest of Eastern Europe, however, brought benefits. Filmmakers used captured German equipment. Agfa colored film stock enabled the director A. Ptushko to make the technically outstanding color film for children, *Stone Flower*. This film was partially made in the famous Prague Barrandov studio. Ivan Pyr'ev made *Tales of the Siberian Land* and Aleksandrov *Spring* in Prague in 1947. As Aleksandrov put it:

The idea of the film was rather complex in a technical sense, and Mosfil'm, as I have already remarked, at the time of the evacuation was taken apart and not yet completely reconstructed. However we quickly found a way out of the difficult situation. The Prague studio, Barrandov-film, offered us its beautifully equipped pavilions [which were, in fact, separate studios] and the work went on quickly.[5]

The same director, as late as 1952, made his colored film, *Composer Glinka*, on Agfa film, once again partially in Prague.[6]

The Party drew up ambitious plans for reconstruction. Ivan Bol'shakov, soon to be named minister of the film industry, wrote in 1945 that plans called for making Mosfil'm the largest studio in Europe, capable within a couple of years of producing 40 films a year. He foresaw that the Soviet Union would produce 80–100 films yearly in the very near future. Optimistically, he called for making the majority of films in color and he wanted the Soviet Union to become the pathfinder in the development of stereofilm.[7] Bol'shakov pointed out that such a planned increase necessitated training more directors and actors. The intention, as in so many similar cases in the past, remained unrealized. Instead of producing more and more films, the studios produced fewer and fewer.

Soon the authorities carried out a strange about-face. A resolution of the

Council of Ministers passed in June 1948 criticized the Ministry of Film industry for "paying too much attention to quantity as opposed to quality." The resolution criticized a large number of films as ideologically weak. It called for producing fewer but "better" films. Every new film was to be a masterpiece, capable of instilling communist consciousness into the masses.[8]

In the post-Stalinist period, Soviet film historians and publicists have argued, the great decline in the number of films made was the result of a conscious decision, albeit an erroneous one. But, in spite of the 1948 resolution, the country produced far fewer films than the leaders wanted. They were obviously not satisfied with the output. In August 1950 *Kul'tura i zhizn'* called for the production of more films, and in the following year the same journal complained that in the previous year the plans called for twenty feature films and the studios produced only six.[9] G. M. Malenkov in his report to the Nineteenth Party Congress mentioned the problems of the film industry and said that it was not using its potential and produced too few good films.[10]

It is easy to understand why so few films were made. The political requirements for a scenario and the difficulties between the acceptance of the literary work and the completion of the film became so extraordinary that scenarists became discouraged; projects remained unfinished. The industry had always suffered from an insufficient number of desirable scripts. The situation became worse and worse. The process of turning a scenario into a film, which had been extraordinarily complex in the 1930s, became even more so. In 1948 the Ministry forbade the studios to conclude agreements with writers. It insisted on a centralized process from the very outset and claimed a monopoly for itself. At the same time it stopped work on 143 manuscripts (out of 203) as politically unacceptable; even out of the 60 acceptable works, only a handful became films.[11]

Kul'tura i zhizn' wrote in August 1950:

One of the weak points of the work of the Ministry of film industry of the USSR and of the Republics is the preparation of scenarios. Deadlines are not fulfilled because of insufficiently prepared scenarios. The scenario departments of the ministries and of the studios do not attract writers and dramatists for this work. Because of the small circle of scenarists such an unhealthy situation is created that on the success or failure of the scenarist depends the enormous collective of the studio with its many sections and departments. The work has to stop and everyone wait for the finished scenario. It is obvious for everyone that the cost of one day of waiting is far greater than the making of many scenarios. The Ministry must greatly expand the preparation of scenarios, must attract authors and carefully work out thematic plans.[12]

The political demands on writers became so stringent that they were almost impossible to satisfy. As a consequence studios stood idle and the managers of cinemas complained about a shortage of films. This shortage occurred at a time when people craved to go to the cinemas. There were few entertainments available and none – aside from vodka – more popular than the cinema. People wanted to get out of their crowded, gloomy apartments. They would go to see almost anything. How did movie houses cope with the shortage? The same films had to be shown for months on end sometimes in all of the cinemas of a city. As a consequence, a new Soviet film had audiences running into the tens of millions. Most of the works of the late 1930s continued to be shown. Films such as *Happy Fellows, Volga-Volga,* and *The Deputy from the Baltic* were not taken off the program. In 1947 *Kul'tura i zhizn'* complained that audiences saw more foreign than Soviet films.[13] Of course, no new Western films were imported; what were then these foreign films about which *Kul'tura i zhizn'* was writing?

Soviet history has always been full of strange contradictions and paradoxes. At a time when Soviet artists could not work because of the heavy hand of censorship and the ever-changing political requirements, audiences did have access to films far more subversive than any native director would have dared to attempt. These films were what audiences at the time called *trofeinye fil'my* (trophy films). When the Red Army occupied Germany and the rest of Eastern Europe, it captured a great many valuables, among them films. Soviet authorities allowed some of these films to be shown, and in the immediate postwar years audiences could see both old and wartime Hollywood Tarzan adventures and German comedies made in the middle of the war. That German films could be shown at all is an interesting testimony to the nonpolitical nature of the bulk of Nazi films. One can only speculate as to why the authorities were willing to show them.[14] They were certainly well aware that any Western film would be subversive. It must have appeared worthwhile to allow the showing of these "frivolous" films in order to take away the attention of the people from their very serious problems and miseries. Ironically, precisely because of the heavy political pressure on the filmmakers, there were so few films available that now the authorities were practically compelled to provide the cinemas with something they could exhibit. The temptation to make money easily must also have been too great to resist.

Soviet periodicals and newspapers never reviewed these films. We have no audience surveys and no data showing how many people saw them. Films such as *His Butler's Sister* and *Sun Valley Serenade* were enormously popular. The evidence we have is largely anecdotal. *Kul'tura i zhizn'* in March 1947 published what purported to be a survey of letters received from readers concerning a German musical comedy made in 1944 and entitled *The Girl of My Dreams* featuring the famous Hungarian-born actress Marika Rokk.[15] If we are to believe the editor who compiled this survey, people absolutely hated the film and protested its showing. A student, S. Bernstein, from Alma Ata wrote in a typical letter: "This film is an example of the worst variant of art without ideas. The film is harmful and unnecessary, and it caters to the basest tastes."

We get an altogether different view from a story written by Bulat Okudzhava and published in *Druzhba narodov* in 1986. For him Marika Rokk was indeed "the girl of his dreams"; but not only for him alone. He writes:

That is, I did not choose the film, it was the one and only in Tbilisi for which everyone went out of their minds, the trophy film, *The Girl of My Dreams*, with the extraordinary and indescribable Marika Rokk in the main role. Normal life stopped in the city. Everyone talked about the film, they ran to see it whenever they had a chance, in the streets people whistled melodies from it, from half-open windows you could hear people playing tunes from it on the piano.[16]

We are entitled to suppose that Okudzhava's fiction is much closer to the truth than excerpts from letters published in *Kul'tura i zhizn'*. We have another bit of evidence showing the popularity of foreign films. On October 4, 1946, *Vecherniaia Moskva* published a harsh criticism of "Dom kino," the clubhouse of the workers of the film industry. M. Chistiakov wrote indignantly that the film workers, who had some autonomy in choosing what to see, in the course of the previous six months had shown sixty foreign films. The managers of "Dom kino" had the poor taste of selecting foreign films "with jazz and foxtrot" to mark the fifth anniversary of the outbreak of the war. Similarly, after Bol'shakov presented his five-year plan, the workers of the film industry instead of enjoying "some of the best products of Soviet film," were exposed to a tasteless (*poshlyi*) Western film.[17] During these bleak years the glimpses from a "decadent" West must have made an extraordinary impression. As the "anticosmopolitan" campaign gathered force, the "trophy" films disappeared. By the early 1950s, aside from a few Eastern European films, foreign films disappeared from Soviet screens.

Bringing movies to the peasantry presented special problems. Here the reconstruction after the devastation of the war was more difficult and progressed more slowly. Before the war the USSR had 9,796 village cinemas and movable projectors. The war cut the network in half. Much of the network before the war was based on movable projectors that traveled the countryside. Such relatively simple technical problems as the unavailability of generators often made projection impossible. A similar problem was that the village network did not have enough trucks. For example in Rostov province in 1947 there were 120 portable projectors, but only twelve trucks. The other machines stood idle.[18]

The war slowed down the effort to exchange silent projectors for ones capable of reproducing sound in the countryside. From the selected districts from which data are available, as late as 1947 about half of the projectors used in the countryside could still show only silent films.[19] Films reached a peasant audience usually a year or a year and a half after they were shown in the large cities. By then the copies were in poor condition.

The difficulties in making films had far-reaching consequences. Because so few films were made, young directors did not have a chance to produce independent work and so an entire generation of talent was lost. In the early 1920s the remarkable feature of Soviet film was the youth of the directors. Young people put their mark on the industry by providing it with innovation, iconoclasm, and effervescence. Now only a few experienced filmmakers had a chance to work.

Many observers had been impressed by the vigor and effectiveness of Soviet propaganda. The history of postwar films does not support such a positive evaluation. Film could not become an important weapon in the propaganda arsenal because not enough films were made and those that were made often did not reach the audiences beyond the cities. The contrast between the early years of the Soviet regime and postwar period could not be greater. During and after the Revolution the Bolsheviks were anxious to spread their message and had great, perhaps excessive, faith in the power of the moving picture as an aid. They encouraged filmmakers to experiment and, considering the circumstances, they gave impressive material support. The Stalinists, by contrast, established a static and repressive regime. There was no room in this world for cinematic art. The Stalinists feared the subversive power of cinema more than they were attracted by the opportunities it offered. The power of Stalinist propaganda was essentially negative. It was powerful because it succeeded in keeping out heterodox thought.

A Great Life

What kind of films should the directors make in the new era? What themes should they deal with? The situation was somewhat similar to that in the early 1930s. As in the time of the "cultural revolution," the first postwar year was a time of uncertainty and groping. For a while directors continued to enjoy a modicum of freedom. When the change came in the summer of 1946, and new restrictions were applied, the change was part of the reconstruction not only of Soviet cultural life but also of the entire sociopolitical order. The Bolshevik leaders welcomed the developing cold war; living in a beleaguered camp justified tightening social discipline, and they felt securer in such a world. Under the circumstances filmmaking did not simply return to the themes and styles of the prewar period. The world had changed and Soviet films were expected to reflect that change.

Of course the leaders could not tell the directors what kind of films they should make, for they did not know themselves. The filmmakers had to find that out by a process of trial and error. Party leaders interfered to the extent of saying yes and no; the "successful" film was held up as a model, and the "failure" was condemned brutally.

In August and September 1946, the Party leadership made several moves that changed the character of Soviet cultural life. This change was presumably engineered by Andrei Zhdanov, a member of the Politburo, Party chief in Leningrad, and the person responsible for ideological matters. The Party now came to be much more demanding: The choice of subjects and the ways in which the artist could deal with them came to be more narrowly defined. The first victims were two major figures of Soviet literature: Zhdanov coarsely and brutally denounced Anna Akhmatova, one of the greatest twentieth-century Soviet poets, and Mikhail Zoshchenko, the humorist. Akhmatova and Zoshchenko were then expelled from the Union of Writers. Following this attack, a resolution of the Central Committee on August 14 ordered the closing down of the literary journal *Leningrad* and the changing of the editorial board of *Zvezda*. On August 26, another resolution condemned the repertoire of theaters for being "apolitical" and for having too many "second-rate" Western plays.[20]

Next month it was the turn of the film industry. On September 4 a Central Committee resolution made an example of the film *A Great Life*, directed by L. Lukov. This film was a sequel to a rather successful work of 1938 about life of miners in the Donbass (*The Miners of Donbass*). The sequel dealt with the postwar period, and the difficulties of reconstruction.

The resolution made three criticisms, all of major significance for the future of the film industry. It criticized the film for paying too much attention to the personal experiences of individuals rather than to social problems. This was a criticism similar to the one leveled at the writers. In other words, a Soviet artist was not to be distracted by private concerns, such as love, jealousy, or death. Second, the resolution criticized the film for not showing modern mining technology but depicting workers living in filthy, dilapidated barracks, and for portraying Soviet people who had cooperated with the German occupiers. Lukov was blamed, in effect, for attempting to give a description of the Soviet world not altogether at variance with reality. This particular point was the most important. The gap between the world as it was and as it was depicted had been wide ever since the time of Stalin's "cultural revolution"; now that gap was to widen further. From this time until the death of Stalin, Soviet films dealing with contemporary themes showed an altogether imaginary country. Third, the resolution criticized the scenarists and director for not paying enough attention to the role of the Party. This issue would be repeated in connection with other works of literature and cinema.

Although the resolution devoted most space to Lukov's film, it also criticized the works of the much better known directors, Eisenstein, Pudovkin, and Kozintsev and Trauberg. Whatever one can say about the Party's attitude to the artists, it must be admitted that this attitude was egalitarian; the Party leaders took on the famous and talented as well as the second-rate. The resolution called *A Great Life* a "depraved film" but Eisenstein's *Ivan the Terrible*, Part II, Pudovkin's *Admiral Nakhimov*, and Kozintsev and Trauberg's *Simple People* were merely described as erroneous. The Party leaders scolded the world-famous artists for being ignorant, for taking a lighthearted attitude to their work, and for not having studied their subject matter. Pudovkin showed too many scenes of balls and not enough of battles. He paid too much attention to the private lives of his heroes, rather than to the accomplishments of Russian armies in the Crimean War. Eisenstein depicted Ivan the Terrible as vacillating and his private army, the *oprichniki*, as a bunch of degenerates, instead of the progressive force that, in the opinion of the Central Committee, it was. The resolution had no specific criticisms of *Simple People*. It appeared from later commentaries that the chief objection to it was the same as it was to *A Great Life:* It depicted the contemporary world too realistically. It showed the evacuation of a factory at wartime as a chaotic event.[21]

The resolution included this threat:

Workers in the arts should understand that those who continue to act irresponsibly and thoughtlessly in connection with their work will easily find themselves outside of the most advanced Soviet art and fall away. The Soviet viewer has grown up and his cultural demands have increased and the party and the state in the future will help to educate in the people good taste and high demands in the realm of arts.[22]

Unlike the attack on Zoshchenko and Akhmatova, the Central Committee resolution was not directed against individuals but against ideas. The resolution explicitly forbade the distribution of *A Great Life,* but the other films criticized could, presumably, be mended. (*A Great Life* was distributed in 1958 and at that time aroused little interest.) Lukov managed to rehabilitate himself. In 1950 he made another film about miners, *The Miners of Donbass,* which showed that he had taken the criticisms to heart. In it the mines are so modern that human beings hardly need to work. Nor did Lukov devote too much attention to "personal problems"; here the hero is the new machinery. If we were to believe Lukov's new version, life in Soviet mines was gay, easy, and free of serious conflicts. He had found the "correct" way of making movies and was properly rewarded with the Stalin Prize.

The denunciation of *Simple People* ended a twenty-year artistic collaboration between Kozintsev and Trauberg. Kozintsev went on making films, but Trauberg became a victim of the later, anticosmopolitan campaign. He returned to work only after the death of Stalin.

Pudovkin alone succeeded in remaking his film to the satisfaction of his critics. He exercised self-criticism. He wrote in *Kul'tura i zhizn'* that his first task was to understand the "dangerousness" of the errors.[23] Within a few months he reconstructed his film. He eliminated the offensive ballroom scenes, left out the episodes concerning the private lives of Nakhimov's officers, and added others showing the heroism of the admiral and of his sailors.[24] The Party rewarded him for his efforts: He too became a winner of the Stalin Prize, first class. After Eisenstein's death in 1948 he was the most prominent Soviet director and, as such, represented his country at festivals abroad; even he, however, had trouble making films. He lived until 1953, but succeeded in completing only two more projects: *Zhukovskii* in 1950 and *The Return of Vasilii Bortnikov* in the year of his death.

Eisenstein's situation was different. Months before the Central Committee resolution, it was evident that *Ivan the Terrible*, Part II, was not a film that in the vastly changed political atmosphere would be allowed to be distributed. On February 7, 1946, a meeting of filmmakers was held to discuss the recently completed work. The director himself could not participate; he had suffered a heart attack a few days before and was in the hospital. In the course of the discussion many of the later criticisms were already voiced. Eisenstein's critics, artists of much lesser talent but with a keener understanding of the politics of the day, understood that Ivan could be presented only as a fully positive character. Just as in the debate concerning *Bezhin Meadow*, I. A. Pyr'ev once again led the attacking pack. In his view Eisenstein did not depict Ivan and his followers as Russians. Others followed his lead. V. G. Zakharov, a conservative folk-music figure, who had also attacked Dmitrii Shostakovich, said:

I very much dislike this film. From the comments of the comrades it would seem that there is much in this film that is good and remarkable, but the film in fact is bad. The film is very boring. There is no Moscow, no people, no nature in it. . . . There is a great deal of formalism. Entirely formalistic are the scenes with color. . . . I did not sense there living people, but actors. Undoubtedly, here it was well said, this is not a Russian film.

A writer, L. S. Sobolev, said:

This is not a Russian film. This was also true about the first part. There is nothing Russian in it. However strange it is, the only person whom I feel to be a Russian, is the cretin Vladimir Staritskii. Ivan the Terrible is not Russian.[25]

The fate of the film was, in fact, decided in August. Bol'shakov showed the film to Stalin, and the dictator did not like it.[26]

There can be no doubt that Eisenstein wanted to satisfy his powerful critics and was willing to make all necessary compromises to make his film acceptable. He responded first by exercising self-criticism. He wrote a letter to the editorial board of *Kul'tura i zhizn'* in October 1946. The tone of this letter is Soviet. One misses in it the ambiguities of his previous self-criticism that followed the banning of *Bezhin Meadow*. Only in one paragraph can we find any attempt at self-justification:

We know Ivan the Terrible as a man with a strong will and firm character. Does that exclude from the characterization of this tsar the possibility of the existence of certain doubts? It is difficult to think that a man who did such unheard-of and unprecedented things in his time never thought over the choice of means or never had doubts about how to act in one time or another. But could it be that these possible doubts overshadowed the historical role of the historical Ivan as it was shown in this film?[27]

At the same time in order to save his work he turned to the highest judge of all, I. V. Stalin. In the past—for example, during the making of *Aleksandr Nevskii*—the Dictator had helped him. Eisenstein therefore thought that Stalin might again come to his aid.

Stalin responded by inviting him and the actor playing Ivan, Nikolai Cherkasov, to the Kremlin. Molotov and Zhdanov were also present. Evidently, Stalin considered that a film made by Eisenstein was worthy of his personal attention. The meeting took place on February 25, 1947, commencing at eleven o'clock at night. The transcript, first published in August 1988 in *Moskovskie novosti,* has a historical significance that transcends Eisenstein's film;[28] this is one of the few instances of recorded conversations with Stalin from the postwar period that have come down to us. Stalin lectured the assembled company on history. It is not surprising to learn that he was ignorant of history; after all, as a politician he had other things to worry about. It is extraordinary, however, to hear the Leader making up history in a most self-confident manner. He undoubtedly believed in what he was saying; after all, there was no one to contradict him. Increasingly, he was living in a world of his own. On this occasion, Eisenstein, understandably, was silent most of the time and Molotov and Zhdanov were merely reinforcing what their frightful chief was saying.[29]

Whether Eisenstein consciously portrayed Ivan on the pattern of the Dictator in his own age, we can never know, but it is evident that Stalin saw himself as the modern-day Ivan the Terrible. He created the figure of Ivan on the basis of his own self-image. His Ivan was a great and progressive figure, free of self-doubt, whose only "error" was not getting rid of his enemies in an even-more resolute manner. In Stalin's view, Ivan's main accomplishment was keeping foreigners out of Russia. From his remarks it is evident that Stalin was obsessed at this time by the danger of foreign influences in his country, and that the later anticosmopolitan campaign and the excesses of Russian chauvinism that characterized intellectual life came out of his own private delusions.

The conversation also had some unintentionally amusing moments. Eisenstein, anxious to save his film, asked the Dictator directly whether he had any other special instructions. Stalin responded: "I do not give you instructions, I merely give you the comments of a viewer." But the film could not be saved. Pudovkin's *Admiral Nakhimov* was an insignificant film, devoid of the individual style that characterized the director's earlier work. Whether changes were introduced in the finished work made little difference from an artistic point of view. By contrast, *Ivan the Terrible* was a masterpiece, the work of a great director at the top of his form. It had all the originality of his previous work, combined with attention to psychological detail, which was new. Eisenstein had never produced as compelling a portrait of a human being as he did here.

Admiral Nakhimov could be saved by cutting and adding new scenes.

The situation was different with *Ivan the Terrible*. First of all, it is difficult to imagine that Eisenstein could make a film, even if he wanted to, that was completely bland stylistically, as was required at the time. Also, what Eisenstein's critics attacked was the very conception of Ivan, a man beset with doubts, a tsar who was ultimately a tragic figure (Fig. 44). In order to change that conception, it would have been necessary to make a different film, a film without subtlety and artistic interest. Ivan the Terrible as a positive hero, a progressive figure in history, as it was demanded of Eisenstein was not only historically altogether false but not a topic for an interesting film.

Eisenstein's illness prevented him from remaking his film. He died in February 1948. The audiences had the first opportunity to see the the great director's masterpiece only ten years after his death.

The anticosmopolitan campaign

The September 4, 1946, resolution of the Central Committee defined the primary characteristics of Soviet film during the last years of Stalin's life. During 1948–9, however, the regime initiated a campaign against "cosmopolitanism" that devastated Soviet intellectual life, arts and sciences alike. Its influence, of course, was also felt in the cinema world. This new outburst of ideological belligerence occasioned some of the strangest aberrations of the late Stalinist age. Paradoxically, Lenin's revolution, carried out in the name of internationalism, within three decades produced the most xenophobic modern society. This xenophobia was born out of insecurity: The leaders considered any contact with foreigners inherently subversive; they saw in any recognition given to the achievements of foreigners an implicit criticism of the Soviet system.

The campaign emphasized two themes. One of these, anti-Semitism, was largely implicit; the other, the insistence on the superiority of Russian ways (past and present), was loud and noisy.

It is impossible to date the appearance of anti-Semitism in Soviet governmental policy. Strange as it may seem, the war against Hitler was a major contributing factor. One can only speculate. It may be that those responsible for propaganda believed that Hitler's identification of "Bolshevik" and "Jewish" was effective and had to be combated. Perhaps the propagandists themselves were influenced by this central aspect of Nazi ideology. As the war was ending, anti-Semitism became an ever stronger force. In the films made in this period, it had only a negative manifestation: Jewish characters did not appear in Soviet films, nor were Jews acknowledged as special victims of Nazism in newsreels and documentaries.

Anti-Semitism, however, touched the lives and careers of individual filmmakers. Surely, in the discussions concerning the second part of *Ivan the Terrible,* the repeated assertions that Eisenstein did not make a "Russian"

Figure 44.   Cherkasov in the role of Ivan: *Ivan the Terrible* (1944–6).

film was a reference to the Jewishness of the director.[30] Romm wrote in 1962:

I am not a Zionist, but a Communist. After 1917 I completely forgot that I was a Jew. I was reminded about it in 1944, when the idea for the project "Russfil'm" arose. This project would have allowed directors Pyr'ev, Aleksandrov, Gerasimov, Savchenko, Babochkin, and Zharov to work in Moscow. But directors Eisenstein, Raizman, Roshal', Romm and others with similar names were to stay in the studios of the national republics, in Alma-Ata and Tashkent. This project was not realized, but in the following years I was frequently reminded by various means that I was Jewish. This took place in connection with cosmopolitanism, in connection with organizing courts of honor, at the time of organizing my filming group and on the occasion of the case of the "killer doctors."[31]

The campaign against, as it was called at the time, groveling (*nizkopoklonstvo*) in front of the West and anti-Semitism were connected. The insistence that Russians had always been the most advanced and progressive people in the world and that foreigners had always wanted to take advantage of them and could not be trusted was aimed at Jews, among others. The Russian people, and at this time also the members of the Soviet hier-

archy, did not regard Jews as their fellow countrymen. Not all the victims
of the anticosmopolitan campaign were Jewish, but, judging on the basis of
their names, most of them were.

The September 1946 resolution scolded erring comrades. In 1948 and
1949 the tone of discourse changed: Those under attack were no longer
called "comrades" but described as agents of the enemy. Ideas and thoughts
were attributed to them that they obviously did not hold, and, of course,
they had no chance to defend themselves.

The campaign consisted of a series of newspaper and journal articles and
meetings that denounced the "cosmopolitans." The defenders of Stalinist
orthodoxy formed a composite picture from the speeches and writings of
their victims and, in Stalinist fashion, held the accused responsible for each
other.[32] The "cosmopolitan" was accused of propagating the idea that there
was a "world cinema" and that artistic standards applied independently of
ideology. The "proof" for such an accusation was a favorable reference to
a Western artist. Because by this time such a favorable reference was extremely rare, the ideological crusaders had to be satisfied with tributes to
two giants of the film art, D. W. Griffith and Charles Chaplin. The incon-
trovertibly correct assertion that Soviet filmmakers had learned from Griffith was now considered to be a proof of lack of patriotism. The Stalinists
were not impressed by the sad irony that at this very time Chaplin's films
could not be shown in the United States because he was considered to be
too much of a leftist and an admirer of the Soviet Union. Another serious
charge against the imaginary cosmopolitan was that he did not appreciate
contemporary Russian films. The publicists dug up criticisms of recent Soviet works by "cosmopolitans" and presented these criticisms as yet other
examples of lack of patriotism: The offenders had elitist tastes and therefore
did not share the "healthy" opinions of "honest" Soviet people.

Among the directors the most prominent victims were Trauberg, who
was most heavily attacked, Dziga Vertov, who had made no films since the
end of the war, and Iutkevich. All three were Jewish. Among the scenarists
and critics, the butt of the most vicious attacks was M. Bleiman, but N.
Kovarskii, N. Otten, V. Sutyrin, and N. Lebedev were also denounced. No
previous services were taken into account. That Trauberg had been the co-
director in the 1930s of the Maxim trilogy, among the most popular films
and made entirely in the Stalinist spirit, did not help. Nor did it count in
Bleiman's favor that he wrote the script for *The Great Citizen,* a film that
justified the purge trials. These prominent directors, scriptwriters, and critics were attacked not for their films but for their writings.

To appreciate the flavor of the attack, it is necessary to quote:

Director L. Trauberg, clearly a formalist, in the course of many years has taken a
hostile position to Soviet art. He grovels before American cinema, and he has viciously attacked all good Soviet films. He made a fully formalist film, *Simple People,*
which was sharply condemned by the Ts. K. VKP (b) [Central Committee of the

Communist Party] and was not allowed to appear in the cinemas. Tauberg started his activity as a lecturer. In his public appearances he slandered Soviet cinema, glorified reactionary American directors, and recommended that we learn from them. In this dirty, antipatriotic activity his collaborators were M. Bleiman and N. Kovarskii. They, just like him, groveled before American film and did not notice the successes of Soviet cinema. In his book about the American director Griffith, Bleiman called this reactionary director, who advocated racist theories in his films, "the father" of world cinematography.[33]

The Soviet political system was effective in finding accomplices. In the spring of 1949, meetings of filmmakers were called in order to denounce the "enemy." *Kul'tura i zhizn'* reported on the meeting of creative workers in cinematography held in Moscow in March 1949:

Director I. Pyr'ev in a brilliant speech showed convincingly that soviet film is a profoundly national, popular art, which grew up and strengthened under the leadership of the Bolshevik Party. Comrade Pyr'ev angrily branded as antipatriot Trauberg and his followers, who are attempting with their dirty hands to prevent the development of Soviet film art. . . . Director V. Pudovkin gave an angry speech in which he unmasked cosmopolitans and aesthetes of all kinds. "We must remove from our work all cosmopolitan and antipatriotic little ideas" – said Comrade Pudovkin. We must demand from all artists, a moral-political cleanliness, a struggle for the creation of new cultural values for our people, and participation in the building of Communism. . . . Instead of helping to carry all over the world the flag of the most advanced Soviet film art – said the writer, K. Simonov in his speech, – these little people got on Hollywood's bandwagon and are allowed to call "art" only what compromised the great name of Soviet film. They attempted to persuade the Soviet people to forget about their national traditions in art.[34]

The anticosmopolitan campaign made a great impact on Soviet cinema: Most films of the era expressed some of the themes of the campaign. The exhibition of patriotic feelings could never be overdone. The films about the admirals Nakhimov and Ushakov showed the heroism of Russian sailors and wisdom of Russian leaders. We learn from other films that Musorgskii and Glinka found inspiration in the music of the folk and that Belinskii attacked his fellow intellectuals for admiring everything Western. The films taught that foreigners should not be trusted. We see in *Przhevalskii* that this Russian explorer of Central Asia was greeted as a friend by the natives, but his work was hindered by the English. *The Fall of Berlin* and *Meeting of the Elbe* demonstrated that foreigners had evil intentions against the fatherland of socialism.

A. Room's film, *The Court of Honor,* made in 1948, was entirely and explicitly devoted to the illustration of the themes of the anticosmopolitan campaign. The film tells the story of two Soviet scientists, who are on the verge of a major scientific discovery. (Rather anticlimactically, the discovery turns out to be only a pain killer.) On the occasion of an American trip the Soviet scientists discuss their work with the foreign press. One of them,

Losev, who turns out to be an unprincipled scoundrel, enunciates the idea against which the entire film is aimed: Science knows no frontiers. In fact, Losev is vain and craves the admiration of foreigners. The Americans are very anxious to get hold of this discovery. They take advantage of the errors of these two men and, masked as scientists but in fact common spies, penetrate the new and beautifully equipped Soviet laboratory. The Americans need more information concerning manufacturing. They, of course, do not succeed: The vigilance of honest Soviet people stops them and they are unmasked. The matter is given over to a court of honor, a Soviet institution of the time. Losev's case is criminal and he cannot be saved, but the other scientist, Dobrotvorskii, who recognizes the magnitude of his errors, is taken back into the bosom of Soviet society.

This is a very revealing film. Russian publicists projected their fears and concerns on the enemy. In reality it was the Russians who were impressed by American science and technology and interested in industrial spying. Here it is inverted: The Americans are amazed how modern and well equipped a Soviet laboratory is. The film also contains amusing little details. A positive character, one whose vigilance foils the spies, castigates her husband, a scientist: "How was this possible? At an official banquet, you took a business card from a foreigner, which had his private number! Just like a child!" Indeed.

The story of *The Court of Honor* was an improbable one. We get a much better sense of the cases which did come under the competence of the "courts of honor" from the memoirs of Mikhail Romm, who tells a Kafkaesque story. In 1945 Romm, carrying out an official instruction from the Society for Contacts Abroad, VOKS, attempted to persuade the famous emigré actor, Mikhail Chekhov, to return to the motherland. Romm, even in 1945, was aware of the delicacy of the task and therefore submitted to his superiors several versions of this invitation. Two years later – ironically at a time when he was making *The Russian Question*, a film about political oppression in America – Bol'shakov, the minister of Film Industry, made a political affair out of the invitation and was planning to submit Romm's case to a "court of honor." Versions of the letter that were never sent in 1947 appeared to be examples of "groveling before the West." Romm was fortunate to be able to save himself. He threatened to implicate Pudovkin, who was to be one of the judges. It turned out that it was Pudovkin who in 1945 entrusted Romm with the writing of the letter. Pudovkin, in order to save himself, prevailed on the minister to drop the case.[35]

After the passage of four decades, life in the Soviet Union during Stalin's last years appears almost surreal. The issues discussed in the press and at meetings seem to us without substance, and the tone so outlandish that they border on the ridiculous. It is difficult for the historian to recapture the atmosphere of those meetings and the feelings of the participants that surface in the record only once in a while. On occasion, however, one can sense the fear that was everywhere and in everyone. We must try to put ourselves in the place of people who were being denounced, even if, on occasion, these were the same people who just a few weeks before were doing the denouncing.

Notes

1 Mira Liehm and Antonin Liehm, *The Most Important Art: Eastern European Film after 1945*, University of California Press, Berkeley, 1977, p. 68.
2 "Bol'she vysokokhudozhestvennykh kinofil'mov!" *Kul'tura i zhizn'*, Oct. 1, 1947.
3 *Sovetskie khudozhestvennye fil'my. Annotirovannyi katalog*, 4 vols. Vol. 2 Iskusstvo, Moscow, 1961–8. Because there is considerable confusion concerning what should be counted as a film, we find different figures in different sources. According to the four-volume history of Soviet films, in 1945 the USSR produced twenty films; in 1946 twenty-one; in 1947 twenty-seven; in 1948 seventeen; in 1949 sixteen; in 1950 fifteen; in 1951 six; in 1952 eighteen. *Ocherki istorii sovetskogo kino. vol 3: 1946–1956*, Iskusstvo, Moscow, 1961, p. 15.
4 *Ocherki* 3: 15.
5 G. V. Aleksandrov, *Epokha i kino*, Politizdat, Moscow, 1983, p. 282. Aleksandrov was the artistic director of Mosfil'm.
6 Jay Leyda, *Kino: A History of Russian and Soviet Film*. Collier Books, New York, 1960, p. 392.
7 "Nashi blizhaishie zadachi," *Iskusstvo kino* 1: 4–5, 1945. Bol'shakov had started his career as a worker in a Tula armament factory. He received Party education in the 1920s. He was named chairman of the Committee on Cinematography in 1939 and Minister of Film Industry in 1946.
8 *Kul'tura i zhizn'*, June 30, 1948.
9 "Bol'she khoroshikh kinofil'mov," *Kul'tura i zhizn'*, Aug. 31, 1950, and Iu Kalashnikov and G. Mdivani, "Vazhnye voprosy proizvodstva kinofil'mov," *Kul'tura i zhizn'*, Jan. 11, 1951.
10 I. Bol'shakov, "Zadachi novogo goda," *Iskusstvo kino* 1: 3, 1953.
11 "Za vysokoe ideino-khudozhestvennoe kachestvo fil'mov," *Iskusstvo kino* 4: 5, 1948. Also, Arkadii Perventsev, "Za dal'neishii pod'em kinodramaturgii," *Kul'tura i zhizn'*, Jan. 11, 1949.
12 "Bol'she khoroshikh kinofil'mov," *Kul'tura i zhizn'*, Aug. 31 1950.
13 "O merakh po uluchsheniiu kinoobsluzhivaniia naseleniia v 1947 godu," *Kul'tura i zhizn'*, May 30, 1947.
14 Maia Turovskaia, a prominent Soviet sociologist of cinema, in a paper presented at a conference of Soviet and American film historians in Washington in December 1990, explained that although on occasion the German films were presented without subtitles and at times were accompanied by propaganda speeches, the audiences, starved of entertainment, flocked to see these films. She organized a film festival of Nazi and Soviet propaganda films in Moscow in July 1989. The catalog of that festival includes thirty-five Nazi films that were shown in the Soviet Union between 1947 and 1949. Judging from the titles, the vast majority of these were mindless entertainment films. *Kino totalitarnoi epokhi, 1933–1945* (in Russian and in German), Moscow, 1989.

15 *Kul'tura i zhizn'*, Mar. 21, 1947, p. 4.

16 Bulat Okudzhava, "Devushka moei mechty," *Druzhba narodov* 10: 43–44, 1986. In this moving short story the young hero's mother returns from a concentration camp. The young man wants to share with his mother what was most valuable in his life and takes her to see this film. The incongruity is overwhelming.

17 *Vecherniaia Moskva*, Oct. 4. 1946, p. 4.

18 "Sel'skim kinoperedvizhkam nuzhny elektrostantsii," *Kul'tura i zhizn'*, March 30, 1947, and N. Cheburakov, "Uluchshit' kinoobsluzhivanie sel'skikh raionov," *Kul'tura i zhizn'*, Mar. 10, 1949.

19 "Bezzabotnoe otnoshenie k rabote sel'skoi kinoseti," *Kul'tura i zhizn'*, Oct. 10, 1947.

20 Werner G. Hahn, *Postwar Soviet Politics: The Fall of Zhdanov and the Defeat of Moderation, 1946–1953*, Cornell University Press, Ithaca, 1982, pp. 58–9.

21 "Za vysokuiu ideinost' sovetskogo kinoiskusstva," an unsigned editorial in *Iskusstvo kino*, Jan. 1947, p. 6.

22 "O kinofil'me 'Bol'shaia zhizn'," *Iskusstvo kino*, Jan. 1947, pp. 1–2.

23 "Uroki postanovki fil'ma 'Admiral Nakhimov,' " *Kul'tura i zhizn'*, Jan. 11, 1947.

24 A Karaganov, *Vsevolod Pudovkin*, Iskusstvo, Moscow, 1983, pp. 227–32.

25 R. Iurenev, *Sergei Eizenshtein. Zamysly: Fil'my. Metod*, vol. 2, *1930–1948*, Iskusstvo, Moscow, 1988, pp. 276–9. Iurenev's material concerning the meeting comes from the central state (TsGALI) archives.

26 Ibid., p. 280.

27 Eisenstein's letter was published in *Kul'tura i zhizn'* on Oct. 20, 1946. This letter was translated and printed in *New Leader*, vol. 29, Dec. 7, 1946, and also in Louis Cohen, *The Cultural-Political Traditions and Developments of the Soviet Cinema, 1917–1972*, Arno Press, New York, 1974, pp. 651–4.

28 *Moskovskie novosti*, Aug. 7, 1988, pp. 8–9.

29 On Stalin identifying himself with Ivan the Terrible, see Robert C. Tucker, *Stalin in Power: Revolution from Above, 1928–1941*, Norton, New York, 1990.

30 To be sure, only Eisenstein's father was Jewish. From the point of view of the anti-Semites, however, he was a Jew.

31 *Sovetskii ekran* 11: 19, 1988. *Sovetskii ekran* published materials from Romm's personal archives. This excerpt was taken from Romm's notes to a letter he wrote to the Central Committee of the Party in November 1962. The "killer doctors" were victims of Stalin's last purge. Prominent doctors, almost all of them Jewish, were accused of attempted medical murder of important Soviet politicians. After Stalin's death, the doctors were freed.

32 "Za sovetskoe patrioticheskoe iskusstvo – protiv kosmopolitiov!" *Iskusstvo kino* 1: 1–3, 1949. V. Shcherbina, "O gruppe estetstvuiushchikh kosmopolitiov v kino," *Iskusstvo kino* 1: 14–16, 1949. A. Abramov, "Rabolepstvuiushchie kosmopolity," *Iskusstvo kino* 1: 17–19, 1949. "Za dal'neishii rastsvet sovetskogo kinoiskusstva," *Kul'tura i zhizn'*, Mar. 10, 1949.

33 "Za dal'neishii raztsvet sovetskogo kinoiskusstva," *Kul'tura i zhizn'*, Mar. 10, 1949.

34 Ibid.

35 M. Romm, "Kak menia predavali sudu chesti," *Sovetskii ekran* 11: 16–18, 1988.

CHAPTER 11

The nadir, 1945–1953

According to the Catalog of Soviet Feature Films, the studios of the USSR made 165 films during 1946–53.[1] However, only 124 of these were feature films as the term is normally used: The rest were films of photographed concerts or theatrical performances and experimental shorts. Many films made in the studios of the national republics received only limited distribution. The remaining films that were widely distributed fell into a few categories; Soviet cinema had become homogeneous.

Tightening the screws of the totalitarian system reduced the number of topics considered fit for discussion. For example, in the 1930s Soviet directors had made a few films about social problems such as the integration of Jews or Gypsies into society. They also had made some movies that were difficult to categorize, such as the surreal *Lieutenant Kizhe,* a genuine oddity, based on a fable by Iu. Tynianov. (This film told the story of a nonexistent soldier in the age of Tsar Paul.) By contrast, in the tightly controlled postwar world there was no room for such works. Perhaps the concerns of the audience had also changed. Flying, a favorite topic before the war, was no longer featured, nor were the adventures of geologists working in exotic terrains. Even the great flood of movies about the Revolution finally came to an end. The only significant film on this topic was M. Chiaureli's *The Unforgettable Year, 1919,* made in 1951. Internal subversion, a favorite topic of scenarists in the 1930s, had clearly lost its appeal by the postwar period.

Even in the 1930s relatively few films had dealt with workers; after the war this aspect of Soviet life almost completely disappeared from view. Among the 124 films there were only 4 dealing with workers, and of these *The Great Life* and *The Fires of Baku* were not distributed. The remaining two films were Lukov's *The Miners of Donbass* and A. Stolper's *Far from Moscow,* a film based on the novel of B. Azhaev. Stolper's film aimed to show that in wartime the production of oil was just as important as fighting the enemy at the front. Postwar films certainly did not celebrate the nominal ruling class, the proletariat.

The peasantry fared somewhat better: Eighteen films had to do with life in the collective farms. Although not widely distributed, several films were made in the republican studios (Latvian, Lithuanian, Estonian, and Ukrainian) depicting the establishment of "socialist agriculture" in these newly conquered territories. The few comedies of this period were mostly set in the countryside. The most famous of these, *Kuban Cossacks* made by Pyr'ev in 1950, purported to show the happy life and competition of two collective farms. In this film the sun is always shining, the peasants live in beautiful, airy, and spacious houses, and they sing and dance a great deal. The conflict between the two farms is resolved by one chairperson marrying the other (Fig. 45).

Another segment of society, the life of the intelligentsia could be glimpsed in seven publicistic films. These celebrated the lives and discoveries of physicians and scientists. However, the only films from this period that we can watch without embarrassment today were made for children. *The Adventures of Nasredin*, made in Tashkent in 1946 and directed by N. Ganiev, was the best and most popular among these. The film amused adults and children by showing the pranks of a Central Asian hero. Two works by Aleksandr Ptushko were also successful: *Stone Flower*, largely made in Prague in 1946, and *Sadko*, which was completed in 1952.

The new age produced new genres. The important, most discussed, and typical films of the period fall into three categories: "artistic documentaries," publicistic films, and film biographies.

"Artistic documentaries": The portrait of Stalin

The subject matter of "artistic documentaries" was the most significant moments of contemporary history. In order to be worthy of their topics, these films were made on a monumental scale. Each had a cast of thousands, and *The Fall of Berlin* and *The Battle of Stalingrad* were so long that they had to be divided into two parts. The viewer was supposed to see history unfolding in front of his eyes. A favorite device, borrowed from Hollywood films of the 1930s, was to begin with the image of an enormous book gradually turning its pages until they come to life.

There were few "artistic documentaries," but these received extremely wide distribution and enthusiastic reviews. The leaders of the regime wanted every Soviet person to see them. Students from schools and workers from factories marched to movie theaters. These films were *The Oath* (1946), *The Third Blow* (1948), *The Fall of Berlin* (1949), and *The Battle of Stalingrad* (1949). Every one of these films depicted World War II and did so from the same perspective. The difficult early period of the war was passed over in silence and only victories were shown. The directors showed the war from the point of view of the headquarters, not the ordinary soldier. Thus the viewer got the impression that in winning the war what mattered was not the heroism of the simple soldier, who remained faceless, but brilliant lead-

Figure 45.   Happy collective farm chairpersons: *Kuban Cossacks* (1950).

ership. We see Stalin and his generals poring over maps, tanks rolling across meadows, guns firing, and houses burning.

These four films were primarily about I. V. Stalin. Interestingly, the Stalin cult in movies developed relatively late and evolved in stages. Although his picture had been carried on posters and in newspapers daily since 1929, and poets and journalists had been competing with one another for words to describe his genius, Stalin did not appear in feature films until the late 1930s. *Lenin in October* (made by Romm in 1937), *The Vyborg Side* (Kozintsev and Trauberg, 1938), *Man with a Gun* (Iutkevich, 1938), and *Iakov Sverdlov* (Iutkevich, 1940) represented the first stage in Stalin's cinematic career.

From the very outset the Stalin cult in movies differed in content and style from Hitler's cult. Hitler loved to harangue the masses and see himself in newsreels. He was an actor. Stalin, by contrast, had little desire for such satisfaction. A pockmarked little man, speaking poor Russian, and an indifferent orator, he apparently did not want to be seen in close-up on the screen. On rare occasions when he did appear, the audience gasped in amazement: This was not the way they had imagined their leader.[2] Because he hardly ever appeared in public after 1945, there is little newsreel footage showing the actual person. Instead Stalin had an idealized image created for himself that bore little resemblance to the historical figure. This imaginary leader fit well into the world of Soviet film, where equally imaginary, happy peasants competed with one another to produce more food for the happy factory workers. It was appropriate that a mythical leader should head a mythical society.

In the films of the late 1930s we can already see many characteristics of the cult at the height of its development.[3] These films dealt with episodes from the Revolution. They vastly exaggerated Stalin's role and depicted him as the closest comrade of Lenin. The directors conveyed to their audience that Stalin was the legitimate heir of Lenin, the Lenin of today. Yet, however much these movies overstated the role of Stalin, they were not about him; he was still not the central figure.

During World War II agitators found it advantageous to underplay Communism in their ideological appeals, but they did not deemphasize the role of the Leader. On the contrary, the cult of Stalin as a surrogate ideology developed further. It was at this time that Stalin became a brilliant general. After all, during the war Soviet soldiers were being sent to battle "For the Motherland and for Stalin." The two wartime films depicting Stalin, *Aleksander Parkhomenko* (Lukov, 1942) and especially *The Defense of Tsaritsyn* (Vasil'ev "brothers" 1942), show him in his capacity as a military leader.

Of all the pre-1945 movies it was M. Chiaureli's *The Great Dawn* (1938) that best anticipated the future image of Stalin. In *The Great Dawn* Chiaureli allowed his fellow Georgian to step out of Lenin's shadow for the first time. It is to him, Stalin, not Lenin, that the revolutionaries look for leadership. Building up his hero, Chiaureli gives Lenin a lesser role.

Among film directors Chiaureli would become the major architect of the Stalin cult. Such a career could hardly have been predicted from his early film, *Khabarda,* a silent film made in Tbilisi in 1931. This film showed a highly individual, even idiosyncratic talent. Not surprisingly, it was attacked at the time for its "formalism." Actually, *Khabarda* was one of the more amusing Soviet silents, satirizing "bourgeois" nationalism and self-important intellectuals. In the Stalinist age, however, irony and idiosyncrasy were rejected in favor of piety and a total subjugation of individual style. Chiaureli made the sacrifice and reached the pinnacle of success.

It is worthwhile to quote extensively from an article he wrote in *Iskusstvo kino* in 1947 to convey the spirit in which he approached his work:

Many Soviet artists saw Comrade Stalin frequently, had conversations with him, heard his voice, looked into his eyes, saw his warm smile, felt his handshake. In the simplicity of his words there is the wisdom of the ages; in his eyes there is the brightness of genius; in his gestures there is self-confidence; in his dealings with you there is the simplicity of a great human being. How to show in art the magnificence of this simplicity? Here in front of you is a person who comprehends with the profundity of a philosopher the complex organism of the universe, our world, the relationship of classes, societies and states. In front of you is a person who comprehends the incomprehensible, who is a carrier of great ideas and the representative of the moving force of history. He calmly and thoughtfully converses with you, and in his appearance there is nothing extraordinary, he does not seem to differ from any Soviet person, worker, peasant, scholar, artist. For all of these people he is close, comprehensible, – a family member. Involuntarily you begin to think that Stalin is more than a human being. This thought arises from the impossibility of comprehending that everything great is simple. Although your mind affirms that this is so, your feelings search for some sort of outward sign of greatness. No! In spite of everything, he is different from ordinary people even in appearance. I long looked at his hands, followed his every movement, wanted to preserve in my mind even the smallest details of his appearance, gestures, every line in his face, his expressions, his way of speaking. And all this time the thought did not leave me that unconsciously I wanted to "bring down to earth" the figure of this great man, to bring his figure into our everyday language. But that very moment I understood the grandiosity of his work and once again felt everything about him is extraordinary: his hands, his smile, his eyes. Please forgive me, my artist colleagues, but none of us has succeeded. None of the portraits of Stalin can be regarded as satisfactory. None of us artists succeeded in transmitting the warm glow in his eyes, the charm of his smile, the hidden, deep humor of his well-chosen words, those hardly noticeable details which belong only to him, which make up the figure, which is simple, but epic.[4]

After the war Chiaureli became the most prominent director of the age because he captured better than anyone the spirit of Stalinism. His film, *The Oath*, which appeared in the movie houses in July 1946, was a turning point in the history of Soviet cinema. The scenario of the film was written by the director together with the prominent writer, P. Pavlenko. *The Oath* set the tone for many others to follow.

The film has neither plot nor characters in the conventional sense. The title refers to Stalin's vow at Lenin's funeral, that the Party would remain faithful to the dead leader's teachings. The film illustrates in a posterlike fashion a Stalinist interpretation of Soviet history from 1924 to 1945. Chiaureli shows us a "typical" Stalingrad family, the Petrovs. The characters represent social types; one son, for example, is a worker, and another is an intellectual. Chiaureli makes not the slightest attempt at individual characterization. The head of the family, a Communist, is murdered by *kulaks*. His wife, Varvara, the central figure, stands for the heroism of Russian women. She sends her sons to fight for the fatherland. The characters have no functions in the development of a nonexistent story. The scenes have no internal logic, but are simple demonstrations of Stalinist themes.

The real hero is Stalin himself. *The Oath* was the first film devoted entirely to him. In the portrayal of Stalin, Chiaureli was a pathfinder. Designing the prototype of Stalin as a film character, Chiaureli made a contribution of great ideological significance: He deified Stalin. This deification was not simply an added element in the ideology of the age; it was its very heart.

Soviet citizens learned that not only individuals but the "masses" also did not matter. The lives of the people were in the hands of Stalin, who was no longer a man, but a god, one who did not appear in person among them but had to be venerated in the form of innumerable busts and pictures, that is, icons.

In *The Oath* it is obviously the Leader who is making history. It is he who inspires people to build new factories and to fight for the fatherland. Giving a speech on Red Square at the time of Lenin's death (a speech that he did not make at that place), Stalin is photographed against the background of the Kremlin, larger than life. In the portrayal of Stalin the director dispensed even with the appearance of realism. During the war the Leader receives Varvara Petrovna in the Kremlin. Although she is only a simple worker of no particular rank or achievement, Stalin explains to her the international situation and the prospects of winning the war. He makes Varvara Petrovna feel at home in the Kremlin.

Pavlenko and Chiaureli surpassed themselves in *The Fall of Berlin* (1949–50) (Fig. 46). This was the ultimate Stalinist film; further than that it was impossible to go. Like *The Oath,* it shows two parallel but connected stories: One is the love and struggles of two simple people, a worker and a teacher, and the other, Stalin's winning of World War II. But even in the first story line, Stalin as an image, as an idea, is always present. Like other war films, the opening scenes depict the wonderful life of the Soviet people before the Nazi invasion. Children sing merrily: "Life is happiness." We see the peaceful, constructive work in a modern steel mill. We learn about the Stakhanovite, Aleksei Ivanov, the typical, heroic Soviet worker. That he is more – or less – than an individual character and has symbolic significance are soon conveyed in a none too subtle fashion: We learn that he was born on November 7, 1917; his name, Ivanov, is also a clue. (In English it might be John Doe.) A teacher, the lovely Natasha, is to give a speech on a festive occasion, to honor Aleksei Ivanov. In fact, she is addressing not her listeners but a portrait of Stalin. There are tears of happiness in her eyes as she looks at the icon. She speaks with religious ecstasy: "Who gave us such a day? The greatest happiness would be ours if He could be with us! Long live Stalin!" We understand that Stalin, if only in the form of an icon, is always present.

We see a sweet love story. Aleksei falls in love with Natasha, but he is a shy man with little self-confidence and does not know how to tell her. He is afraid that she prefers a concert pianist, who is also interested in her. These scenes are followed by a sequence, which, in retrospect, is the most unconsciously amusing in all Stalinist films. Aleksei, the Stakhanovite, is summoned to Stalin's presence. The icon now comes to life in a hagiographic episode. Stalin is tending his fruit trees (Fig. 47). Birds are singing. In the background we hear the soft singing of women – surely they must be angels. Understandably, Aleksei is dumbstruck; he wants to run away. We in the audience sympathize; we could do no better. But Comrade Stalin comes up

Figure 46.   Stalin smiling in *The Fall of Berlin* (1949).

Figure 47.   Stalin tending his garden in *The Fall of Berlin* (1949).

to him and, with his simple, fatherly manner, immediately puts him at ease. There can be no secrets left in Aleksei's heart, and as one would talk to God, he tells the Supreme Leader about his love for Natasha. Stalin utters these memorable lines: "She will love you, but if not, just let me know about it." And, of course, the love story turns out well. The two young people confess their love to each other.

Now the mood of the film changes: The Germans attack; wheat fields burn; the little town is bombed and later occupied by the Nazis. Aleksei and Natasha continue to figure in the story, but from this point on they recede into the background: Enslaved in Germany, she symbolizes the suffering, endurance, and constancy of the Soviet people, while the wounded Aleksei represents the courage, patriotism, and strength of the Soviet soldier. He is present at the battle of Moscow and at Stalingrad, and he says to General Chuikov: "It is rumored that Comrade Stalin is here." Chuikov answers: "Comrade Stalin is always with us!" (This very same sentence is spoken by Malenkov in *The Battle of Stalingrad* as he addresses workers going into battle.) It is Aleksei's unit that liberates the camp in which Natasha is kept, and, of course, he is present in the final battle for the Reichstag in Berlin.

The war is Stalin's. It is his genius alone that matters. The generals report to him, and he alone makes strategy. He tells Zhukov how many artillery pieces the army must deploy per square mile. The generals turn to him with questions, and he answers them in a slow but decisive manner. They can only mutter to themselves: "Yes! I see! Brilliant." But the enemy is also in awe of Stalin's genius. The German generals tell Hitler that a war against Stalin is hopeless. At the end of the film when Hitler is confronted with the inevitable end, he delivers his final accolade: "Stalin has defeated every-one!" The film concludes with Stalin literally descending from on high. As he steps from the plane, the soldiers shout "Hurray," and their shouts blend with victorious music. People from all nations greet him. Natasha runs up to him and kisses him.

According to Pavlenko and Chiaureli, the Soviet Union was fighting not only against Nazi Germany, but against Hitler's covert allies, the United States, Great Britain, and the Vatican. As the representative of the Vatican brings greetings from the pope, Hitler tells him that he would look well in a Nazi uniform. From this film we learn that the British supplied Germany through Sweden with chrome and wolfram, essential raw materials for the war industry. The British, just like the Nazis, feared Stalin and were im-mensely impressed by his military talent. Hitler in the last minutes of his life still hoped that he would be saved from the Russians by the Americans.

Although no other films matched let alone surpassed *The Fall of Berlin* in Stalinist piety, the figure of Stalin in films such as *The Third Blow* and *The Battle of Stalingrad,* played by different actors, nevertheless is recogniz-ably the same person (Fig. 48). The image allowed only small variations. In every film Stalin speaks slowly, thus conveying the weight of his every utter-

Figure 48.   Stalin and Malenkov in *The Battle of Stalingrad* (1949).

ance. He is always calm, he is always working tirelessly, and he can always tell the next move of the enemy. He is surrounded by people whose eyes light up at every new manifestation of his genius.

In *The Fall of Berlin* Stalin was played by M. Gelovani, who played the same role in approximately twenty other films.[5] His interpretation came to be regarded as the definitive one, and he received the Stalin Prize for it. But he was not the only one to play Stalin. In *Iakov Sverdlov* it was A. Koba-ladze, in *Lenin in October* and *Aleksandr Parkhomenko* it was S. Gol'd-shtab (a Jewish Stalin!), and in *The Battle of Stalingrad* and *The Third Blow* it was A. Dikii. However, aside from some mannerisms of speech and gesture, it mattered little who was the actor. Playing the Supreme Leader imposed severe limitations on the work of the artist. Given the need to calculate carefully every gesture, given the pompous, wooden lines they had to utter, it is impossible to blame the actors for not portraying a believable character.

Publicistic film: The portrait of the enemy

The postwar Soviet regime did not hold purge trials. As those murderous spectacles disappeared from public life, so did the fixation on spies, saboteurs, and internal enemies of various sorts. Judging purely on the basis of contemporary films, the regime that murdered millions of its citizens ruled over a conflictless society. The "enemy," so very important both for good drama and also for the cohesion of the Soviet order, was now almost always foreign. In those postwar films that were made as contributions to various Soviet propaganda campaigns, the Soviet hero always defeated a foreign enemy.

There were few publicistic films, but these were important because they received wide distribution and extensive discussion in the press. Films such as *The Court of Honor* (Romm, 1948), *The Russian Question* (Romm, 1947), *The Conspiracy of the Doomed* (Kalatozov, 1950), *Meeting on the Elbe* (Aleksandrov, 1949) and *The Secret Mission* (Room, 1950) were among the best-known works of the period. These films necessarily differed from one another more than the "artistic" documentaries did. They each dealt with a contemporary issue: *The Court of Honor* was a contribution to the struggle against "cosmopolitans"; *The Russian Question* showed how anti-Sovietism was created and encouraged by American imperialists; *Conspiracy of the Doomed* was a peculiar, Soviet version of the political struggles that had recently occurred in occupied Eastern Europe (Fig. 49); and *The Secret Mission* dealt with Anglo–American treachery during the past war. In spite of their widely different topics, the message was always the same: Russian ways were superior, the Soviet people were courageous, patriotic, and handsome, and foreigners were treacherous and infinitely mean and cruel.

The most ambitious of the publicistic films was *Meeting on the Elbe*, which gave the Soviet version of the events leading to the outbreak of the cold war.[6] The film contrasts the two worlds at the moment of victory over Hitler and in the immediate postwar period. One would not expect subtlety in such a juxtaposition, and indeed, there is none. In Aleksandrov's version the Red Army brought peaceful reconstruction to the inhabitants of an imaginary German town, Altenstadt. In the Soviet zone the munition factories are converted to the production of consumer goods. Soviet soldiers are ready to help in all sorts of good causes. As the Soviet general puts it: "We must find a way to the heart of the German people!" This general gives machine-gun oil to the nuns for making candles. The soldiers and officers are heroic, physically attractive, and immensely proud of their nation. They suffer from homesickness. There is no need to worry that the Red Army would impose communism on the unwilling Germans. As the Soviet officer explains to his American interlocutor: "You must deserve the Soviet system!"

Far more interesting than the Soviet figures, all knights in shining armor, are the Americans. During World War II Soviet directors had always depicted Germans as evil. By contrast, the Americans were now presented as a varied lot: The simple Americans love and admire the Russians and want

Figure 49.   Eastern European Communist leaders in *The Conspiracy of the Doomed* (1950).

peace above all. They well understand that it was the Russians, rather than the Western Allies, who won the war. The enemy is the capitalists and their hirelings. Obviously, Soviet scenarists and directors knew little about America, and they made no effort to expose the genuine failings of capitalist society. They created an image of an enemy that bore as little similarity to reality as did their version of the new Soviet man.

The directors put together their picture of the Americans from various sources. Some features of that picture go back to the earliest days of the Soviet regime. For example, the notion of debauchery has always fascinated Soviet observers. Many of them imagined modern-day America as Rome just before its fall. In *Meeting on the Elbe*, as in many others, the capitalist chomps on his cigar, listens to jazz, and is entertained by scantily dressed young women. (In this era jazz is always a symptom of corruption.) The idea that sexual seduction is a weapon in the hands of the class enemy is one that goes back to the first Soviet films. In *Meeting on the Elbe*, needless to say, our Soviet hero indignantly rejects the approach of the beautiful spy-journalist, played by the director's wife, Liubov' Orlova (Fig. 50).

This film is interesting because it is so unconsciously self-revelatory; the director projected on the enemy what he knew the Red Army was doing or was accused of doing. In the 1930s the Soviet regime successfully cut off its own people from the outside world. The war broke down the barriers, and millions of Soviet citizens came to learn something about the way of life of foreigners and their high standard of living. From the point of view of the Soviet authorities contacts between their own people and Europeans and Americans were dangerously subversive and had to be minimized. *Meeting on the Elbe* starts out with a depiction of a joyful meeting of Soviet and American soldiers. The American general, watching the scene, remarks: "This is the most unfortunate consequence of the war." He is afraid that Americans, getting to know Russians, would become immune to capitalist, anti-Soviet propaganda. The Russians, encountering Westerners, especially Americans, have always been painfully conscious of their technological backwardness. In this film it is the Americans who envy Soviet achievements in optics and steal a German invention in order to turn it to military use. The choice of optics is a particularly interesting example, because the most famous Russian military booty was the famous Zeiss factory, which was moved from Jena to the Ukraine, lock, stock, and barrel. Hundreds of thousands of Soviet citizens were sent to camps because of their dangerous exposure to Western ways. In this film the decent American officer, Major Hill, who befriended his Russian counterpart, is excluded from the U.S. Army and sent home to face the committee investigating un-American activities. The Soviet Union was in the embarrassing situation of having to explain why millions of its citizens after the end of the war did not want to return home. Here we see an American soldier of Ukrainian background, who forever pines for his abandoned motherland.

The most frequently heard – and justified – charge against Soviet occupation forces was that they looted and raped. In this film, of course, it is the Americans who loot. The wife of General McDermot says to her husband:

Be a man, and not a chicken in uniform. You are not in a general's uniform in order to nurse the Germans. There is a beautiful forest around us and the leaves murmur like dollars. Cut down the forest and sell the wood to the British before it is too late!

It is, of course, especially demeaning that it is a woman, a Lady Macbeth, who gives commands to her husband. (We also see how American soldiers abuse and exploit German women.)

The Germans in this film have a dramatic role. They have to choose between the two ways of life: the Soviet way, which represents the future, or the American, which is the past. The ex-Nazis, the criminals, feel more at home with the Americans. The Communists, the most progressive people, identify with the Soviet Union to such an extent that we see them coming

Figure 50.   Liubov' Orlova as an American spy in *Meeting on the Elbe* (1949).

out of prison, singing in Russian. The battle is for the allegiance of the non-Communist, decent Germans. Otto Dietrich, the mayor of the town and a scientist, stands for the soul of Germany. This honest and elderly professor had opposed the fascists, but, unlike his son, did not sympathize with the Communists. Now he sees the constructive work that is going on in the Soviet zone; he understands that Soviet policy aims at the unification of Germany under democratic rule; and he becomes fully conscious of the corruption and viciousness of the Americans. He wholeheartedly chooses the Soviet side.

This relatively positive portrayal of the recent enemy almost got the film into trouble. When the completed work was shown to the Artistic Council of the Ministry of Film Industry (i.e., the censorship committee), it was heavily criticized. The next day the film was shown to the entire Central Committee of the Communist Party of the Soviet Union. Stalin once again came to the aid of Aleksandrov. He uttered a single sentence: "This film was made with great knowledge of the material."[7] The success of the film was assured.

Film biographies: The portrait of the hero

Between 1946 and 1953 seventeen film biographies were produced in the Soviet Union. Each film simply bore the name of its hero: *Admiral Nakhi-*

*mov, Glinka, Pirogov, Michurin, Academician Ivan Pavlov, Aleksandr Po-
pov, Rainis, Zhukovskii, Musorgskii, Belinskii, Przhevalskii, Taras Shevchenko, Composer Glinka Rimskii-Korsakov, Admiral Ushakov* (Parts I and
II), and *Dzhambul*. Composers got four films, scientists six, admirals three,
and literary figures four. It is noteworthy that not one of these films was
devoted to the life of a revolutionary figure. A partial exception was *Hostile
Storms* whose hero was Felix Dzherzhinskii. This film, however, made in
1953, was not publicly shown until 1956. Dealing with the careers of revolutionaries evidently posed too many difficulties.

Why the biography genre appealed so much to Soviet directors is easy to
understand. First of all, it was an excellent vehicle for conveying the most
important propaganda messages: In history it has always been the individual hero who mattered. These films, indirectly, contributed to the Stalin
cult. They also expressed in the clearest form the xenophobic message of
Stalinist ideology. Russian scientists, musicians, and admirals have always
been the greatest; and Russian talent and virtue have always shone. The
films, therefore, bolstered patriotism. Second, by focusing on a nineteenth-
or early twentieth-century figure, the director could avoid dealing with the
touchy issues of the present. Third, and perhaps most important, the industry developed a pattern. All the director had to do was to fit his material
into it. This way he could be almost certain to be able to avoid problems
with the censorship, which struck down the most innocuous attempts at
individual expression.

The mind-numbing uniformity of the biography film was not entirely the
result of the pusillanimity of the directors; it was imposed on them. Their
superiors required the elimination of all episodes that would have revealed
individuality. The important criticism of *Admiral Nakhimov* by the Central
Committee of the Party implied that much. Pudovkin was attacked for
showing what was "not essential," such as balls and love affairs. R. Iurenev,
writing in *Iskusstvo kino* in 1947, developed this point:

> If we recall the almost forgotten film about Pushkin *Travel to Arzrum*, it becomes
> clear that the attempt to characterize the great Russian poet on the basis of material
> that is unimportant, on the basis of accidental episodes from his life, is bound to be
> unsuccessful. The film did not give an understanding of the great poet and it failed.[8]

Iurenev described the scenes that were removed from the first version of
Admiral Nakhimov. Scenes that showed the admiral helping the love affairs
of his officers had to be cut, Iurenev argued, for in these Nakhimov behaved
like a "good-hearted uncle" rather than a "fighting admiral."[9] In a Soviet
film an admiral was to act like an admiral.

These considerations produced a uniformity that is hard to imagine. There
is no reason to choose a typical plot, for the story line of all these films was
the same. One could tell who the hero of the film was only by looking at his
clothes: If he wore a uniform, he was an admiral. The sound track also

helped: Bombardment signified admiral, music implied composer, and the reading of poetry meant a literary figure. But without such obvious aids the viewer was lost: The heroes looked alike, they had the same facial expressions, they struggled against the same problems, and the dialogues were virtually interchangeable.

The first characteristic of the synthetic Soviet hero is that he never changes. We never see a Belinskii, a Michurin, or a Pirogov develop. As geniuses they have great ideas and correct attitudes to everything from the first moment of our meeting them. Circumstances may change. But even the Great October Socialist Revolution is able to make a difference only in the material life of a Michurin or a Pavlov; their mental world and characters demand no further improvement. This requirement of stasis is not only contrary to reality, and good drama, but also to a genuinely materialist view of history. These films have more in common with the ancient lives of saints than with Marxism. Development is possible only in a world of shades of gray. Admitting the possibility that a good person might have unpleasant traits or that someone might change his ideas from bad to good or from good to bad seemed subversive to the Stalinists.

The synthetic hero always faces a hostile environment. Such portrayal serves two functions. First of all, by showing the difficulties the hero has to overcome, the audience understands better the magnitude of his accomplishments. Further, since all of these films are placed entirely or almost entirely in the past, the director can illustrate the superiority of the Soviet present to the tsarist past. It is noteworthy that in this age of heightened patriotism the Soviet publicists held against the previous rulers not so much that they had exploited the people but that they did not protect Russian national interest and pride.

Aside from tsarist bureaucrats and capitalists, the hero meets lack of understanding among his colleagues. The main fault of these people is that they also do not trust sufficiently domestic talent and they show too much admiration for foreign ways, whether in music, in military hardware, or, most frequently, in science. In the age of the struggle against "rootless cosmopolitans," the films are shamelessly presentist and anachronistic.

The hero is one with the common people. Glinka, Musorgskii, Rimskii-Korsakov get their inspiration by listening to the music of the folk. Popov, for example, explains electromagnetism to simple fishermen, who do not merely understand him but also come up with brilliant suggestions for further work. The opponent of Michurin, a made-up figure, Kartashev, talks about genes, chromosomes, and mutations. The purpose of the director, A. Dovzhenko, is to ridicule the scientist. Michurin answers Kartashev: "It is time for biology to get off the pedestal. It should speak the language of the people, and not get lost in fog." The simple people understand the magnitude of Michurin's accomplishments and the breadth of his thinking. Soviet films made about scientists were profoundly antiscience and antiintellectual.

Michurin makes a point that is implied also in other films: Science that does not have immediate use is useless.

Aside from the simple people it is the foreigners who are best in appreciating Russian talent. Unlike native bureaucrats and scientists they are in awe of the accomplishments of Russian genius. They use every means, fair or foul, to get hold of Russian inventions and to prevent accomplishments in geographic discovery, military power, and anything that might add to prestige. Foreigners try to prevent I. D. Zhukovskii's epoch-making work in the development of the airplane. Americans attempt to persuade Michurin and Pavlov to leave their native land and continue their valuable work in the United States. They propose to buy Popov's marvelous invention, the radio (Fig. 51). But Popov speaks for all Russian heroes when he answers: "My work belongs to my fatherland. I am a Russian person, and I have the right to give all my knowledge, all my work, and all my accomplishments only to my fatherland." Because he cannot be bought, foreigners are forced to steal his invention. According to this film, Marconi is no better than a common thief. He is an ignorant, insignificant person, who contributed nothing but his name. The innocent scientific work of the great Russian geographer, Przhevalskii, beloved by the natives in Central Asia, arouses fear and hostility among the British. Even the British prime minister, Disraeli, takes note of Przhevalskii's accomplishments. The film hints darkly that the English secret service would have liked to kill him. Przhevalskii prevails in spite of the intrigues of the British.

All remnants of the directors' individual styles had disappeared by this time. Pudovkin learned from his experience with *Admiral Nakhimov;* the making and showing of *Zhukovskii* caused no problems. Dovzhenko, on the other hand, had a great deal of trouble in making *Michurin.* It took four years, in the course of which innumerable changes in the script had to be made. The final product was undoubtedly his worst film. Admirers of Dovzhenko argued that the film had gone through so many changes that were forced on the director that the final product should not be included in his oeuvre.[10]

Even contemporary observers pointed out that the biography film genre became so schematic that different films used not merely the same situations but almost the same words. In *Aleksandr Popov,* Makarov, the progressive admiral, is attempting to persuade the conservative officers of the Ministry of the Navy to develop Popov's invention. The official says: "I already told you. We will find firms that will deliver what we need. Most likely an English firm." Makarov: "Why English?" Official: "Well, French." Makarov: "We should start something ourselves. But we will. By God, we will!" In *Zhukovskii* the inventor says to the reactionary official: "The military authorities should understand, colonel, that we ourselves can make airplanes. And you suggest that we should order them from abroad. Why? Why?"[11]

Figure 51.   Popov explains his invention: *Aleksandr Popov* (1949).

The end of the Stalin era

During the worst years in the history of Soviet culture, cinema, as a form of art, died. This was not because films were expected to convey a political message; first-rate films can be intensely political. Art of any kind, however, could not be reconciled with the forcible elimination of individual style, and the repudiation of irony, complexity, and ambiguity. Further, the principles of Stalinist filmmaking went contrary to the fundamental requirement of cinema; cinema, in order to be worthy of the name, must be visual, yet Stalinist publicists insisted on the primacy of the word, of the scenario. The scenarist could be controlled more easily than the director. One-dimensional meaning could be approximated more easily in words than in pictures.

During the last year of Stalin's life, the leaders of the Party recognized that Soviet culture had become barren. The leaders were concerned that novels, plays, and films would no longer serve the agitational needs of the Party, and therefore took a few hesitant steps away from orthodoxy. For the state of Soviet culture, they blamed not their own previous policies but unnamed critics and filmmakers. In April 1952, *Pravda* published an important editorial: "Overcome the lag in dramaturgy."[12] The article criticized plays, and by implication films, for being boring, for having no conflict, and for having one-dimensional characters. (When in 1948–9 critics made similar assertions, they had been denounced as "cosmopolitans" and enemies of art for the people.) G. M. Malenkov, who gave the major report to the Nineteenth Party Congress in October 1952, devoted some of his speech to the problems of Soviet culture. His ideas were later elaborated by innumerable publicists.[13]

One of the themes of the new campaign was that the country needed more films. When Malenkov called for making more films, he implicitly repudiated the previous position of the leadership that insisted on making only "masterpieces." The problem was such a formulation was best expressed by Mikhail Romm: "To make a few films turned out to be by no means easier than to make many. The idea that we must concentrate our attention on a few works (as if this way it would be possible to produce only excellent quality) turned out to be utopian."[14] The decision to produce more films once again had far-reaching consequences. It meant that the republican studios that had been neglected could be revived; that perspectives would open to young talents; that the studios would stop concentrating on spectaculars and instead would make more modest films; that the decision to make mostly colored films was at best premature; and that genres that had almost disappeared should be resurrected. Malenkov expressed special concern for the lack of Soviet comedies. As he put it: "We need Soviet Gogol's and Shchedrins, who with the fire of satire would eliminate from our lives everything negative, unpleasant, and dead, everything that slows down our movement forward."[15] Following Malenkov, dozens of publicists decried the lack of Soviet comedy, and quoted the Politburo member on the need for "Gogol's and Shchedrins."

The second major theme of the critics was that many Soviet films lacked conflict. Without conflict films were bound to be boring. According to N. Kriuchenikov, the source of the trouble was a misunderstanding. He wrote:

The defenders of the lack of conflict theory in order to support their position frequently point to the fact that in our society there are no contradictions that could be the basis of dramatic conflicts. Indeed, in Soviet socialist society in which the exploiting classes have already been liquidated, there are no antagonistic contradictions. But this does not at all mean that our society develops without overcoming contradictions.

The scenarist had to be able to distinguish between antagonistic and nonantagonistic contradictions. Kriuchenikov gave an example of the "wrong" type of conflict: Lukov's *A Great Life*, criticized by the Central Committee resolution in 1946, showed backwardness, destruction, and Russians cooperating with Germans. The successful scenarist had to be able to find "genuine" conflicts (i.e., between the remnants of the old and the new) and be able to show the victory of the new.[16]

The most telling and justified criticism of Soviet films was that they were stereotyped, full of schematic characters and situations. A. Solov'ev in a sharp article in *Iskusstvo kino* wrote that many Soviet films were based on formulas, presented characters in a superficial manner, contained no conflict, and therefore were boring.[17] No Soviet critic, of course, was able to point to the source of the problem. Because of terror the scenarist and the director sought security in following preestablished patterns. Directors could not be expected to become more courageous as long as they lived under a bloody tyranny.

The changes of 1952–3 affected not the films themselves but only publicistic writings. In the Soviet Union it took a considerable amount of time to see a film project through from its first stages to its premiere in the movie houses, and therefore what actually appeared in the cinemas during 1952–3 was just as dreary as before. Under the circumstances, did the campaign matter at all? One can imagine that the decision to make more films would have had beneficial consequences. On the other hand, the fundamental problems of Soviet film, and of Soviet culture, could not have been solved within the framework of the existing system.

The precondition of genuine change was the removal of the tyrant by death, in March 1953. This was followed by profound changes in the political order. The revival of Soviet film came remarkably quickly; it was a part of the thaw that benefited every component of Soviet culture. In the mid-1950s many of the old restrictions were lifted. The output of the industry grew impressively. Directors who had done interesting work in the distant past once again took advantage of the opportunity and returned to experimentation. New and talented directors had a chance to show what they could do. Artists turned to genuine issues and expressed themselves with passion. Cinema became heterogeneous. Because the Soviet system politicized all aspects of life and claimed credit for all achievements, a film that depicted the world more or less realistically, and thus pointed to problems, was inherently subversive. Although Soviet cinema never again achieved the worldwide acclaim it had enjoyed in the late 1920s, films once again became worth watching.

Notes

1 *Sovetskie khudozhestvennye fil'my. Annotirovannyi katalog*, 4 vols., Iskusstvo, Moscow, 1960–8, vol. 2.

2 Information from M. Chudakova, interview in June 1989.

3 There is some evidence to show that at least in the early stages of the Stalin cult the Dictator had an ironic attitude to it. I. Babel described an episode to a Hungarian friend. Babel and Gorky were visiting Stalin. Stalin's daughter, Svetlana, came in. Stalin said to her: "Tell the Father of the peoples, the Leader of the world

proletariat, what you learned in the school today?" Ervin Sinko, *Egy Regeny Regenye. Moszkvai Naplojegyzetek, 1935–1937,* Magveto, Budapest, 1988, p. 540.

4 "Voploshchenie obraza velikovo vozhdia," *Iskusstvo kino* 1: 8, 1947.

5 Jay Leyda, *Kino: A History of the Russian and Soviet Film.* Collier Books, New York, 1960, p. 352.

6 There were two extensive review articles of this film. N. Gribachev wrote one in *Kul'tura i zhizn'*, Mar. 10, 1949, p. 3, and A. Mar'iamov published a review in *Iskusstvo kino* 2: 8–12, 1949, "Bor'ba za mir."

7 G. V. Aleksandrov, *Epokha i kino*, Politizdat, Moscow, 1983, pp. 297–8. Aleksandrov, writing in 1983, still believed that this film was honest and a contribution to the "struggle for peace."

8 "Admiral Nakhimov," *Iskusstvo kino* 1: 15, 1947.

9 Ibid., p. 17.

10 On *Michurin*, see Vance Kepley, *In the Service of the State: The Cinema of Alexander Dovzhenko*, University of Wisconsin Press, Madison, 1986, pp. 135–47.

11 A. Solov'ev, "Protiv skhematisma i shtampa v biograficheskikh stsenariakh," *Iskusstvo kino* 5: 84, 1952.

12 "Preodelet' otstavanie dramaturgii," *Pravda*, Apr. 7, 1952.

13 For example, A. Shtein, "Tvorcheskii dolg dramaturga," *Iskusstvo kino* 2: 8–17, 1953; V. Turkin, "Dramaticheskii konflikt i kharakter," *Iskusstvo kino* 2: 18–28, 1953; I. Maseev, "Tipicheskoe i konflikt v dramaturgii," *Iskusstvo kino* 3: 12–28, 1953. These articles make the same two or three points again and again.

14 M. M. Romm, "Pered shirokim razvorotom kinoiskusstva," *Iskusstvo kino* 9: 15, 1954.

15 I. Bol'shakov, "Zadachi novogo goda," *Iskusstvo kino* 1: 3–10, 1953.

16 N. Kriuchenikov, "O konflikte v stsenarii," *Iskusstvo kino* 6: 91, 1952.

17 Solov'ev, p. 83.

Conclusions

In this book we have touched on three important issues: the role of cinema as a propaganda instrument; the connection between political oppression and artistic achievement; and the role of artists in the creation and maintenance of the Soviet system. Let us examine them once again.

The Bolsheviks have always been convinced that cinema was a powerful tool for political "education," and therefore from the very beginning of their rule they attempted to use it. To the question How successful were they? there is no clear-cut answer.

The Bolshevik regime between 1917 and 1953 went through enormous changes. As the political context changed, so did the propaganda themes, methods, and expectations of the activists. During the Civil War, for example, the most significant Bolshevik venture in this field was sending trains and ships into the countryside, equipped with projectors and hastily and poorly made short agitational films. The revolutionaries correctly expected that the peasant audience would be attracted by what must have seemed to them as a miracle, a moving picture. Once the peasants assembled, and were exposed to the primitive message of the films about the wickedness of the White enemy and the bright future that awaited workers and peasants, they were addressed by trained agitators who conveyed the important and somewhat more complex propaganda themes. At this point, cinema was hardly more than a fairground attraction.

After the conclusion of the devastating Civil War, Soviet studios were not in the position to produce feature films in sufficient numbers as to be a significant component of the overall propaganda effort; Soviet theaters almost exclusively showed foreign and prerevolutionary films. It is clear from a letter written by Lenin in 1922 (see Chapter 2) that the Bolshevik leader still thought of films primarily as a means for attracting an audience, and expected that the propaganda message would be delivered by newsreels and by agitators. He did not realize that the feature film itself could become the most valuable instrument.

Only in the second half of the 1920s was the Soviet film industry sufficiently well developed as to be able to become a significant component of

247

the political "education" system. The Bolsheviks insisted ever-more strongly that every Soviet-made film should instruct in the spirit of socialism. The task was new, the demands unclear and contradictory, and it is not surprising that the situation occasioned passionate debates. The activists were disappointed and not at all pleased with the performance of the Soviet film industry in its most glorious age. If we accept the self-evaluation of activists, film propaganda was a failure.

The greatest change in the character of Soviet film occurred, as in all other aspects of Soviet life, with the introduction of collectivization, industrialization, urbanization, and "cultural revolution." From this time on, until the end of the Stalin era, the main task of Soviet cinema was – though it was never articulated as such – to create an "alternate reality," that is, to show people not how life was, but how life should have been. This was as much a negative as a positive role: The task of art was to deny reality, to cover up how people really lived, what really concerned them, and what they really thought. Because of the camera's ability to create an appearance of reality, cinema was especially powerful. The overall effect of Soviet films on the viewers was confusion; people in some recesses of their minds started to doubt their own perceptions.

It is difficult to measure the success of Soviet film propaganda partly because at different times it had different tasks and partly because the ambition and nature of the themes varied greatly: Some films were made to persuade people to buy lottery tickets, to wash their hands, or to participate in sports; other, more ambitious movies aimed to increase patriotism, to encourage people to work harder, and to turn people into new "socialist human beings." Propagandists were more likely to succeed when people had no direct ways to check the truthfulness of the message. The industry produced many films, for example, that showed the desperate plight of the unemployed in the West, and many Soviet people came to believe that the workers in capitalist countries lived in constant uncertainty. On the other hand, it was hardly possible to convince collective farm peasants that their life was gay and easy and that food was abundant. Furthermore, it is obviously easier to sell ideas that are consistent with beliefs and values that people already hold than those that are not. During World War II, for example, cinema made a great contribution to raising the morale of the Soviet peoples. On the other hand, in the age of Gorbachev, it is clear that the attempts to create a new humanity with the help of propaganda, or to persuade them to work harder for the benefit of community and for the "glory of work," obviously failed. "Socialist humanity" has not been born.

Although it is not possible to give a simple and unequivocal evaluation of the power of Soviet film propaganda, we may make a few observations. The politicians have always been dissatisfied with the results, because like most people, they tended to overestimate the power of propaganda. They believed that it would be possible to change humanity, if they just tried a little harder, if they just carried out the work a little differently. The fact, however, that the activists have not achieved their most ambitious goals does not mean that films did not make an impact on the audiences.

It is naïve to think of propagandists as a small group of people, standing outside of society, consciously and successfully manipulating the views of the majority, while they themselves remain immune. The only way to approach the question of propaganda, film propaganda included, is to place it within the larger context of the Soviet polity. The particular style of Soviet film propaganda could not have existed within another political system on the one hand; on the other, it is difficult to imagine Soviet society without its means of mass communications. Each depended on the other. Propaganda was an essential component of the Soviet system, not so much because it convinced people to do what they did not want to do but because it helped to define what the Soviet political system was. Propaganda was inseparable from a style of discourse; it taught people how to express themselves; it helped to define subjects that were fit for discussion in the public sphere.[1]

In examining the history of Soviet film from the time of the Revolution through the end of the Stalin era, a second question arises. What was the relationship between art and politics? That is, could artistically worthwhile films be made at a time of oppression? This is an easier question to answer than the first one, for the historical record is unambiguous.

Although in the late 1920s the Soviet state was authoritarian and intellectual life was hardly free, nevertheless cinema flourished. This golden age of cinema could develop, because the politicians – though they often interfered in small and large issues of the film industry – possessed an attitude that was not altogether inimical to the production of art.

For an appreciation of the mentality of Bolshevik politicians Lenin's writings are the most important. The Bolshevik leader again and again stressed the importance of raising the cultural level of the people and defined the task as a political one, for in his view socialism could be achieved only after the people became more cultured. On the question of autonomy of literature (and by extension, all arts) he expressed himself ambiguously. In an important article written in 1905, "Party organization and party literature," he argued that the neutrality was always only a pretense and all writing served a political purpose. It was not clear, however, whether he had in mind only publicistic writings or also belles lettres.[2] His followers interpreted his thoughts according to their own political purposes. Lenin's actions, however, were more consistent with the view that he had only publicistic writings in mind. As long as he was in power he made no attempt to stop the publication of writers unless they were explicitly hostile to the Bolsheviks.

Lenin and his comrades brought with themselves to a greater extent than they themselves realized the traditions of the nineteenth-century intelligentsia, even when they were rebelling against some of those traditions. They regarded "culture" and art with respect and admiration, and aimed to bring them to the Russian people for they optimistically assumed that artists were working for the same goals as they were: the betterment of humanity. It followed from this attitude that the revolutionaries were willing to leave a degree of autonomy to artists. The first set of Bolshevik leaders might not on occasion appreciate or like the work of avant-garde artists, but nevertheless they allowed them to do more or less what they wanted to.

Indeed, one may plausibly argue that those directors who became best known in the West and produced art films for an elite audience could do their best work because they had been freed from commercial considerations that almost always exist in capitalist societies. These Soviet directors had a better chance to produce innovative and experimental art than their Western colleagues. A few directors, though not many, may even have been genuinely inspired to express a Bolshevik and revolutionary ideology.

At the end of the 1920s the new generation of leaders who came to power with Stalin saw matters differently. They believed that art that was many layered and complex – as all first-rate art must be – was a dangerous opponent. The worldview that they propagated was a simple one that tolerated only black and white; and art that included complexity, irony, and ambiguity undermined such a worldview. The Bolsheviks set out to destroy the autonomy of culture; they defined politics so broadly as to subsume all aspects of life, including culture.

In the intervention of the 1930s, oppression increased and as a result artistic experimentation came to an end, the quality of the work greatly declined, and films became much less interesting. It is striking, however, that in spite of the extraordinary oppression, some watchable films (such as the Gorky autobiographical trilogy, *Chapaev*, and *Aleksandr Nevskii*) could still be made. The regime required conformity and prescribed precise story lines and types of characters; nevertheless, here and there – at times in the work of actors, at times in an unexpected story development or in the depiction of a minor character – artistic talent could still shine through. The bear could on occasion still dance, even though the shackles were increasingly heavy.

As oppression further increased during Stalin's last years, however, cinema art died. Intervention became so all-encompassing and minute, the topics that could be treated so few, the permitted style so bland that it became close to impossible to make movies in the Soviet Union.

After the death of Stalin, as restrictions loosened, though by no means disappeared, Soviet artists quickly regained their talents and once again made some good films. At this time a curious development took place. Films were made that treated life more or less realistically and thereby explicitly contradicted the claims of ideology. The best Soviet films, instead of serving as propaganda tools, became subversive. Because the Soviet state claimed credit for all aspects of existence, it had to accept responsibility for all failures. An

American film showing prostitution was simply a film about prostitution; a Soviet film about prostitution was an attack on the regime. In the era of Khrushchev and Brezhnev many films were made that could not be shown in movie houses, but some that did appear were particularly exciting to watch because the viewer could sense the controlled passion of the director, conscious of making a political statement.

A third issue was raised at the outset of this conclusion: What was the role of the artists in the creation of the Stalinist system? In the early twentieth century in Western Europe, but also to a lesser extent in Imperial Russia, the simple people became consumers of art and literature and were particularly attracted to the cinema. Naturally, studios catered to the taste of the ill-educated. The best and most innovative young directors despised the results and blamed the philistine taste of the bourgeoisie. They hated the bourgeoisie for its smug self-satisfaction; they wanted to destroy all conventions; they desired a clean break with the old world. At the time of the Revolution and for some years afterward the artists deluded themselves, by believing that they were the equivalents of the Bolsheviks in their own sphere.

The Bolsheviks fought their revolution against the old order, and they talked about and visibly believed in the creation of an altogether different life. They fought in the name of the proletariat, which, on the basis of their Marxist learning, they regarded as the "universal class." As time went on, however, it became clear that the political ideas of real-life workers coincided less and less with those of their new rulers. The Bolsheviks responded by creating an ideal "proletariat," a proletariat that possessed proper revolutionary consciousness, was willing to make sacrifices for a better future, and was conscious of its "internationalist obligations." The only problem was that this "proletariat" was an abstraction that never existed and, indeed, could never exist anywhere and at any time. The avant-garde film directors behaved exactly the same way. They wanted to create a new style of art for the workers. Only the blind could not see, however, that real-life workers preferred melodramas, comedies, crime stories – exactly those films that the "petite bourgeoisie" was supposed to want. To the extent that the avant-garde directors found an audience, they found it among the intelligentsia and the despised bourgeoisie.

The avant-garde artists were interested in their art and were not deeply political. They had little knowledge of who the Bolsheviks really were and would have found the study of Marxism boring. Without fully comprehending, they liked Bolshevism's least attractive components: antidemocratic, antipopulist, and antiliberal politics. The misunderstanding – that artists and revolutionaries were fighting the same fight – was bound to be cleared up sooner or later. When it happened it had tragic and ironic consequences: The Bolsheviks ultimately imposed on the artists the most philistine style imaginable, and the artists did not merely have to endure it, but adjust their work accordingly, and heap praise on "socialist realism."

The cult of genius is widespread among us; most of us tend to idealize the artist. We are attracted to the image of the lone artist struggling against a repressive system and ultimately falling victim to the tyrant. This image is not altogether false, for, indeed, the directors — if not as individuals at least as artists — did fall victims and their art was destroyed. However, even a cursory examination will show that the artists were not simply victims but also architects of the system that destroyed them. The Soviet system succeeded in making everyone, or almost everyone, into an accomplice.

The moral content of most films made during the reign of Stalin was reprehensible. The directors, almost without exception, lent their talents to propagating an odious ideology. We have no recorded incidents, though it may have happened, of a director using one pretext or another to refuse an assigned topic. The talented were no different from the second-rate. Pudovkin, the maker of *Mother* and *The Heir of Genghis Khan,* played a prominent role in the anticosmopolitan campaign. The great Dziga Vertov, the most radical iconoclast of the 1920s, made a fawning contribution to Stalin's personality cult in 1937 with *Lullaby.* This effort, by the way, did not save him from falling into disfavor. Nor did Bleiman, the scriptwriter of the odious *The Great Citizen,* receive gratitude for his services: At the time of the "anticosmopolitan" campaign he was among the victims. Ermler, Pyr'ev, Eisenstein, and Dovzhenko, among others, made films that justified the terror and encouraged people to denounce each other and be suspicious of those who were closest to them. Whether they believed in the Stalinist ideology — most likely they themselves did not know — does not matter. Each individual case is complex: The same person who on one occasion showed courage and resisted great pressure at another time behaved reprehensibly. No easy and clear separation of decent and despicable people is possible.

Like all Soviet people at the time, the high and the low, filmmakers participated in the ritual denunciation of one another. Here we do see differences among people. Reading in between the lines of their speeches, it is easy to see that some were pained, and carried out the distasteful task because they had to and compromised others as little as possible, whereas other people were venomous. We do not have all the evidence available to make a judgment, nor is it the task of the historian to judge the behavior of people who lived under very different and very difficult circumstances. Nevertheless, the few examples of courage and decency shine through the record. One thinks of Kuleshov making his extraordinary, anti-Stalinist film, *The Great Consoler* or, even more remarkably, of Pavlenko, who would go on writing scripts for Chiaureli's most distasteful films but who alone came to the defense of Eisenstein in 1937, at a time when famous directors competed with one another to heap abuse on the maker of *Bezhin Meadow.*

The record is incontrovertible. As a group, artists were like everyone else,

neither better nor worse, neither less nor more courageous. What right do
we have to expect anything else?

Stalinist cinema was like no other for it served a regime that was altogether novel in world history. Up to that time there never had existed a
political order that had such far-reaching goals in restructuring society and
even remaking humanity, and one that was so much without moral scruples
in destroying its own citizens. Soviet cinema was a part of this system; it
was an accomplice in building the edifice of Stalinism.

Notes

1 I have developed these themes in greater detail in my book, *The Birth of the
Propaganda State: Soviet Methods of Mass Mobilization, 1917–1929*, Cambridge
University Press, 1985.

2 V. I. Lenin, *Polnoe sobranie sochinenii*, Politizdat, Moscow, 5th ed., vol. 12,
pp. 99–105.

Glossary

agitka	short agitational film
Glavrepetkom	State Repertoire Committee
GUK/GUKF	State Directorate for Cinema and Photo Industry ("Photo" added in 1937)
Goskino	State Cinema Organization
KPSS	Communist Party of the Soviet Union
kolkhoz	collective farm
Komsomol	Communist Youth Organization
Mezhrabpom	International Workers' Aid, the source of financial support for Mezhrabpom–Rus' and later Mezhrabpomfil'm studios (existed until 1936)
NEP	New Economic Policy
NKVD	People's Commissariat for Internal Affairs
Narkomfin	People's Commissariat for Finance
Narkompros	People's Commissariat of Enlightenment
Narkomtorg	People's Commissariat of Trade
ODN	Society "Down with Illiteracy"
ODSK	Society of Friends of Soviet Cinema
PUR	Political Administration of the Revolutionary Military Council
politprosvet	political education
Proletkul't	Proletarian Culture, social-educational movement in the 1920s
RAPP	Russian Association of Proletarian Writers
Rabkrin	Workers' Peasants' Inspectorate
Rossark	Russian Association of Revolutionary Cinematography

254

Soiuzdetfil'm	Union Children Film (children's film studio)
Sovkino	Soviet Cinema Organization
TsK	Central Committee
VFKO	Photo and Cinema Section of Narkompros
Vostokkino	Cinema organization for the Soviet Far East
VSNKh	Supreme Council of the National Economy
VTsSPS	Central Council of the Trade Union
VUFKU	Ukrainian Photo and Cinema Organization

Bibliography

The most important written primary sources for this study were the following newspapers and journals, all published in Moscow:

Iskusstvo kino	*Novyi lef*
Iz istorii kino	*Novyi mir*
Izvestiia	*Ogonek*
Izvestiia Tsentral' nogo Komiteta	*Pravda*
Kino	*Proletarskoe kino*
Kino i kultura	*Sovetskii ekran*
Kino i vremia	*Sovetskoe kino*
Kino i zhizn'	*Vecherniaia Moskva*
Kul'tura i zhizn'	*Voprosy istorii*
Kommunisticheskaia revoliutsiia	*Voprosy kinoiskusstva*
Literatura i iskusstvo	*Zhizn' iskusstva*

Akselrod, L., "Dokumenty po istorii natsionalizatsii russkoi kinematografii." *Iz istorii kino* 1: 25–37, 1958.

Aleksandrov, G. V. *Epokha i kino*. Politizdar, Moscow, 1983.

"Amerikanskie fil'my v sovetskom prokate." *Kino i vremia*, 1960.

Arlazorov, Mikhail. *Protazanov*. Iskusstvo, Moscow, 1973.

Aumout, J. *Montage Eisenstein*. Indiana University Press, Bloomington, 1987.

Bagaev, B. *Boris Shumiatskii*. Krasnoiarsk, 1974.

Balázs, Béla. *Theory of the Film*. B. Dobson, London, 1952.

—A Lathato Ember: A Film Szelleme. Gondolat, Budapest, 1984.

Barabas, Iurii. *Dovzhenko. Nekotorye voprosy estetiki i poetiki*. Khudozhestvennaia literatura, Moscow, 1968.

Barna, Yon. *Eisenstein*. Secker and Warburg, London, 1973.

Bazin, André. *What Is Cinema?* University of California Press, Berkeley, 1967.

Bleiman, M. *O kino. Svidetel'skie pokazaniia*. Iskusstvo, Moscow, 1973.

Bratoliubov, S. *Na zare Sovetskoi kinematografii*. Iskusstvo, Leningrad, 1976.

Brown, Edward J. *The Proletarian Episode in Russian Literature, 1928–1932*. Octagon, New York, 1971.

Buchanan, George. *My Mission to Russia and Other Diplomatic Memories*. Little, Brown, Boston, 1923.

Budiak, L. M., and V. P. Mikhailov. *Adresa Moskovskogo kino*. Moskovskii rabochii, Moscow, 1987.

Buss, Robin. *The French through Their Films*. Ungar, New York, 1988.

256

Carter, Huntley. *The New Theater and Cinema of Soviet Russia.* Chapman and Dodd, London, 1924.

Cherchi, Paolo, et al. (eds.). *Silent Witnesses: Russian Films, 1908–1919.* BFI, London, 1989.

Chernyshev, A. *Russkaia dooktiabr' skaia kinopublitsistika.* MGU, Moscow, 1987.

Christie, Ian, and Richard Taylor. *The Film Factory: Russian and Soviet Cinema Documents, 1896–1939.* Harvard University Press, Cambridge, 1988.

Clark, Katerina. *The Soviet Novel.* University of Chicago Press, Chicago, 1981.

Cohen, Louis. *The Cultural-Political Traditions and Developments of the Soviet Cinema, 1917–1972.* Arno Press, New York, 1974.

Dart, P. *Pudovkin's Films and Film Theory.* Arno, New York, 1974.

Dovzhenko, Aleksandr. *Sobrannye sochineniia.* Iskusstvo, Moscow, 1966–9.

—*The Poet as Film Maker: Selected Writings.* Ed. Marco Carynnyk. MIT Press, Cambridge, 1973.

Drobashenko, Sergei. *Prostranstvo ekrannogo dokumenta.* Iskusstvo, Moscow, 1986.

Druzhnikov, Iu. I. *Vosnesenie Pavlika Morozova.* Overseas Publications, London, 1988.

Dunham, Vera. *In Stalin's Time: Middleclass Values in Soviet Fiction.* Cambridge University Press, 1976.

Dzigan, E. *Zhizn' i fil'my.* Iskusstvo, Moscow, 1981.

Eikhenbaum, Boris (ed.). *Poetika kino.* Kinopechat', Moscow, Leningrad, 1927.

Eisenstein, Sergei. *The Film Form and the Film Sense.* Meridian, New York, 1957.

—*Notes of a Film Director.* Dover, New York, 1970.

—*Immoral Memories.* Houghton Mifflin, Boston, 1983.

Ezhegodnik Sovetskoi kinematografii za 1938 god. Goskinoizdat, Moscow, 1939.

Feldman, Seth. *Evolution of Style in the Early Works of Dziga Vertov.* Arno, New York, 1977.

Ferro, Marc. *Cinema et Histoire.* Denoel/Gonthier, Paris, 1977.

Fitzpatrick, Sheila (ed.). *Cultural Revolution in Russia, 1928–1931.* Indiana University Press, Bloomington, 1978.

"Frantsuskie fil'my v sovetskom prokate." *Kino i vremia,* 1965.

Gerasimov, Sergei. *Vospitanie kinorezhissera,* Iskusstvo, Moscow, 1978.

Ginzburg, S. *Kinematografiia dorevoliutsionnoi Rossii.* Iskusstvo, Moscow, 1963.

Goriachev, Iu. *Istoriia stroitel'stva sovetskoi kinematografii (1917–1925).* VGIK, Moscow, 1977.

Gromov, E. *Lev Vladimirovich Kuleshov.* Iskusstvo, Moscow, 1984.

Hahn, Werner G. *Postwar Soviet Politics: The Fall of Zhdanov and the Defeat of Moderation, 1946–1953.* Cornell University Press, Ithaca, 1982.

Hull, David S. *Film in the Third Reich: A Study of German Cinema, 1933–1945.* University of California Press, Berkeley, 1969.

Hunnings, Neville. *Film Censors and the Law.* Allen and Unwin, London, 1967.

Istoriia sovetskogo kino, 1917–1967. 4 vols. Iskusstvo, Moscow, 1969–1978.

Iurenev, R. *Kratkaia istoriia sovetskogo kino.* SK SSSR BPSK, Moscow, 1979.

—*Sergei Eizenshtein. Zamysly. Fil'my. Metod.* 2 vols. Iskusstvo, Moscow, 1985–8.

—*Novatorstvo sovetskogo iskusstva.* Prosveshchenie, Moscow, 1986.

Iz istorii kino. Akad. nauk SSSR, Moscow, 1958.

James, C. Vaughan. *Soviet Socialist Realism: Origin and Theory.* St. Martin's Press, New York, 1973.

Karaganov, A. *Sovetskoe kino.* Politizdat, Moscow, 1977.

—*Vsevolod Pudovkin.* Iskusstvo, Moscow, 1983.

Katsigras, A. *Kinorabota v derevne.* Kinopechat', Moscow, 1926.

Kenez, Peter. *The Birth of the Propaganda State: Soviet Methods of Mass Mobilization, 1917–1929.* Cambridge University Press, 1985.

Kepley, Vance. *In Service of the State: The Cinema of Alexander Dovzhenko.* University of Wisconsin Press, Madison, 1986.

Khanzhonkov, A. "Pervyi mul'tiplikator." *Iz istorii kino,* vol. 7.

—*Pervye gody russkoi kinematografii.* Iskusstvo, Moscow, 1937.

Kinematograf. Sbornik statei. Gosizdat, Moscow, 1919.

Kino. Entsiklopenicheskii slovar'. Sovetskaia entsiklopediia, Moscow, 1987.

Kinospravochnik. Ed. G. M. Boltianskii. Kinoizdatel' stvo, Moscow, 1926.

Kleberg, Lars. "The Audience as Myth and Reality: Soviet Theatrical Ideology and Audience Research in the 1920's." *Russian History* 9: 227–41, 1982.

Kozintsev, G. *Glubokii ekran.* Iskusstvo, Moscow, 1971.

—*Vremia i sovest'.* Propaganda Bureau of Soviet Film Art, Moscow, 1981.

Kracauer, Sigfried. *From Caligari to Hitler: A Psychological Study of Germany Cinema, 1933–1945.* Princeton University Press, Princeton, 1947.

Kresin, M. "Iz vospominanii starogo kinorabotnika." *Iz istorii kino* 1: 92–6, 1958.

Kuleshov, Lev. *Gody tvorcheskikh poiskov.* Propaganda Bureau of Soviet Film Art, Moscow, 1969.

—*Kuleshov on Film.* Ed. R. Levaco. University of California Press, Berkeley, 1974.

—*Filmmuveszet es Filmrendezes.* Gondolat, Budapest, 1985.

—*Vospominaniia.* 2 vols. Iskusstvo, Moscow, 1987–8.

Kushnirov, Mark. *Zhizn' i fil'my Borisa Barneta.* Iskusstvo, Moscow, 1977.

Lary, N. *Dostoevsky and Soviet Film: Visions of Demonic Realism.* Cornell University Press, Ithaca, 1986.

Latyshev, A. "Stalin i kino." In *Surovaia drama naroda,* ed. Iu. P. Senokozov, pp. 489–507. Politizdat, Moscow, 1989.

Lawton, Anna. "Cinema and the Russian Avant-garde." *Occasional Papers.* Kennan Institute, Washington, D.C., 1986.

Lebedev, N. A. *Ocherk istorii kino SSSR.* Iskusstvo, Moscow, 1947.

—*Ocherki istorii kino SSSR. Vol. 1: Nemoe kino 1917–1934.* Iskusstvo, Moscow, 1965.

—"Boevye dvatsatye gody." *Iskusstvo kino* 12: 85–99, 1968.

Lenin, V. I. *Polnoe sobranie sochinenii.* Politizdat, Moscow, 1958–70.

Leyda, Jay. *Kino: A History of Russian and Soviet Film.* Collier Books, New York, 1960.

Liehm, Mira, and Antonin Liehm. *The Most Important Art: Eastern European Film After 1945.* University of California Press, Berkeley, 1977.

Likhachev, B. S. "Materialy k istorii kino v Rossii, 1914–1918." In *Iz istorii kino.* Vol. 3. Akademiia Nauk, Moscow, 1960.

Lunacharskii, A. V. *Kino na zapade i u nas.* Tea-kino pechat', Moscow, 1928.

—*O kino: Stat'i.* Iskusstvo, Moscow, 1965.

Mally, Lynn. *Culture of the Future: The Poletkult Movement in Revolutionary Russia.* University of California Press, Berkeley, 1990.

Mamatova, L. *Mnogonatsionalnoe sovetskoe kinoiskusstvo.* Znanie, Moscow, 1982.

—*Vetvi moguchei krony.* Iskusstvo, Moscow, 1986.

Mayne, Judith. *Kino and the Woman Question: Feminism and Soviet Silent Film.* Ohio State University Press, Columbus, 1989.

Messer, R. *Geroi sovetskoi kinematografii.* Iskusstvo, Moscow, 1938.

Nemeskurty, Istvan. *A Keppe Varazsolt Ido.* Magveto, Budapest, 1983.

—*A filmmuveszet Uj Utjai.* Magveto, Budapest, 1986.

"Nemetskie fil'my v sovetskom prokate." *Kino i vremia,* 1965.

Ocherki istorii sovetskogo kino. 3 vols. Iskusstvo, Moscow, 1956–61.

Ol'khovyi, B. (ed.). *Puti kino: Pervye vsesoiuznoe soveshchanie po kinematografii.* Tea-kino pechat', Moscow, 1929.

Pisarevskii, D. *Bratiia Vasil'evy.* Iskusstvo, Moscow, 1981.

Preobrazhenskii, N. "Vospominaniia o rabote VFKO." *Iz istorii kino* 1: 85–91, 1958.

Pudovkin, Vsevolod. *Film Technique and Film Acting.* Lear, New York, 1948.

Pyr'ev, Ivan. *Izbrannye proizvedeniia.* 2 vols. Iskusstvo, Moscow, 1976–8.

Repertuarnyi ukazatel'. Kinofotoizdat, Moscow, 1936.

Richter, Hans. *The Struggle for the Film.* St. Martin's Press, New York, 1986.

Rimberg, John. *The Motion Picture in the Soviet Union, 1918–1952: A Sociological Analysis.* Arno Press, New York, 1973.

Rimberg, John, and Paul Babitsky. *The Soviet Film Industry.* Praeger, New York, 1955.

Robinson, David. *The History of World Cinema.* Stein and Day, New York, 1981.

Romanov, A. *Kinoiskusstvo i sovremennost'.* Iskusstvo, Moscow, 1968.

—*Liubov' Orlova.* Iskusstvo, Moscow, 1987.

Roshal', L. *Dziga Vertov.* Iskusstvo, Moscow, 1982.

Rubailo, A. I. *Partiinoe rukovodstvo razvitiem kinoiskusstva, 1928–1937 gg.* MGU, Moscow, 1976.

Samoe vazhnoe iz vsekh iskusstv: Lenin o kino. Iskusstvo, Moscow, 1963.

Samoe vazhnoe iz vsekh iskusstv: Lenin o kino. 2nd ed. Iskusstvo, Moscow, 1973.

Seton, Marie. *Sergei M. Eisenstein.* A. A. Wyn, New York, 1952.

Shklovskii, Viktor. *Eizenshtein.* Iskusstvo, Moscow, 1976.

—*Za 60 let. Raboty o kino.* Iskusstvo, Moscow, 1985.

Shumiatskii, Boris. *Kinematografiia millionov.* Kinofotoizdat, Moscow, 1935.

Sinko, Ervin. *Egy Regeny Regenye. Moszkvai naplojegyzetek, 1935–1937.* Magveto, Budapest, 1988.

Smith, Paul (ed.). *The Historian and Film.* Cambridge University Press, 1976.

Sobolev, R. *Aleksander Dovzhenko.* Iskusstvo, Moscow, 1980.

Sokolov, I. *Istoriia sovetskogo kinoiskusstva zvukogo perioda.* Goskinoizdat, Moscow, 1946.

Sovetskie khudozhestvennye fil'my. Annotirovannyi katalog. 4 vols. Iskusstvo, Moscow, 1961–1968.

Soviet Writers' Congress, 1934: The Debate of Socialist Realism and Modernism. Lawrence and Wishart, London, 1977.

Stites, Richard. *Red Dreams: Utopian Vision and Experimental Life in the Russian Revolution.* Oxford University Press, Oxford, 1989.

Sychev, M., and V. Perlin. *Kino v Krasnoi Armii.* Teakinopechat', Moscow, 1929.

Taylor, R., and K. R. M. Short. "Soviet Cinema and the International Menace, 1928–1939." *Historical Journal of Film, Radio and Television* 2: 131–56, 1986.

Taylor, Richard. *Film Propaganda: Soviet Russia and Nazi Germany*. Croom Helm, London, 1979.

—"Boris Shumyatsky and the Soviet Cinema in the 1930s: Ideology as Mass Entertainment." *Historical Journal of Film, Radio and Television* 6: 43–60, 1986.

—*The Politics of Soviet Cinema, 1917–1929*. Cambridge University Press, 1979.

Tertz, A. *On Socialist Realism*. Pantheon, New York, 1960.

Trauberg, Leonid. *Izbrannye proizvedeniia*. 2 vols. Iskusstvo, Moscow, 1988.

Trotsky, Leon. *Literature and Revolution*. University of Michigan Press, Ann Arbor, 1960.

—*Problems of Everyday Life*. Monad Press, New York, 1973.

Tucker, Robert C. *Stalin in Power: The Revolution from Above, 1928–1941*. Norton, New York, 1990.

Turovskaia, Maia. *Pamiati tekushchego mgnoveniia*. Sovetskii pisatel', Moscow, 1987.

Vas, Zoltan. "A kelet-Europai barati kapcsolatok." *Latohatar*, Budapest, June 1989.

Vertov, Dziga. *Kino-eye: The Writings of Vertov Dziga*. Ed. Annette Micchelson. University of California Press, Berkeley, 1984.

Vorontsov, Iurii, and Igor Rachuk. *The Phenomenon of Soviet Cinema*. Progress, Moscow, 1980.

Williams, Alan. "The Lumière Organization and 'Documentary Realism.' " In John L. Fell (ed.), *Film before Griffith*. University of California Press, Berkeley, 1983.

Youngblood, Denise. *Soviet Cinema in the Silent Era, 1918–1935*. UMI Press, Ann Arbor, Mich., 1985.

—"Cinema as Social Criticism: The Early Films of Fridrich Ermler." In Anna Lawton (ed.), *Red Screen: Image Making and Social Impact*. Harper Collins, New York, 1991.

Zak, Mark. *Mikhail Romm i traditsii sovetskoi kinorezhissury*. Iskusstvo, Moscow, 1974.

—*Fil'my o Velikoi Otechestvennoi Voine*. Znanie, Moscow, 1978.

—*Mikhail Romm i ego fil'my*. Iskusstvo, Moscow, 1988.

Zakhri, A. *Moi debiuty*. Iskusstvo, Moscow, 1985.

Zhdan, V. (ed.). *Kratkaia istoriia sovetskogo kino*. Iskusstvo, Moscow, 1969.

Zorkaia, N. M. *Sovetskii istoricheskii fil'm*. Akad. Nauk, Moscow, 1962.

—"Iakov Protazanov i sovetskoe kinoiskusstvo 20-kh godov." *Voprosy kinoiskusstva* 6: 165–91, 1962.

—*Portrety*. Iskusstvo, Moscow, 1966.

—*Na rubezhe stoletii. U istokov massovogo iskusstva v Rossii 1900–1910 godov*. Nauka, Moscow, 1976.

—*The Illustrated History of the Soviet Cinema*. Hippocrene Books, New York, 1989.

Zsuffa, Joseph, *Béla Balazs: The Man and the Artist*. University of California Press, Berkeley, 1987.

Filmography

The first part of this Filmography lists only those prerevolutionary and Soviet films that I have seen myself. Most of the prerevolutionary films were viewed in the Hungarian Film Archives in Budapest. The Pacific Film Archives in Berkeley, California, was my best source for Soviet silent films. I saw most of the films from the 1930s, 1940s, and 1950s at the Hungarian Film Archives and at the Soviet Film Archives in Moscow. Some films were also made available for my viewing at the Hoover Institution at Stanford, California, and at the Library of Congress and the National Archives in Washington, D.C. The second part of this Filmography lists additional cited films and is largely based on *Sovetskie khudozhestvennye fil'my: Annotioravannyi katalog*, 4 vols., Iskusstvo, Moscow, 1960–4.

Soviet and prerevolutionary Russian films seen by the author

Academician Ivan Pavlov (*Akademik Ivan Pavlov*), dir. G. Roshal' (Lenfil'm, 1949)

Actress (*Aktrisa*), dir. Leonid Trauberg (TsOKS/Alma-Ata, 1943)

Admiral Nakhimov, dir. Vsevolod Pudovkin (Mosfil'm, 1946; first shown 1947)

Adventures of Nasredin, The (*Pokhozhdeniia Nasredina*), dir. N. Ganiev (Tashkent and Soiuzdetfil'm, 1946; first shown 1947)

Aelita, dir. Iakov Protazanov (Mezhrabpom–Rus', 1924)

Aerograd (a/k/a *Air City*), dir. Aleksandr Dovzhenko (Mosfil'm and Ukrainfil'm, 1935)

Aleksandr Nevskii, dir. Sergei Eisenstein (Mosfil'm, 1938)

Aleksandr Popov, dir. G. Rappaport (Lenfil'm, 1949)

Alisher Navoi, dir. K. Iarmatov (Tashkent, 1947; first shown 1948)

Alone (*Odna*), dir. G. Kozintsev and L. Trauberg (Soiuzkino/Leningrad, 1931)

Anton Ivanovich Is Angry (*Anton Ivanovich serditsia*), dir. A. Ivanovskii (Lenfil'm, 1941)

Arsenal, dir. Aleksandr Dovzhenko (VUKFU, 1929)

At Six o'Clock after the War (*V shest' chasov vechera posle voiny*), dir. Ivan A. Pyr'ev (Mosfil'm, 1944)

At the Bluest Sea (*U samogo sinego moria*), dir. Boris Barnet (Mezhrabpom and Azerfil'm, 1935; first shown 1936)

261

Battle of Stalingrad, The (Stalingradskaia bitva), Parts I–II, dir. V. Petrov (Mosfil'm, 1949)

Battleship Potemkin (Bronenosets Potemkin), dir. Sergei Eisenstein (Mosfil'm 1925; theatrical release 1926)

Bear's Wedding, The (Medvezh'ia svad'ba), dir. K. Eggert (Mezhrabpom–Rus', 1925; first shown 1926)

Bogdan Khmel'nitskii, dir. I. Savchenko (Kiev, 1941)

Borderlands (a/k/a Patriots; Okraina), dir. Boris Barnet (Mezhrabpom, 1933)

Bountiful Summer (Shchedroe leto), dir. Boris Barnet (Kiev, 1950; first shown 1951)

Brigade Commander Ivanov (Kombrig Ivanov), dir. A. Razumnyi (Proletkino, 1923)

By the Law (a/k/a Dura Lex; Po zakonu), dir. Lev Kuleshov (Goskino, 1926)

Captain Grant's Children (Deti kapitana Granta), dir. V. Vainshtok (Mosfil'm, 1936)

Cavalier of the Golden Star (Kavaler zoloti zvezdy), dir. Iu. Raizman (Mosfil'm, 1950; first shown 1951)

Chapaev, dir. Sergei and Georgii Vasil'ev (Leninfil'm, 1934)

Chess Fever (Shakhmatnaia goriachka), dir. Vsevolod Pudovkin (Mezhrabpom–Rus', 1925)

Child of the Big City (Ditia bol'shogo goroda), dir. Evgenii Bauer (Khanzhonkov, 1914)

Childhood of Maksim Gorkii, The (a/k/a Childhood of Gorky; Detstvo Gor'kogo), dir. Mark Donskoi (Soiuzdetfil'm, 1938); Part I of Gorky trilogy

Cigarette Girl from Mosselprom, The (Papirosnitsa iz Mossel'proma), dir. Iu. Zheliabuzhskii (Mezhrabpom–Rus', 1924)

Circus (Tsirk), dir. G. Aleksandrov (Mosfil'm, 1936)

Composer Glinka, dir. G. Aleksandrov (Mosfil'm, 1952)

Conspiracy of the Doomed, The (Zagovor obrechennykh), dir. M. Kalatozov (Mosfil'm, 1950)

Conveyor Belt of Death, The (Konveier smerti; a/k/a Tovar Ploshchadei), dir. Ivan A. Pyr'ev (Soiuzfil'm, 1933)

Counterplan (Vstrechnyi), dir. Sergei Iutkevich and Fridrich Ermler (Rosfil'm, 1932)

Courageous Seven, The (Semero smelykh), dir. Sergei Gerasimov (Lenfil'm, 1936)

Court of Honor, The (Sud chesti), dir. Abram Room (Mosfil'm, 1948; first shown 1949)

Days and Nights (Dni i nochi), dir. A. Stol'per (Mosfil'm, 1944; first shown 1945)

Death Ray, The (Luch smerti), dir. Lev Kuleshov, sc. Vsevolod Pudovkin (Goskino, 1925)

Defense of Sevastopol, The (Oborona Sevastopolia), dir. Vasilii Goncharov and A. Khanzhonkov (Khanzhonkov, 1911)

Departure of the Grand Old Man (Ukhod velikovo startsa), dir. Iakov Protazanov (Thiemann and Reinhardt, 1912)

Deputy from the Baltic, The (Deputat Baltiki), dir. A. Zakhri and I. Kheifits (Lenfil'm, USSR, 1936; first shown 1937)

Deserter (Dezertir), dir. Vsevolod Pudovkin (Mezhrabpom, 1933)

Devil's Wheel, The (*Chertovo koleso*), dir. Grigori Kozintsev and Leonid Trauberg (Leningradkino, 1926)

Diplomatic Pouch, The (*Teka dypkuryera* [Ukr.]; *Sumka dipkurera* [Russ.]), dir. Aleksandr Dovzhenko (VUKFU, 1927)

Don Diego and Pelagea (*Don Diego i Pelageia*), dir. Iakov Protazanov (Mezhrabpom–Rus', 1927; first shown 1928)

Dying Swan, The (*Umiraiushchii lebed'*), dir. Evgenii Bauer (Khanzhonkov, 1916)

Earth (*Zemlia*), dir. Aleksandr Dovzhenko (VUKFU, 1930)

End of St. Petersburg, The (*Konets Sankt-Petersburga*), dir. Vsevolod Pudovkin (Mezhrabpom–Rus', 1927)

Engineer Prite's Project (*Proekt Inzhenera Praita*), dir. Lev Kuleshov (Khanzhonkov, 1918)

Extraordinary Adventures of Mr. West in the Land of the Bolsheviks (*Neobychainie prikliucheniia Mistera Vesta v strane Bol'shevikov*), dir. Lev Kuleshov (Goskino, 1924)

Fall of Berlin, The (*Padenie Berlina*), Parts I–II, dir. M. Chiaureli (Mosfil'm, 1949; first shown 1950)

Fall of the Romanov Dynasty, The (*Padenie dinastii Romanovykh*), dir. Esther Shub (Sovkino, 1927; first shown 1928)

Far from Moscow (*Daleko ot Moskvy*), dir. A. Stol'per (Mosfil'm, 1950)

Father Sergius (*Otets Sergii*), dir. Iakov Protazanov (Ermolev, 1917; first shown 1918)

Fifteen-Year-Old Captain (*Piatnadtsatiletnyi kapitan*), dir. V. Zhuravlev (Soiuzdetfil'm, 1945; first shown 1946)

First Glove, The (*Pervaia perchatka*), dir. A. Florov (Mosfil'm, 1946; first shown 1947)

First-Year Student (*Pervoklassnitsa*), dir. I. Frez (Soiuzdetfil'm, 1948)

Flyers (*Letchiki*), dir. Iu. Raizman (Mosfil'm, 1935)

Forty-First, The (*Sorok pervyi*), dir. Iakov Protazanov (Mezhrabpom–Rus', 1926; first shown 1927)

Forward, Soviet! (*Shagai sovet!*), dir. Dziga Vertov (Sovkino, 1926)

Fragment of an Empire (*Oblomok imperii*), dir. Fridrich Ermler (Sovkino/Leningrad, 1929)

Frontier (*Granitsa*), dir. M. Dubson (Lenfil'm, 1935)

Fruit of Love, The (a/k/a *Love's Berry; Iagodka liubvi*), dir. Aleksandr Dovzhenko (VUKFU, 1926)

Gay Canary, The (*Veselaia kanareika*), dir. Lev Kuleshov (Mezhrabpom, 1929)

Girlfriends (*Podrugi*), dir. L. Arnshtam (Lenfil'm, 1935; first shown 1936)

Glinka, dir. L. Arnshtam (Mosfil'm, 1946; first shown 1947)

Glumov's Diary (*Kinodnevik Glumova*), dir. Sergei Eisenstein (short inserted in production of Ostrovsky's *Enough Folly in a Wise Man*, Proletkult Theater, Moscow, 1923)

Golden Lake (*Zolotoe ozero*), dir. V. Schneiderov (Mezhrabpom, 1935)

Golden Mountains (Zlatye gory), dir. Sergei Iutkevich (Sovkino/Leningrad, 1931)

Grasshopper and the Ant (*Strekoza i muravei*), dir. W. Starewicz (Khanzhonkov, 1912)

Great Citizen, The (*Velikii grazhdanin*), Parts I–II, dir. Fridrich Ermler, sc. M. Bleiman (Lenfil'm, 1937–9; Part I first shown 1938)

Great Consoler, The (*Velikii uteshitel'*), dir. Lev Kuleshov (Mezhrabpom, 1933)

Great Life, A (*Bol'shaia zhizn'*), dir. L. Lukov (Kiev, 1939; first shown 1940)

Grunia Kornakova, dir. N. Ekk (Mezhrabpom, 1936)

Happiness (*Schast'e*), dir. A. Medvedkin (Mosfil'm, 1935)

Happy Fellows (*Veselye rebiata*), dir. G. Aleksandrov (Moskinokombinat, 1934)

Heir of Genghis Khan, The (a/k/a *Storm over Asia; Potomok Chingis-khana*), dir. Vsevolod Pudovkin (Mezhrabpom, 1928; first shown 1929)

His Call (a/k/a *Broken Chains; Ego prizyv*), dir. Iakov Protazanov (Mezhrabpom–Rus', 1925)

Horizon – The Wandering Jew (*Gorizont*), dir. Lev Kuleshov (Mezhrabpom, 1932; first shown 1933)

House in the Snowdrift, The (*Dom v sugrobakh*), dir. Fridrich Ermler (Sovkino/Leningrad, 1928)

How the Steel Was Tempered (a/k/a *Heroes Are Made; Kak zakalialas' stal'*), dir. Mark Donskoi (Kiev and Ashkhabad, 1942)

Inspector General, The (*Revizor*), dir. V. Petrov (Mosfil'm, 1952)

Ivan, dir. Aleksandr Dovzhenko (Ukrainfil'm, 1932)

Ivan the Terrible (*Ivan Groznyi*), Parts I–II, dir. Sergei Eisenstein (TsOKS/Alma-Ata, 1944–6; Part I first shown 1945; Part II first shown 1958)

Karo, dir. A. Ai-Artian (Armenkino, 1937)

Katka's Reinette Apples (*Kat'ka bumazhnyi ranet*), dir. Fridrich Ermler (Sovkino/Leningrad, 1926)

Khabarda, dir. M. Chiaureli (Goskino Gruzii, 1931)

Kino-Eye (*Kino-glaz*), dir. Dziga Vertov (Goskino, 1924)

Kiss of Mary Pickford, The (*Potselui Meri Pikford*), dir. S. Komarov (Mezhrabpom–Rus', 1927)

Komsomolsk, dir. Sergei Gerasimov (Lenfil'm, 1938)

Kuban Cossacks (*Kubanskie kazaki*), dir. Ivan A. Pyr'ev (Mosfil'm, 1949; first shown 1950)

Last Camp, The (*Poslednyi tabor*), dir. E. Shneider (Mezhrbpom, 1935; first shown 1936)

Lenin in 1918 (*Lenin v 1918 godu*), dir. Mikhail Romm (Mosfil'm, 1939)

Lenin in October (*Lenin v Oktiabr*), dir. Mikhail Romm (Mosfil'm, 1937)

Lieutenant Kizhe (*Poruchik Kizhe*), dir. A. Faintsimmer (Belgoskino, 1934)

Life in Death (*Zhizn' v smerti*), dir. Evgenii Bauer (Khanzhonkov, 1914)

Little Red Devils, The (*Krasnye diavoloiata*), dir. I. Perestiani, sc. P. A. Bliakhin (Georgian Narkompros, 1923)

Locksmith and Chancellor (*Slesar' i kantsler*), dir. Vladimir Gardin, co-sc. Vsevolod Pudovkin (VUFKU, 1923)

Lone White Sail (*Beleet parus edinokii*), dir. V. Legoshin (Soiuzdetfil'm, 1937)

Man from the Restaurant, The (*Chelovek iz restorana*), dir. Iakov Protazanov (Mezhrabpom–Rus', 1927)

Man with a Gun, The (*Chelovek s ruzhem*), dir. Sergei Iutkevich (Lenfil'm, 1938)

Man with the Movie Camera, The (*Chelovek s kinoapparatom*), dir. Dziga Vertov (VUKFU, 1929)

Marionettes (*Marionetki*), dir. Iakov Protazanov (Mezhrabpom, 1934)

Mashenka, dir. Iu. Raizman (Mosfil'm, 1942)

Meeting on the Elbe (*Vstrecha na El'be*), dir. G Aleksandrov (Mosfil'm, 1949)

Member of the Government (*Chlen pravitel' stva*), dir. A. Zakhri and I. Kheifits (Lenfil'm, 1939; first shown 1940)

Mess-Mend, Parts I–III, dir. F. Otsep and Boris Barnet (Mezhrabpom–Rus', 1926)

Michurin, dir. Aleksandr Dovzhenko (Mosfil'm, 1948; first shown 1949)

Miners, The (*Shakhtery*), dir. Sergei Iutkevich (Lenfil'm, 1937)

Miracle Worker, The (a/k/a *Beauty and the Bolshevik; Chudotvorets*), dir. Aleksandr Panteleev (Sevzapkino and First Petrograd Committee of Film Artists, 1922)

Mother (*Mat'*), dir. Vsevolod Pudovkin (Mezhrabpom–Rus', 1926)

Musorgskii, dir. G. Roshal' (Lenfil'm, 1950)

My Apprenticeship (a/k/a *Among People; V liudiakh*), dir. Mark Donskoi (Soiuzdetfil'm, 1939; first shown 1940); Part II of Gorky trilogy

My Grandmother (*Maia babushka*), dir. K. Mikaberidze (Goskino Gruzii, 1929; unclear whether publicly exhibited)

My Universities (*Moi universitety*), dir. Mark Donskoi (Soiuzdetfil'm, 1939; first shown in 1940); Part III of Gorky trilogy

New Babylon, The (*Novyi Vavilon*), dir. Grigori Kozintsev and Leonid Trauberg (Sovkino/Leningrad, 1929)

Oath, The (a/k/a *The Vow; Kliatva*), dir. M. Chiaureli (Tbilisi, 1946)

October (a/k/a *Ten Days That Shook the World; Oktiabr'*), dir. Sergei Eisenstein, (Sovkino, 1927)

Old and the New, The (a/k/a *The General Line; Staroe i novoe* [a/k/a *Generalnaia linia*]), dir. Sergei Eisenstein (Sovkino, 1929)

Once Upon a Time There Lived a Little Girl (*Zhila byla devochka*), dir. V. Eismont (Soiuzfil'm, 1944)

Parisian Cobbler, The (*Parizhskii sapozhnik*), dir. Fridrich Ermler (Sovkino/Leningrad, 1927; first shown 1928)

Party Card (*Partiinyi bilet*), dir. Ivan A. Pyr'ev (Mosfil'm, 1936)

Peasant Women of Riazan, The (*Baby riazanskie*), dir. Olga I. Preobrazhenskaia (Sovkino, 1927)

Peasants (*Krestiane*), dir. Fridrich Ermler (Leninfil'm, 1934; first shown 1935)

Peter the First (*Petr Pervyi*), Parts I–II, dir. V. Petrov (Lenfil'm, 1937–8; Part II first shown 1939)

Pirogov, dir. Grigori Kozintsev (Lenfil'm, 1947)

Private Life of Peter Vinogradov, The (Chastnaia zhizn' Petra Vinogradova), dir. Aleksandr Macheret (Moskinokombinat, 1934; first shown 1935)

Proletarians of the World Unite! (Proletarii vsekh stran, soediniates'!), dir. B. Sushkevich (Moscow Film Committee, 1919)

Rainbow, The (Raduga), dir. Mark Donskoi (Kiev, 1943; first shown 1944)

Return of Maxim, The (Vozvrashchenie Maksima), dir. Grigori Kozintsev and Leonid Trauberg (Lenfil'm, 1937); Part II of Maxim trilogy

Return of Nathan Becker, The (Vozvrashchenie Neitana Bekkera), dir. B. Shpis and R. Mil'man (Belgoskino/Leningrad, 1932)

Return of Vasilii Bortonikov, The (Vozvrachenie Vasiliia Borotnikova), dir. Vsevolod Pudovkin (Mosfil'm, 1952; first shown 1953)

Revenge of the Cameraman, The (Mest' Kinematograficheskogo operatora), dir. W. Starewicz (animated short; Khanzhonkov, 1912)

Rich Bride, The (Bogataia nevesta), dir. Ivan A. Pyr'ev (Ukrainfil'm, 1937; first shown 1938)

Rising of the Fishermen, The (Vosstanie rybakov), dir. Erwin Piskator (Mezhrabpom, 1934)

Road to Life, The (Putevka v zhizn'), dir. N. Ekk (Mezhrabpom, 1931)

Russian Question, The (Russkii vopros), dir. Mikhail Romm (Mosfil'm, 1947; first shown 1948)

S.V.D. – Union of the Great Cause, The (a/k/a *S.V.D. – The Club of the Big Deed; S.V.D. – Soyuz Velikogo Dela),* dir. Grigori Kozintsev and Leonid Trauberg (Sovkino, 1927)

Sadko, dir. Aleksandr Ptushko (Mosfil'm, 1952; first shown 1953)

Satan Triumphant (Satana likuiushchii), dir. Iakov Protazanov (Ermolev, 1917)

Secretary of the District Committee, The (Sekretar' raikoma), dir. Ivan A. Pyr'ev (TsOKS/Alma-Ata, 1942)

Shchors, dir. Aleksandr Dovzhenko (Kiev, 1939)

She Defends the Motherland (Ona zashchishchaet rodinu; in the United States shown as *No Greater Love),* dir. Fridrikh Ermler (TsOKS/Alma-Ata, 1943)

Shepherd and the Tsar, The (Pastukh i tsar'), dir. A. Ledashchev (Mosfil'm, 1934)

Shining Path (Svetlyi put'), dir. G. Aleksandrov (Mosfil'm, 1940)

Simple Case, A (Prostoi sluchai), dir. Vsevolod Pudovkin (Mezhrabpom, 1930)

Son of the Regiment, The (Syn polka), dir. V. Pronin (Soiuzdetfil'm, 1946)

Sons (Synov'ia), dir. A. Ivanov (Lenfil'm and Riga, 1946)

Spring (Vesna), dir. G. Aleksandrov (Mosfil'm, 1947)

Stenka Razin, dir. V. Romashkov (Drankov, 1908)

Stepan Razin, dir. Olga I. Preobrazhenskaia (Mosfil'm, 1939)

Stone Flower (Kamennyi tsvetok), dir. Aleksandr Ptushko (Barrandov [Prague], Czechoslovakia, and Mosfil'm, 1946)

Strict Young Man, A (Strogii iunosha), dir. Abram Room (Ukrainfil'm, 1934; never publicly exhibited)

Strike (Stachka), dir. Sergei Eisenstein (Goskino and Proletkul't, 1925)

Swineherd and Shepherd (Svinarka i pastukh), dir. Ivan A. Pry'ev (Mosfil'm, 1941)

Tailor from Torzhok, The (Zakroishchik iz Torzhka), dir. Iakov Protazanov (Mezhrabpom–Rus', 1925)

Tale about a Real Man, A (Povest' o nastoiashchem cheloveke), dir. A. Stol'per (Mosfil'm, 1948)

Taras Shevchenko, dir. I. Savhenko (Kiev, 1951)

Teacher (Uchitel'), dir. Sergei Gerasimov (Lenfil'm, 1939)

Third Blow, The (Tretii udar), dir. I. Savchenko (Kiev, 1948)

Third Meshchanskaia Street (a/k/a/ *Bed and Sofa; Tretia meshchanskaia*), dir. Abram Room (Sovkino, 1927)

Thirteen, The (Trinadstat'), dir. Mikhail Romm (Mosfil'm, 1937)

Three Million Case, The (Protsess o trekh millionakh), dir. Iakov Protazanov (Mezhrabpom–Rus', 1926)

Toward Meeting Life (Navstrechu zhizni), dir. N. Lebedev (Lenfil'm, 1952)

Tractorists (Traktoristy), dir. Ivan A. Pry'ev (Modfil'm, 1939)

Two Buldis, The (2-Bul' di-2), dir. Lev Kuleshov (Mezhrabpom, 1929; first shown 1930)

Two Days (Dva dnia), dir. G. Stabovoi (VUFKU, 1927)

Unforgettable Year, 1919, The (Nezabyvaemyi 1919 – i god), dir. M. Chiaureli (Mosfil'm, 1951; first shown 1952)

Village Schoolteacher, A (a/k/a *Varvara, An Emotional Education; Sel'skaia uchitel'nitsa*), dir. M. Donskoi (Soiuzdetfil'm, 1947)

Volga-Volga, dir. G. Aleksandrov (Mosfil'm, 1938)

Vyborg Side, The (a/k/a *New Horizons; Vyborgskaia storona*), dir. Grigori Kozintsev and Leonid Trauberg (Lenfil'm, 1938; first shown 1939); Part III of Maxim trilogy

Wait for Me (Zhdi menia), dir. A. Stol'per (TsOKS/Alma-Ata, 1943)

We Are from Kronstadt (My iz Kronshtata), dir. E. Dzigan (Mosfil'm, 1936)

Wedding (Svad'ba), dir. I. Annenskii (Tbilisi, 1944)

Young Guard (Molodaia gvardiia), Parts I–II, dir. Sergei Gerasimov (Gorkii, 1947)

Young Lady and the Hooligan, The (Baryshnia i khuligan), dir. E. Slavinskii, sc. Vladimir Maiakovskii (Neptune, 1918)

Young Woman Hurries to the Rendezvous, The (Devushka speshit na svidanie), dir. M. Verner (Belgoskino, 1936)

Youth of Maxim, The (Iunost' Maksima), dir. Grigori Kozintsev and Leonid Trauberg (Leninfil'm, 1934; first shown 1935); Part I of Maxim trilogy

Zhukovskii, dir. Vsevolod Pudovkin (Mosfil'm, 1950)

Zoia, Dir. L. Arnshtam (Soiuzdetfil'm, 1944)

Zvenigora ([Ukr.] *Zvenyhora*), dir. Aleksandr Dovzhenko (VUKFU, 1927; first shown 1928)

Additional cited films (USSR unless otherwise noted)

Admiral Ushakov, dir. Mikhail Romm (Mosfil'm, 1953)

Aleksandr Parkhomenko, dir. L. Lukov (Kiev, 1942)

Among the Bullets of German Barbarians (pre-1917)

Antosha Rybkin (3rd kinosbornik), dir. K. Iudin (Mosfil'm, 1941)

Antosha Rybkin, dir. K. Iudin (Alma-Ata, 1942)

Arshin-Mal-Alan, dir. R. Takhmasib (Baku, 1943)

Battle for Our Soviet Ukraine, The (Bytva za nashu radiansku Ukrainu), dir. Aleksandr Dovzhenko (Newsreel studio, 1943)

Belinskii, dir. Kozintsev (Lenfil'm, 1950)

Bezhin Meadow (Bezhin lug), dir. Sergei Eisenstein (unfinished; Mosfil'm, 1935–7)

Cabin in the Cotton (a/k/a *The Betrayal of Marvin Blake*), dir. Michael Curtiz (Warner Bros., USA, 1932)

Cabinet of Dr. Caligari, The (Das Kabinett des Dr. Caligari), dir. Robert Wiene (Germany, 1919)

Cagliostro, dir. Reinhold Schunzel (Germany, 1920)

Casablanca, dir. Michael Curtiz (Warner Bros., USA, 1942)

Children – The Flower of Life (Deti – tsvety zhizni), dir. Iu. Zheliabuzhskii (VFKO, 1919)

Civilized Barbarians (Tsivilirozvannye varvary) (Russia, 1914)

Cooperatives in Normandy (French, date unknown)

Cossacks of the Don, The (Donskie kozaki) dir. Olga I. Preobrazhenskaia (Pathé, but made in Russia, 1908)

Cross and the Mauser, The (Krest i mauzer), dir. Vladimir Gardin (Goskino, 1925)

Dark Forces (Temnye sily) (Russia, 1917)

Daughter of the Night, dir. Elmer Clifton (USA, 1924)

David Bek, dir. A. Bek-Nazarov (Erevan, 1944)

Day of the New World, A (Den' novogo mira), dir. M. Ia. Slutskii (Newsreel studio, 1940)

Day of the War, A (Den' voiny), dir. M. Ia. Slutskii (Newsreel studio, 1942)

Defeat of the German Armies Outside Moscow, The (a/k/a *Moscow Strikes Back; Razgrom nemetskikh voisk pod Moskvoi),* dir. L. V. Varlamov and I. P. Kopalin (Newsreel studio, 1942)

Defeat of Iudenich, The (Razgrom Iudenicha), dir. P. Petrov-Bytov (Lenfil'm, 1941)

Defense of Tsaritsyn, The (Oborona Tsaritsyna), dir. Sergei Vasil'ev and Georgii Vasil'ev (Lenfil'm, 1942)

Don Q, Son of Zorro, dir. Donald Crisp (Elton, USA, 1925)

Down with the German Yoke

Dr. Mabuse, the Gambler (Dr. Mabuse, der Spieler), dir. Fritz Lang (Germany, 1922)

Dream, The (Mechta), dir. Mikhail Romm (Mosfil'm and Tashkent, 1943)

Dubrovskii, dir. A. Ivanovskii (Lenfil'm, 1936)

Dzhambul, dir. Ie. Dzigan (Alma-Ata, 1952)

1812, dir. Vasilii Goncharov (Khanzhonkov, Russia, 1912)

Elixir of Courage (Eliksir bodrosti), dir. Sergei Iutkevich (7th kinosbornik) (Soiuzdetfil'm, 1941)

Elusive Ian (Neulovimyi Ian), dir. V. Petrov (Tbilisi, 1942)

Enthusiasm: Symphony of the Don Basin (Entuziasm: Simfonia Donbassa), dir. Dziga Vertov (Ukrainafil'm, 1931)

Eternal Jew, The (Der ewige Jude), dir. Ministry of Propaganda of the Third Reich, under supervision of Fritz Heppler (Germany, 1940)

Evdokiia Rozhnovskaia, dir. S. Mitrich (Goskino, 1924)

Fall of Nations, The (origin unclear: perhaps *The Fall of a Nation,* dir. Bartley Cushing [USA, 1916])

Father and Son (Otets i syn), dir. I. Perestiani (Khanzhonkov, 1919)

Father and Son (Otets i syn), dir. Margarita A. Barskaia (Soiuzdetfil'm, 1937, never exhibited)

Feast in Zhirmunka (Pir v Zhirmunke), dir. Vsevolod Pudovkin, sc. Leonid Leonov (6th kinosbornik) (Mosfil'm, 1941)

Film-Truth (Kino-pravda), dir. Dziga Vertov (newsreel series, Goskino, 1922–5)

Fires of Baku, The (Ogni Baku), dir. A. Zakhri and I. Kheifits (Baku, 1950; first shown in 1958)

Flags Wave Triumphantly (Gordo viotsia znamia) (Russia, no date)

For the Red Flag (Za krasnoe znamia), dir. V. Kasianov (Neptune, 1919)

For Tsar and Fatherland (Za Tsaria, za rodinu) (Russia, 1914)

Frightened Burzhui, The (Zapugannyi burzhui), dir. M. Verner (Kiev, 1919)

Front, The (Front), dir. Sergei Vasil'ev and Georgii Vasil'ev (TsOKS Alma-Ata, 1943)

Georgii Saakadze, dir. M. Chiaureli (Tbilisi, 1942)

Ghost That Will Not Return, The (Prividenie, kotorye ne vozvrashchaetsia), dir. Abram Room (Sovkino, 1930)

Girl from the Other Side, The (Devushka s togo berega), dir. Esakia (Tbilisi, 1941)

Girl No. 217 (Chelovek No. 217), dir. Mikhail Romm (Mosfil'm Tashkent, 1944)

Girl of My Dreams (Die Frau meine Träume), dir. Georg Jacoby (Germany, 1944)

Girl with the Hatbox, The (Devushka s korobkoi), dir. Boris Barnet (Mezhrabpom, 1927)

Glory to Us – Death to the Enemy (Slava nam – smert' vragam), dir. E. Bauer (Khanzhonkov, Russia, 1914)

Gold Rush, The, dir. Charles Chaplin (Chaplin/United Artists, USA, 1925)

Golden Road, The (Zolotaia doroga), dir. Gomarteli (Tbilisi, 1945)

Governmental Deception (Gosudarstvennyi obman) (Russia, 1917)

Great Dawn, The (Velikoe zavero), dir. M. Chiaureli (Tbilisi, 1938)

Great Land (a/k/a *The Mainland; Bol'shaia zemlia),* dir. Sergei Gerasimov (Mosfil'm, 1944)

His Butler's Sister, dir. Frank Borzage (Universal, USA, 1943)

His Career (a/k/a *Provocator; Ego Kar'era. Provokator*), dir. Turin (Yalta VUFKU, 1927)

Hostile Storms (*Vikhri vrazhdebnye*), dir. M. Kalatozov (Mosfil'm, 1953; first shown in 1956)

How a German General Signed a Pact with the Devil (*Kak nemetskii general podpisal' dogovor's diavolom*) (Russia, 1914)

How Snooky Became a Capitalist (country of origin and date unknown)

Hunger . . . Hunger . . . Hunger . . . (*Golod . . . golod . . . golod . . .*), dir. Vladimir Gardin and Vsevolod Pudovkin, photog. Edward Tisse (Goskino, 1921)

Iakov Sverdlov, dir. Sergei Iutkevich (Soiuzdetfil'm, 1940)

In the Clutches of Judas (*V lapakh Iudy*) (Russia, 1917)

In the Fire of the Storm (*V ogne storma*) (Russia, 1914)

In the Sentry Box (*V storozhevoi budke*), dir. D. Antadze (Tbilisi, 1941)

Incident at the Telegraph Office (*Sluchai na telegrafe*), dir. L. Arnshtam and Grigori Kozintsev (2nd kinosbornik) (Lenfil'm, 1941)

Intolerance, dir. D. W. Griffith (USA, 1916)

Ivan Nikulin – Russian Sailor (*Ivan Nikulin – Russkii matros*), dir. Ivan Savchenko (Mosfil'm, 1944)

Jobs and Men (*Dela i liudi*), dir. Aleksandr Macheret, asst. dir. Mikhail Romm (Soiuzkino, 1932)

Karl Brunner, dir. Masliukov (Odessa, 1936)

Kastus Kalinovskii, dir. V. Gardin (Belgoskino and Sovkino, 1928)

Khveska, dir. A. Ivanovskii (Rus' and VFKO, 1920; first shown in 1923)

Kid, The, dir. Charles Chaplin (Chaplin/AFN, USA, 1921)

King of the Beasts (country of origin and date unknown)

King, Law, Freedom (*Korol', zakon, svoboda*) (Russia, 1914)

Knights of the Dark Nights, The (*Rytsary chornykh nochei*) (country of origin and date unknown)

Kotovskii, dir. A. Faintsimmer (TsOKS Alma-Ata, 1942)

Kutuzov, dir. V. Petrov (Mosfil'm, 1944)

Lady of the Summer Resort Fears Not Even the Devil, The (*Dama kurorta dazhe chorta ne boitsia*) (country of origin and date unknown)

Law of Life, The (*Zakon zhizni*), dir. A. Stol'per (Mosfil'm, 1940)

Liberation of the Serfs, The (*Osvobozhdenie krepostnykh*) (Russia, date unknown)

Living Corpse, The (*Zhivoi trup*), dir. Ch. Sabinskii (Kharitonov, 1918)

Lucky Ten Ruble Piece, The (*Shchastlivyi chernovets*), dir. Dmitriev (Mezhrabpom–Rus', 1928)

Lullaby (*Kolibel'naia*), dir. Dziga Vertov (Mosfil'm, 1937)

Malakhov Kurgan (*Malakhov kurgan*), dir. Zakhri and Kheifits (Tbilisi, 1944)

Mark of Zorro, The dir. Fred Niblo (Fairbanks/UA, USA, 1920)

Meeting, The (*Vstrecha*), dir. V. Feinberg (2nd kinosbornik) (Lenfil'm, 1941)

Miners of the Donbass, The (*Donetskie shakhtery*), dir. L. Lukov (Gorkii, 1950)

Minin and Pozharskii, dir. Vsevolod Pudovkin (Mosfil'm, 1939)

Moscow Sky (Nebo Moskvy), dir. Raizman (Mosfil'm, 1944)

Murderers Are on Their Way (Ubiitsy vykhodiat na dorogu), dir. Vsevolod Pudovkin (Combined studios, 1942)

Mysterious Murder in Petrograd on December 16 (Tainoe ublistvo v Petorgrade, Dek. 16) (Russia, 1917)

New Adventures of Schweik (Novye pokhozhdeniia Shveika), dir. Sergei Iutkevich (Stalinabad, 1943)

Nishchaia (a/k/a *Podaite, Khrista radi, ei; The Lowest. Give, in the Name of Christ),* dir. Iakov Protazanov (Ermolev, Russia, 1916)

Oppenheim Family, The (Semia Oppenheim), dir. G. Roshal (Mosfil'm, 1939)

Our Moscow (Nasha Moskva), dir. M. Ia. Slutskii (Mosfil'm, 1941)

Peace to the Shack and War to the Palace (Mir khizhinam – voina dvortsam), dir. M. Bonch-Tomashevskii (Kiev, 1919)

Perils of Pauline, dir. Donald Mackenzie (serial; USA, 1914)

Pet'ka (original title: *Peter*) (Hungary, 1934)

Polikushka, dir. Aleksandr Sanin (made in 1919; first shown in 1922)

Power of Darkness, The (Vlast' tmi), dir. Ch. Sabinskii (Ermolev, 1918)

Prisoners (Zakliuchennye), dir. E. Cherviakov (Mosfil'm USSR, 1936)

Professor Mamlok, dir. Minkin and G. Rappaport (Lenfil'm, 1938)

Przhevalskii, dir. Sergei Iutkevich (Mosfil'm, 1951)

Pugachev, dir. P. Petrov-Bytov (Mosfil'm, 1937)

Queen of Spades, The (Pikovaia dama), dir. Iakov Protazanov (Ermolev, Russia, 1916)

Quiet, My Sorrow, Quiet (country of origin and date unknown)

Rainis, dir. Iu. Raizman (Riga, 1949)

Red Tanks (Soviet documentary collection as shown in the USA in 1942)

Rimskii-Korsakov, dir. G. Roshal (Lenfil'm, 1953)

Robin Hood, dir. Allan Dwan (Fairbanks/UA, USA, 1922)

Schweik in the Concentration Camp (English title of 7th kinosbornik, *Novye rasskazy bravogo soldata shveika),* dir. Sergei Iutkevich (Soiuzdetfil'm, 1941)

Searchers for Happiness (Iskateli shchastia), dir. V. Korsh-Sablin (Belgoskino, 1936)

Secret Mission, The (Sekretnaia missiia), dir. Abram Room (Mosfil'm, 1950)

Secret of the German Embassy (Taina nemetskogo posol'stva) (Russia, 1914)

Siberians, The (Sibiriaki), dir. Lev Kuleshov (Soiuzdetfil'm, 1940)

Sickle and the Hammer, The (Serp i molot), dir. Vladimir Gardin, photog. Edward Tisse (Goskinoshkola and VFKO, 1921)

Sil'va (a/k/a *Gypsy Princess),* dir. A. Ivanovskii (Sverdlov, 1944)

Simple People (a/k/a *Plain People; Prostye liudi),* dir. Grigori Kozintsev and Leonid Trauberg (Lenfil'm, 1945; first shown in 1958)

Skull of the Pharaoh's Daughter (Germany, no date)

Spiders (Pauki), dir. Leonard Trauberg (11th kinosbornik) (Tashkent, 1942)

Star, The (*Zvezda*), dir. A. Ivanov (Lenfil'm, 1949; first shown in 1953)

Sun Valley Serenade, dir. H. Bruce Humberstone (20th C.–Fox, USA, 1941)

Suvorov, dir. Vsevolod Pudovkin and M. Doller (Mosfil'm, 1941)

Swedish Match, The (*Shvedskaia spichka*), dir. Aleksandr S. Kurbas (VUFKU Odessa, 1922; first shown in 1924)

Tales of the Siberian Land (*Skazanie o zemle Sibirskoi*), dir. Ivan A. Pyr'ev (Barrandov, Czechoslovakia, and Mosfil'm, 1947)

Tears of Destroyed Poland

Thief of Baghdad, The, dir. Raoul Walsh (Fairbanks/UA, USA, 1924)

Thief, but Not from Baghdad, The (*Vor, no ne Bagdadskii*), dir. V. Feinberg (Goskino, 1926)

Three in a Shell Hole (*Troe v voronke*), dir. I. Mutanov (1st kinosbornik) (Mosfil'm, 1941)

Torn Boots (*Rvannye bashmaki*), dir. Margarita A. Barskaia (Mezhrabpom, 1933)

Trading House of Romanov, Rasputin, Sukhomlinov, Miasoedov, Protopopov and Co., The (*Torgovoi dom Romanov, Rasputin, . . .*), dir. Saltykov (Kino-alpha, Russia, 1917)

Travel to Arzrum (*Puteshestvie v Arzrum*), dir. M. Levin (Lenfil'm, 1937)

Turksib (*Turksib*), dir. V. Turin (Vostokkino, 1929)

Two Warriors (*Dva boitsa*), dir. L. Lukov (Tashkent, 1943)

Under the Roofs of Paris (*Sous les toits de Paris*), dir. René Clair (Tobis/Images, France, 1930)

Vendetta (*Vendetta*), dir. Aleksandr S. Kurbas (VUFKU, Odessa, 1924)

Victory Will Be Ours (*Pobeda budet za nami*) (title of a series of *kinosborniki*; USSR, 1941)

White Eagle, The (*Belyi orel*), dir. Iakov Protazanov (Mezhrabpom, 1928)

Wolf's Duty, The (*Volchii dolg*) (Odessa, 1921)

Your Acquaintance (a/k/a *Journalist; Vasha znakomaia. Zhurnalist*), dir. Lev Kuleshov (Sovkino, 1927)

Index

Illustrations are indicated by italic page numbers.

273